The South West Coast Path Association is a Registered Charity, number 1163422, and a volunteer led organisation governed by Trustees. It was formed by Philip and Mary Carter in 1973.

There is a volunteer Path Committee made up of Area and Local Reps who walk and survey the Path and who ensure funds raised are spent where they are most needed.

Staff members undertake the rest of the work, ensuring that the Business Plan set out by the Trustees is delivered and that the volunteers are supported in their endeavours.

If you would like to contact the Association the details are as follows:

South West Coast Path Association, Bowker House, Lee Mill Bridge, Ivybridge, Devon, PL21 9EF

Chairman: chair@southwestcoastpath.org.uk
Secretary: secretary@southwestcoastpath.org.uk
Treasurer: treasurer@southwestcoastpath.org.uk
Director: esther.pearson@southwestcoastpath.org.uk
Administration: hello@southwestcoastpath.org.uk

Published by: The South West Coast Path Association
ISBN: 9 780907 055235

© South West Coast Path Association 2016
Designed by Ingrid Kendall, Paignton. Printed by Latimer Trend, Plymouth

Cover photography:
Wheal Coates by Jim Tarbox

Welcome

Come to the beach anywhere in the South West of England, turn left or right and you'll be on the South West Coast Path and on the edge of an amazing experience. Where else can you walk along 630 miles of such superb coastline which make up the longest National Trail in the UK? The heritage, wildlife, geology and scenery along the way are truly inspirational and every day walking brings stunning new experiences.

Whether you're looking for an afternoon stroll to take you to a beautiful view, or for a challenge like no other in hiking the entire 630 miles from Somerset's Minehead around to the shores of Poole Harbour in Dorset, you've come to the right place to start your journey.

This Guide is produced by the South West Coast Path Association, the voice and heart of the Path. Our aim is to promote and protect the Path and we are really lucky to have a huge range of supporters who help us to deliver our promises and look after the Path, conserving it for future generations and promoting it for the enjoyment of everyone.

We have a membership base of well over 5,000 dedicated South West Coast Path lovers, a handful of these members have been supporting us since the very beginning in 1973. Some are individual members and some joint, we also have a number who live overseas and want to enable us to continue the good work from afar. Whatever the reason for being a member, you are always welcome to join us.

We also have some wonderful business supporters, one of which is South West Water who have been contributing to the Coast Path since 2014. Other business supporters include Toad Hall Cottages and hotels such as the Thurlestone, Mullion Cove, South Sands, Yarn Market and more.

In addition, a range of local businesses support us through our business membership scheme which offers advertising for businesses, support for them to be walker friendly and much more. South West Coast Path walkers spent £468 million in 2014, mostly in local businesses, which supports the equivalent of 10,600 full-time jobs, so we understand the opportunities this gives local business.

All the listings in this Guide are Business Members, to ensure that they continue to support the Path and advertise with us, please support them and in turn help support the Path!

Thank you! In 2015 we were able to invest over £500,000 in Path improvements.

Bridge at South Milton
Repaired thanks to the South West Coast Path Association

Photographs courtesy of:
Adrian Ballisat, Alexis Gilbert, Andreas Byrne, Andrew Bolton, Angie Latham, Ann-Marie Clapham, Anthony Grimley, Audrey Rowlatt, Barry Lockwood, Bob Small, Chris Parker, Christian Schoter, Colin Milner, Cynthia Snowdon, Dan Martin, Dave Westcott, David Carvey, David Curry, Deena Drees, Doug Chinnery, Ginny Stevens, Howard Marples, Jaap Gassenbeek, James Uglow, Jennifer Rowlandson, Jon Mills, Kingsley Scott, Lawrence Hunt, Mark Camp, Mike Mayor, Mike Pike, Nicola Clark, Peter Shepheard, Pontus Henningsohn, Ray & Dot Culmer, Ray Lainsbury, Rebecca Avant, Rob Kendall, Rosie Spooner, Sarah Skinner, Steve Pattemore, Steve Rumming, Steve Tew, Ted Forman, Tim Barker, Tim Foster, Veronica Hall

East Portlemouth bench

www.southwestcoastpath.org.uk

The South West Coast Path is a 630-mile adventure around the coastline of the south west peninsula. From Minehead in Somerset all the way round to Poole Harbour in Dorset, it is simply the best way to enjoy the scenery, wildlife and heritage of this wonderful coastline.

The sheer variety of the South West Coast Path means that there are plenty of gentle stretches as well as dramatic headlands and steep coastal valleys where the going can be strenuous and demanding. Relaxation, challenge, tranquility or inspiration – the choice is yours!

The South West Coast Path is one of the country's 15 National Trails, walking (and sometimes riding) routes through the nation's finest scenery and heritage. This means it receives a high standard of care and is regarded as one of the flagships of the country's path network.

The Coast Path is a total of 630 miles (1,014km) in length, making it the longest of the National Trails by far. But this does not mean it is not possible to enjoy shorter lengths. To help you, the South West Coast Path Association's website – www.southwestcoastpath.org.uk – includes a distance calculator with nearly 200 locations so that you can pick your own length of path and know the distance.

Clearly, given the nature of the coastline of the South West, the Coast Path is not flat, and to help you plan your trip this Guide includes the amount of climbing involved in each of the sections. It is interesting to note that those who do complete all 630 miles will have climbed a total of 115,000 feet (35,024m), just a little short of climbing the height of Mount Everest four times!

The South West Coast Path passes through some of the finest coastal scenery anywhere, and has an enormous variety and contrast from bustling resorts to quiet coves, airy cliff tops to wooded estuaries. No other walking route has quite this contrast and variety.

The South West Coast Path Association – dedicated to helping everyone enjoy the Path

The Association, a registered charity, was formed in 1973 by a group of enthusiasts to encourage the development and improvement of the South West Coast Path. This is still one of the main aims of the Association, and it works closely with Natural England, the local authorities and the National Trust to achieve the best possible Coast Path. As part of this role the Association is a formal member of the South West Coast Path Partnership, the body whose role is to take collective responsibility for providing a high quality trail meeting national Quality Standards.

Since its foundation the Association has continuously campaigned for maintenance, signing and alignment improvements. There have, over the years, been many such improvements, and the Association has been involved in many of these. It was also instrumental in the placing of markers at each end of the trail, and also a half-way marker, all of which are landmarks appreciated by walkers and which feature in many a celebratory photograph!

Today one of the Association's functions is to help and advise all those who wish to walk along this wonderful coastline – whether in short, relaxing strolls around a headland or by more demanding long distance walks lasting several days or even by heroic attempts at covering the whole length of 630 miles in one go! This Guide is part of this function, and it is hoped that Coast Path walkers find it useful for planning their walks. The Association also provides detailed descriptions of each of the lengths set out in the Guide for those who need such information (see p.10).

Of increasing importance to the Association is the raising of funds for improvements and repair work. Funding for the Coast Path has traditionally come from Natural England, the Government body responsible for the National Trails, and from the local

So here it is – England's longest and most beautiful walking trail. Give yourself a treat and give it a try!

highway authorities. However, substantial budget reductions for these bodies have meant consequent reductions in spending on the Coast Path. This has coincided with expenditure needed to address the considerable storm damage which occurred in the winters of 2012-13 and 2013-14. As a result, the Association has taken on the role of raising funds to try and plug these gaps, something which, as a charity whose focus is on the Coast Path, it is uniquely well placed to do.

All of the tasks the Association undertakes are for the benefit of ALL Coast Path users, not just the hardy long-distance walkers, and it is ALL Coast Path users that the Association represents. Whether you plan to walk all 630 miles, or have already done so, or are happy to stroll along the coast on a sunny afternoon or spend a couple of days a year when on holiday, if you love the Coast Path the Association is for you.

As a member you give us a voice, with more members we have a stronger voice and a stronger voice helps us to gain more funding for the Path.

The Association's formal Objectives

As a registered charity, the Association has a formal set of Objectives. These are:-

1. To secure the protection, improvement and conservation of the South West Coast Path and public access to it in order to improve the health and wellbeing of the general public.

2. To educate the general public to a greater knowledge of, respect and care for, the coast and countryside by promoting the South West Coast Path.

It is to achieve these formal Objectives that the Association undertakes all the works outlined above.

Membership

You're probably already a member but if not please join us or encourage a friend to sign up.

It costs at least £1,000 per year for every mile of this glorious Path to be kept open, maintained and clearly signed, we're asking for your support to help us look after and love the Path.

Our members are great supporters of the Path, if you would like to join us prices for 2016 are:

Individual Membership	**£20**
Joint Membership	**£25**
International Membership	**£25**

Payment may be made at **www.southwestcoastpath.org.uk** or by telephoning **01752 896237** or by using a cheque or postal order made payable to the South West Coast Path Association.

Padstow

Members' Certificate Presentation

Planning Your Walk

Most people planning to walk on the Coast Path will not be undertaking a long distance walk. The vast majority of Coast Path users are walking for a few hours, half a day or perhaps a full day. Such walkers will have an idea of their capabilities and not require any advice. However, it is as well to remember that some lengths of the Coast Path can be quite arduous, with frequent repeated climbs and descents or, occasionally, awkward terrain, and it is not always possible to calculate the time or effort to be taken for a length purely on the distance. The degree of difficulty has to be considered so check in this Guide for the grading – easy, moderate, strenuous or severe – of any length it is intended to walk for an idea of what to expect.

Long Distance Path Walking

For those who are contemplating a walk along the Coast Path spanning more than a day, it might be helpful to consider the points set out below. These words are not for those who have the gear, have done other long-distance walks and know what to expect. We receive letters every year from those who have not ventured on long-distance paths before and are seeking advice. For such walkers, the following pointers may be useful.

Newcomers to the Coast Path

Most people planning a longer walk on the Coast Path have probably already taken some day walks along it. If not, this is a good way of getting an idea of what coastal walking is about. Perhaps start with a length graded 'easy' or 'moderate' in the Guide – start at one end and turn back when still feeling quite fresh to avoid fighting fatigue at the end. Alternatively, walk a section shown as having convenient public transport. If doing so, try to use the public transport at the start and walk back to your base. This avoids having to race the clock to catch a bus at the end of the walk.

Don't forget, if walking alone make sure someone knows your destination and estimated time of arrival.

While there is little need for special kit on the 'easy' sections – good shoes and a rainproof jacket will probably be enough – once you progress further decent boots and a rucksack for food and drink and other bits and pieces will be needed. And although it is unlikely you will get lost many walkers like to have the appropriate map to keep track of where they are, what is around them, etc.

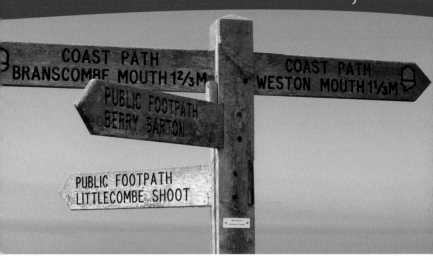

Sign at Berry Barton near Branscombe

Long Distance Coast Path walking

If you have not undertaken walking for more than a day at a time, bear in mind that you will not be able to accomplish the same distance day after day as you do in a one-off day walk. The first reason for this is that you will be carrying more gear than usual, including a change of clothes and possibly footwear, nightwear and toilet kit, all in a bigger rucksack than usual. Secondly, there is the 'wear' factor – for the first few days especially it is simply more tiring having to walk each day. And finally, there is the 'interest' factor – the walk is likely to take you through new places and new scenery; there is more to see and you will need more time to look round.

These factors will influence your planning. Not being too optimistic about what you can achieve each day will be important if booking accommodation ahead. It can be easy to become tied to a treadmill which you cannot get off and which takes all the enjoyment out of the walk. Booking ahead does have the advantage of knowing you have a bed for the night, which can be important in the south west in the summer. On the other hand, it does mean that even if you are tired, have developed blisters and the weather is awful, you have to keep going. Check the grading in the Guide for the length you will be walking – the time and effort for a 'severe' length can be the same as twice that distance on an 'easy' section.

Some Practical Details

While you will have to carry more gear than usual, think long and hard about every item you think you will need and travel as light as possible. Also remember that rucksacks are very rarely waterproof. A plastic liner, used as an additional inner layer, will prevent arriving at your accommodation after a day in the rain to find that your change of clothes is wet. In fact, it is recommended that items such as clothing are kept in further plastic bags within the liner to ensure dryness.

Another practical point to be aware of is the availability of refreshments. You are recommended to carry water whenever out walking on the coast. Nevertheless, during the summer season, refreshments are quite widely available except for the relatively few remote lengths which are highlighted in the Guide. However, out of the holiday season refreshments can be quite far apart on long stretches of coast and you should take your own food supplies as well as water.

Walking Alone

The Association has long had a scheme that enables single female members who are a little nervous about walking alone to team up with other single female members.

Contact hello@southwestcoastpath.org.uk for details.

Walking Guides

These Walking Guides provide detailed instructions for shorter sections of the Path, laid out in both directions. They include maps and photos as well as offering interesting facts, history, wildlife and geological information. Available to buy through our online shop, **www.southwestcoastpath.org.uk** or by calling us on **01752 896237**.

1	Minehead to Porlock Weir 9.5 miles / 15.3 km		**27** **Part 1**	St Ives to Zennor 6.5 miles / 10.4 km
2	Porlock Weir to Lynmouth 12.3 miles / 19.8 km		**27** **Part 2**	Zennor to Pendeen Watch 7.0 miles / 11.2 km
3 **Part 1**	Lynton to Hunter's Inn 6.3 miles / 10.1 km		**28**	Pendeen Watch to Sennen Cove 9.1 miles / 14.6 km
3 **Part 2**	Hunter's Inn to Combe Martin 7.5 miles / 12 km		**29**	Sennen Cove to Porthcurno 6.6 miles / 10.6 km
4	Combe Martin to Ilfracombe 5.3 miles / 8.5 km		**30**	Porthcurno to Lamorna Cove 5.5 miles / 8.8 km
5	Ilfracombe to Woolacombe 7.3 miles / 11.7 km		**31**	Lamorna Cove to Penzance to Marazion 9.4 miles / 15.1 km
6	Woolacombe to Croyde Bay 6.3 miles / 10.2 km		**32** **Part 1**	Penzance to Marazion to Praa Sands 9.0 miles / 14.5 km
7	Croyde Bay to Braunton 8.8 miles / 14.0 km		**32** **Part 2**	Praa Sands to Portleven 4.5 miles / 7.2 km
8	Braunton to Barnstaple 5.6 miles / 9.1 km		**33**	Porthleven to Poldhu Cove 5.2 miles / 8.3 km
9	Barnstaple to Bideford 10.4 miles / 16.7 km		**34**	Poldhu Cove to The Lizard 8.7 miles / 14.0 km
10	Bideford to Westward Ho! 8.7 miles / 14.0 km		**35**	The Lizard to Coverack 10.5 miles / 16.9 km
11	Westward Ho! to Clovelly 11.2 miles / 18.0 km		**36**	Coverack to Helford 13.1 miles / 21.1 km
12	Clovelly to Hartland Quay 10.3 miles / 16.6 km		**37**	Helford to Falmouth (Ferry) 10.0 miles / 16.1 km
13 **Part 1**	Hartland Quay to Morwenstow 8 miles / 12.9 km		**38**	St Mawes (Ferry) to Portscatho 6.2 miles / 9.9 km
13 **Part 2**	Morwenstow to Bude 7.4 miles / 12.0 km		**39**	Portscatho to Portloe 7.5 miles / 12 km
14	Bude to Crackington Haven 10.2 miles / 16.4 km		**40**	Portloe to Mevagissey 12.3 miles / 19.8 km
15	Crackington Haven to Boscastle 6.8 miles / 10.9 km		**41**	Mevagissey to Charlestown 7.2 miles / 11.6 km
16	Boscastle to Tintagel 4.6 miles / 7.4 km		**42**	Charlestown to Fowey 10.3 miles / 16.6 km
17	Tintagel to Port Isaac 9.1 miles / 14.7 km		**43**	Fowey to Polperro 7.1 miles / 11.5 km
18	Port Isaac to Padstow 11.7 miles / 18.9 km		**44**	Polperro to Looe 5.0 miles / 8.0 km
19	Padstow to Harlyn Bay 6.8 miles / 11.0 km		**45**	Looe to Portwrinkle 7.6 miles / 12.2 km
20	Harlyn Bay to Porthcothan 6.6 miles / 10.6 km		**46** **Part 1**	Portwrinkle to Cawsand 9.6 miles / 15.4 km
21	Porthcothan to Newquay 11.1 miles / 17.9 km		**46** **Part 2**	Cawsand to Cremyll (Plymouth Ferry) 3.5 miles / 5.6 km
22	Newquay (Harbour) to Holywell Bay 6.3 miles / 10.2 km		**47** **Part 1**	Admiral's Hard (Plymouth) to The Barbican 3.5 miles / 5.6 km
23	Holywell Bay to Perranporth 4.5 miles / 7.2 km		**47** **Part 2**	The Barbican to Mount Batten 5.0 miles / 8.0 km
24 **Part 1**	Perranporth to Trevaunance Cove St Agnes 3.9 miles / 6.3 km		**48**	Mount Batten to Warren Point (Yealm Ferry) 7.3 miles / 11.7 km
24 **Part 2**	Trevaunance Cove (St Agnes) to Portreath 8.3 miles / 13.3 km		**49**	Noss Mayo (Yealm Ferry) to Mothecombe 9.5 miles / 15.3 km
25	Portreath to Hayle 12.5 miles / 20.1 km		**50**	Mothecombe to Thurlestone 9.1 miles / 14.6 km
26	Hayle to St Ives 6.1 miles / 9.8 km		**51**	Thurlestone to Salcombe 9.5 miles / 15.3 km

52	Salcombe to Torcross 12.9 miles / 20.8 km
53	Torcross to Dartmouth 10.2 miles / 16.4 km
54	Dartmouth (Kingswear) to Brixham 10.8 miles / 17.3 km
55 Part 1	Brixham to Paignton 5.5 miles / 8.8 km
55 Part 2	Paignton to Babbacombe 7.5 miles / 12.0 km
56	Babbacombe to Teignmouth 6.4 miles / 10.3 km
57	Teignmouth to Exmouth 7.9 miles / 12.7 km
58	Exmouth to Budleigh Salterton 6.2 miles / 9.9 km
59	Budleigh Salterton to Sidmouth 6.9 miles / 11.1 km
60 Part 1	Sidmouth to Branscombe 7.0 miles / 11.2 km
60 Part 2	Branscombe to Seaton 3.5 miles / 5.6 km
61	Seaton to Lyme Regis 6.8 miles / 11.0 km
62	Lyme Regis to West Bay 11.4 miles / 18.3 km
63	West Bay to Abbotsbury 9.0 miles / 14.5 km
64	Abbotsbury to Weymouth 13.5 miles / 21.7 km
65	The Isle of Portland 13.2 miles / 21.3 km
66	Weymouth to Lulworth Cove 14.1 miles / 22.7 km
67	Lulworth to Kimmeridge 7.3 miles / 11.7 km
68	Kimmeridge to Worth Matravers 5.2 miles / 8.3 km
69	Worth Matravers to Swanage 8.1 miles / 13.1 km
70	Swanage to South Haven Point 7.6 miles / 12.2 km

These Walking Guides are all available to buy from £1.50 to £2 at **www.southwestcoastpath.org.uk** or call us on **01752 896237**.

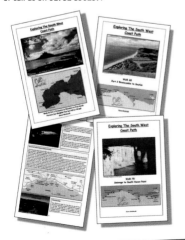

The Reverse Guide

A useful guide providing directions of the whole 630 miles of Coast Path from Poole (Dorset) to Minehead (Somerset). Price £5.50 from our web site.

Maps

The Coast Path is very well signposted. However we do understand that many people like to walk with a map – finding out what else is around you, peace of mind and of course access to the Coast Path.

A-Z Adventure Maps

The A-Z Map Company has now mapped the entire 630 miles of the South West Coast Path and covered the entire route in five and convenient Adventure Maps.

The maps use 1:25 000 and are in a booklet format making them very user friendly – as you walk along to Coast Path you can simply turn the page. There are QR barcodes providing up to date details on public transport, the weather, tides and other tourist information.

Map 1	North Devon & Somerset
Map 2	North Cornwall
Map 3	South Cornwall
Map 4	South Devon
Map 5	Dorset

The maps cost £10 including P&P and are available from **www.southwestcoastpath.org.uk**

Harvey Maps

You will need all three maps to cover the whole South West Coast Path each one giving around two weeks of walking. The maps are waterproof and are supplied in a clear plastic wallet at a scale of 1:40 000.

Also included is information on finding accommodation, camping, food and directions to the start. Also included are Ranger Service contact numbers and enlargements of towns and villages showing facilities available and tips on weather and clothing.

Map 1	Minehead to St Ives
Map 2	St Ives to Plymouth
Map 3	Plymouth to Poole Harbour

The maps are £13.95 each or £38.85 for the set of 3 and are available on their web site at **www.harveymaps.co.uk**

Ordnance Survey Maps

1:50 000

The Landranger series covering the Coast Path are numbered as follows and cost £7.99 or £13.99 for a waterproof version:

181	Minehead & Brendon Hills
180	Barnstaple & Ilfracombe
190	Bude & Clovelly
200	Newquay & Bodmin
203	Land's End & Isles of Scilly
204	Truro & Falmouth
201	Plymouth & Launceston
202	Torbay & South Dartmoor
192	Exeter & Sidmouth
193	Taunton & Lyme Regis
194	Dorchester & Weymouth
195	Bournemouth & Purbeck

1:25 000

The Explorer and Outdoor Leisure maps cost £8.99 or £14.99 for a waterproof version and come with a code for mobile downloads.

- **Outdoor Leisure 9** Exmoor
- **Explorer 139** Bideford, Ilfracombe and Barnstaple
- **Explorer 126** Clovelly and Hartland
- **Explorer 111** Bude, Boscastle and Tintagel
- **Explorer 109** Bodmin Moor (depicts Coast Path from Boscastle to Portgaverne)
- **Explorer 106** Newquay and Padstow
- **Explorer 104** Redruth, St Agnes, Camborne and Perranporth
- **Explorer 102** Land's End
- **Explorer 103** The Lizard
- **Explorer 105** Falmouth and Mevagissey
- **Explorer 107** St Austell and Liskeard
- **Explorer 108** Lower Tamar Valley and Plymouth (depicts Coast Path from Downderry to Heybrook Bay
- **Explorer OL20** South Devon
- **Explorer 110** Torquay and Dawlish
- **Explorer 115** Exmouth and Sidmouth
- **Explorer 116** Lyme Regis and Bridport
- **Outdoor Leisure 15**
- **Outdoor Leisure 44** Torquay and Dawlish (was Explorer 110)

Books

There are other books which describe the South West Coast Path and also a series of circular walk books.

Circular Walks

There are 8 books in this series covering Studland to Padstow with 16 to 18 walks described in each one. An estimated walk time is given along with distance, ascent, a written description of the walk and an aerial shot giving the route. They are all available from **www.southwestcoastpath.org.uk**

National Trail Guides

The Coast Path is split in to 4 sections in this series published by Aurum Press in association with Natural England. It features many colour photographs and has background information on local history and wildlife. It is not so much a walking guide as a complete companion to the landscape of the Path, whether you are a dedicated long-distance walker or a weekend stroller.

Minehead to Padstow by Roland Tarr

Padstow to Falmouth by John Macadam

Falmouth to Exmouth by Brian le Messurier

Exmouth to Poole by Roland Tarr

Minehead to South Haven Point

Published by Cicerone this pocket size book is a handy guide and splits the Coast Path in to 45 different sections. It is available from **www.cicerone.co.uk**

Railways

To plan your train journey and book your tickets to the South West you can visit **www.thetrainline.com** or **www.nationalrail.co.uk** or **www.traveline.info**

Throughout the year there is a regular service linking London Paddington with Taunton, Exeter St. David's, Newton Abbot, Plymouth and Cornwall. There are also regular services linking Birmingham, the North West, North East and Scotland with Taunton, Exeter St. David's, Plymouth, Cornwall and Bournemouth.

There is also an overnight sleeper service between Paddington and Penzance.

There is a half hourly South West Trains service linking London Waterloo, Woking, Basingstoke and Southampton with Bournemouth, Poole, Wareham (for Swanage), Dorchester (for Bridport and Lyme Regis) and Weymouth for those intending to walk the Dorset end of the Coast Path.

East Devon is also served by South West Trains with an hourly service from London Waterloo to Exeter St David's calling at Woking, Basingstoke and Salisbury to Axminster (for Lyme Regis & Seaton), Honiton (for Sidmouth), and Exeter Central (for Exmouth branch).

The long distance trains link Cardiff and Bristol with Exeter, Penzance, Plymouth, Portsmouth, Salisbury, Southampton and Weymouth. Local services on the branch lines do connect with the GWR and ACC services.

Bus Services

For information on buses to the South West, visit **www.travelinesw.com** or to buy tickets go to **www.nationalexpress.com** or **uk.megabus.com**

Tourist Information Centres (TICs) can be very helpful with bus enquiries. For details of all coastal TICs see page 155.

Access to the start of the Path

Access to the start of the Path can be made locally and from outside the region, with a bus service linking Minehead to the mainline railway station at Taunton.

Airports

There are airports in or near towns close to the Coast Path. In Path order, they are:

Newquay Airport

Daily flights from London Gatwick and year round flights from Manchester and Isles of Scilly. Many more seasonal destinations. St Mawgan, Newquay TR8 4RQ
info@newquaycornwallairport.com
Tel: **01637 860600**
www.newquaycornwallairport.com

Land's End

For flights to the Isles of Scilly: Information from Isles of Scilly Travel, Steamship House, Quay Street, Penzance TR18 4BZ
Tel: **0845 710 5555**
www.islesofscilly-travel.co.uk

Exeter

Exeter International Airport, Exeter, EX5 2BD
www.exeter-airport.co.uk

Bournemouth

Bournemouth Airport Ltd., Christchurch, Bournemouth BH23 6SE
Tel: **01202 364000**
www.bournemouthairport.com

Sea Transport & Coastal Cruises

Brittany Ferries provide a ferry link as follows to the South West Coast Path: Plymouth/Roscoff; Poole/Cherbourg (Not Dec - Feb); Plymouth/Santander.

Tel: **0330 159 7000**

email: **reservations@brittanyferries.com**

www.brittany-ferries.co.uk, or contact by mail to Brittany Ferries, Millbay, Plymouth, Devon, PL1 3EW

The famous pleasure steamers Waverley and Balmoral provide both cruises and transport, to and from the Exmoor Coast.

From May until September these sea-going ships provide transport to South Wales, Bristol, North Somerset, Lundy Island and the Exmoor and Jurassic Coast.

Sailings are to and from Ilfracombe and Minehead and information is available on their web site at
www.waverleyexcursions.co.uk
0845 130 4647 or
info@waverleyexcursions.co.uk

Sea Tractor at Burgh Island

Planning your walking holiday in the south west can be helped at www.travelinesw.com or telephone 0871 200 2233.

Bus Information

Listed below, in path order, are details of services and information available from County Councils and local bus operators; it is intended for guidance use only. All information provided is correct at the time of going to print; responsibility for any inaccuracies or changes cannot be accepted by County Councils or bus operators. For up to date bus service information, telephone the relevant numbers given in the following paragraphs.

Somerset

For service 28 or 18 from Taunton to Minehead and services 30/30A from Taunton to Lyme Regis and Weymouth via Axminster (change buses to X54 for Axminster to Lyme Regis and X53 Axminster to Weymouth) contact First, The Bus Station, Tower Street, Taunton, TA1 4AF

Tel: **0871 200 2233**

www.firstgroup.com

For service 18 from Taunton to Minehead, service 10 from Minehead to Porlock contact **sales@webberbus.com**

0800 096 3039 or **01278 452086**

www.webberbus.com

Somerset County Council can send you a free paper copy of the timetables'
Tel: **0845 345 9155**

Email: **generalenquiries@somerset.gov.uk**

www.somerset.gov.uk

North Devon

The North Devon coast has a range of bus services which may be of use to coastal walkers. The greatest choice of coastal destinations is provided from Barnstaple.

Devon & Cornwall's First Buses are useful for those walking between North Devon and North Cornwall.

For timetable enquiries telephone Traveline on 0871 200 2233 or go online at **www.travelinesw.org.uk**

Alternatively the Devon County Council web site has a variety of options. There is an interactive bus map to look at and also Area Bus Timetable Booklets to download:

www.journeydevon.info They do advise that previously printed timetables will vary from these digital guides, but that the digital guides are the most up to date.

If you find yourself at a bus stop and want to know when the next bus is coming along, find the 8 letter reference number on the stop and text it to 84268. You will receive a reply with the times of the next 3 buses to come past that stop.

Cornwall

Cornwall Council have an informative web site at **www.cornwallpublictransport**. info with up to date and full timetables and frequency guides for all the different operators. There are weekday, evening and weekend timetables. You can also call **0300 1234 222** if you prefer. On the site there is an Interactive Cornwall County Map, which shows all the bus lines and their numbers. All the main towns have bus routes to and from them but do check the times especially out of the main holiday times. We have not listed as much detail here as in previous years simply due to the changing nature of the timetables and technology making the information more readily available to people.

Traveline: **0871 200 2233**

www.travelinesw.org.uk

Also local bus operator First:
www.firstgroup.com. Their information is included on the Cornwall Council site too.

Stagecoach run service 6A from Exeter to Bude, if you are coming to the South West by train this may be useful.

South Devon

The coastline between Plymouth and Exeter is accessible by bus from many inland towns. As for North Devon, the Devon County Council web site has a variety of options. There is an interactive bus map to look at and also Area Bus Timetable Booklets to download: **www.journeydevon.info**

Also as for North Devon, when you are at a bus stop, use the 8 letter reference number on the bus stop and text it to 84268. You will receive a reply with the times of the next 3 buses to come past that stop.

For more timetable enquiries telephone Traveline on **0871 200 2233** or go online at **www.travelinesw.org.uk**

The main operators are Stagecoach, First Group and Tally Ho. For Plymouth Citybus map and services go to **www.plymouth.gov.uk** and follow links for the transport section.

East Devon

The East Devon coastline is accessible by bus from Exeter, Ottery St. Mary, Honiton and Axminster. Trains are also available from London Waterloo stop at Axminster, Honiton and Exeter or the quicker train from London Paddington stops at Exeter as do trains coming from Bristol.

Please note, as previously, that the summer and winter timetables do vary a lot.

Dorset

The Dorset Coast is accessible by bus from various inland points with train connections for the distant traveller. For a complete and up to date list of bus routes, timetables and bus numbers go to **www.dorsetforyou.com** and follow the links for Transport. You can download the timetables for local services whose operators are as follows - First Hampshire & Dorset **0870 010 6022**, Damory Coaches **01258 452545**, Morebus **0845 0727 093** and Yellow Buses **01202 636110**.

There is also a helpful map of where to find the bus stops. The main towns from which the transports leaves are Lyme Regis, Weymouth, Poole, Dorchester, Swanage, Bournemouth and Wareham.

SOUTH WEST WATER

South West Water is delighted to team up with the South West Coast Path Association to support one of the region's major tourist attractions.

The South West Coast Path offers a fantastic walking experience, scenic views of some of Europe's cleanest beaches and coastal waters, as well as access to many of those beaches and waterways.

Over the last two decades South West Water has undertaken a massive clean-up of Devon and Cornwall's bathing waters and this has helped to transform the fortunes of tourism in the region. Last year, we spent a further £20million to deliver even cleaner seas at nine beaches in the south west.

Our renewed partnership with the South West Coast Path Association fits with our aim of supporting local communities and protecting the natural environment. We look forward to helping to promote this jewel in the region's tourism crown and the good work done by the Association.

Transforming our region's bathing waters from polluted seas 25 years ago to some of the finest beaches in Europe today has been our focus for a quarter of a century. We continue to make improvements to ensure we meet the ever-higher standards set by the European Union for bathing water cleanliness. But nowadays, we love seeing people enjoy the fruits of that work: walking the Coast Path, playing on the beaches, swimming in the sea and taking advantage of all the opportunities afforded by our stunning coastline.

The South West Coast Path is the path to the sea, giving access and enjoyment to millions. It feels very natural for us to support the Association and help it go from strength to strength as it protects this precious asset for the future.

Ferries & River Crossings

The nature of the Coast Path means that many ferries must be used to cross estuaries along the length of the path. It is recommended the ferry operator be contacted direct for the service to be used. Please do this especially when a fairly late timing is expected and it is necessary to confirm the time of the last run. Also do this when using outside the main tourist season or if use by a party of walkers is planned.

All information correct at time of going to print. Ferries can be subject to change due to weather conditions and tides.

We have attempted to list those directly necessary. The ferry crossings encountered, in path order, are: River Torridge (Instow/Appledore) (optional); River Camel (Rock/Padstow); River Gannel (Newquay/Crantock); Helford River (Helford/Helford Passage); Fal Estuary (Falmouth/St Mawes and St Mawes/Place); River Fowey (Fowey/Polruan); River Tamar (Cremyll/Plymouth); River Yealm (Wembury/Noss Mayo); River Avon (Bigbury-on-Sea/Bantham); River Dart (Dartmouth/Kingswear); River Teign (Shaldon/Teignmouth); River Exe (Starcross/Exmouth, Turf/Topsham); Weymouth Harbour.

Instow/Appledore (River Torridge)

www.appledoreinstowferry.com
email: contact@appledoreinstowferry.com

This service is an optional means of crossing the Torridge without passing through Bideford. Since the ferry is bound by tides, operating times vary daily so walkers are urged to check the website for operating times, but it generally runs for 2 hours either side of high tide.

The ferry will operate from early April 2016 until October.

Padstock/Rock (River Camel)

01841 532239
www.padstow-harbour.co.uk
email: padstowharbour@btconnect.com

The ferry will depart from one of two points in Padstow depending on tides. On big spring tides ferry may disembark at Daymer Bay over the extreme low water period.

Ferry runs every 20 minutes from Padstow starting at 08:00am.

November to 31 March the last ferry from Padstow: 4.50pm and from Rock: 4.30pm. April to 31 May the last ferry from Padstow: 5.50pm and from Rock: 5.30pm. June to mid July and first two weeks in September last ferry from Padstow: 6.50pm and from Rock: 6.30pm. Mid July to 31 August the last ferry from Padstow: 7.50pm and from Rock: 7.30pm.

Water taxi

An evening water taxi service operates between Rock and Padstow between 19:00 and midnight from Easter to end October, weather and tides permitting.

01208 862815 (9am to 5pm)
www.rock-watertaxi.co.uk
email: info@rock-watertaxi.co.uk
Or contact the boat direct on 07778 105297.

Newquay/Crantock (River Gannel)

Fern Pit Café & Ferry, Fern Pit, Riverside Crescent, Newquay, Cornwall TR7 1PJ
01637 873181
www.fernpit.co.uk
email: mail@fernpit.co.uk

Ferry operates as follows: 23rd May to mid September continuous, 7 days a week, 10:00-18:00. Weather dependant.

Gillan Creek

Anthony Jenkin 01326 231357
www.stanthony.co.uk
Email: info@stanthony.co.uk

Ferry operates April 1st to October 31st on demand during normal office hours. It runs approx 3 hours either side of high tide when the stepping stones are submerged.

Helford River

River Boats, Helford Passage, Falmouth, Cornwall TR1 5HP
01326 250770
www.helford-river-boats.co.uk
email: ian@helford-river-boats.co.uk

Ferry operates Good Friday/1st April to 31st October 09:30 to 17:00 daily on demand. July & August ferry may run into the evening. It is possible to use local taxi services if the ferry is not operating. Autocabs: 01326 573773
Trebleone Taxis: 01326 210111.

Falmouth/St Mawes (River Fal)

Cornwall Ferries
01326 741194
www.falriver.co.uk

Ferry operates all year. June-October 3 ferries per hour, fewer at other times. Ferries operate from Falmouth Prince of Wales Pier all year and Custom House Quay summer only.

St Mawes/Place (Percuil River)

Cornwall Ferries (see above)
01326 741194
www.falriver.co.uk
info@falriver.co.uk

1 June – 30 September from 09:00 – 17:00 running every ½ hour, subject to demand.

Falmouth Water Taxi service also operates between Falmouth and St Mawes or Place, weather permitting, between March and October, 9am – 6pm (until 10.30pm May-Sept). If needed, it is advisable to telephone 2-3 days in advance in the Summer.

Tel: 07522 446659 www.falmouthwatertaxi.co.uk

St Mawes Kayaks also offer a water taxi service: Telephone 07971 846786 or visit www.stmaweskayaks.co.uk

Fowey/Polruan (River Fowey)
01726 870232
www.ctomsandson.co.uk
email: enquiries@ctomsandson.co.uk
Polruan Ferry Co Ltd, Toms Yard, East Street Polruan-by-Fowey, Cornwall PL23 1PB
Ferry operates all year at 10-15 min intervals.
07:00 to 23:00 1st May-30th September (Saturdays 07:30 start, Sundays 09:00 start)
07:00 to 19:00 1st October-30th April (Saturdays 07:30 start, Sundays 10:00 to 17:00).
During winter months and summer evenings, ferry runs to Town Quay (centre of Fowey).
During summer months, daytime service runs to Whitehouse slipway (situated on the Esplanade).

Cremyll/Plymouth
Cremyll Ferry, Cremyll Quay, Cremyll, Torpoint, Cornwall PL10 1HX
01752 822105
www.cremyll-ferry.co.uk
The ferry operates depending on weather, tides and other circumstances permitting.
All year round at 30 minute intervals.
Summer Service from 1st April to 30th September.
From Mt Edgcumbe:
Weekdays 06:45 to 20:30, Saturdays 08:00 to 21:30, Sundays 09:00 to 21:00.
From Plymouth:
Weekdays 07:15 to 20:45. Saturdays 08:15 to 21:45, Sundays 09:15 to 21:15.
Winter Service from 1st October to 31st March.
From Mt Edgcumbe: Weekdays 06:45 to 18:30.
Saturdays 08:00 to 18:30. Sundays 09:00 to 18:00.
From Plymouth: Weekdays 07:15 to 18:45.
Saturdays 08:15 to 18:45. Sundays 09:15 to 18:15.
Closed Christmas, Boxing & New Year's Days
We urge you to contact the ferry operator direct if you are relying on this service, particularly if you are anticipating a fairly late finish and need to confirm the time of its last run.

Sutton Harbour/Mount Batten
Mount Batten Ferry 0751 537 0000
www.mountbattenferry.co.uk
email: mountbattenferry@gmail.com
All year round, every ½ hour.
Summer weekdays 07:45 to 23:00, Saturday 08:45 to 22:30 and Sunday 08:45 – 18:15

Winter weekdays 07:45 – 18:15, Saturday 08:45 - 23:00 and Sunday 08:45 – 18:15
We urge you to contact the ferry operator direct if you are relying on this service, particularly if you are anticipating a fairly late finish and need to confirm the time of its last run.

Wembury (Warren Point)/Noss Mayo (River Yealm)
Bill Gregor: 07817 132757
Ferry operates the Monday before Good Friday until last Sunday in Sept, 10:00 to 16:00.
In bad weather, school term-time & weekdays, ferry may be restricted to 10:00 – 12:00 & 15:00 – 16:00, BUT use the signal board to call ferry if required.
Eco-Taxi based in Kingsbridge will carry walkers between Plymouth and Dartmouth and from all estuaries in South Devon.
Tel: 07811 385275.
Alternatively, **Ivy Cabs** may also carry walkers round the South Hams estuaries.
Tel: 01752 696969

Bigbury/Bantham (River Avon)
Marsh Dawes, The Boathouse, Bantham, Kingsbridge, Devon
01548 561196
07837 361306
Ferry operates 25 April – 17 September daily except Sundays, 10:00 to 11:00 and 15:00 to 16:00.
Eco-Taxi based in Kingsbridge will carry walkers between Plymouth and Dartmouth and from all estuaries in South Devon **07811 385275**
Alternatively, **Ivy Cabs** may also carry walkers round the South Hams estuaries **01752 696969**

Salcombe to East Portlemouth Ferry
The Salcombe Ferry
01548 842061/07769 319375
Simon Shortman
Ferry operates all year: November – March every half hour and continuously April – October. Please note that the ferry point is Jubilee Pier in summer & Whitestrand Pontoon in winter. We urge you to contact the ferry operator direct if you are relying on this service, particularly if you are anticipating a fairly late finish and need to confirm the time of its last run.

Dartmouth/Kingswear (River Dart)
Sat Nav Codes – Kingswear TQ6 0AA
Dartmouth TQ6 9AP
01803 752342
www.southhams.gov.uk
DartmouthLowerFerry
Email: pat.webb@southhams.gov.uk
Ferry operates all year on a continuous service 07:00 to 22:45, Sundays 08:00 to 22:45

Dartmouth Passenger Ferry
(River Dart)
Dartmouth Steam Railway & River Boat Co.
5 Lower Street, Dartmouth TQ6 9AJ
01803 555872
www.dartmouthrailriver.co.uk
Ferry operates all year on a continuous service 07:30 to 23:10, Sundays 09:00 to 23:10.
Check web for specific times.

Shaldon/Teignmouth
Ferry operated by Greg Allen
07896 711822
www.teignmouthshaldonferry.co.uk
email: captgreg28@yahoo.com

April – mid July	08:00 to 18:00
Mid July – end August	08:00 to 20:30
September – October	08:00 to 18:00
*November – January	08:00 to 16:30
February – March	08:00 to 17:00

Closed Mon & Tues in December & January. Please note ferry operates 09:00 at weekends April – end of October, and 10:00 November-end of March.
If operating, the ferry runs from the beach opposite the Ferry Boat Inn.

Starcross/Exmouth (River Exe)
Exe to Sea Cruises, Mr Mark Rackley
01626 774770 / 07974 022536 / 07974 772681 / 07779 157280
Ferry operates mid-April – end October, hourly, 7 days a week. From Starcross,on the hour from 10:10 until 16:10, until 17:10 (mid-May to mid September). From Exmouth, on the half hour from 10:40 until 16:40 (Easter and October), until 17:40 (mid-May and June-mid September).

Turf/Topsham (River Exe)
Steve Garrett Tel: 07778 370582
www.topshamtoturfferry.co.uk
email: seadreamferry@btinternet.com
Ferry operates weekends Easter - end May. Daily June – August. Weekends in September, from Turf 11:45 to 15:00 and from Topsham 11:30 to 14:15. In peak season ferry runs until 16:00 from Turf and 15:15 from Topsham.

Topsham Ferry (River Exe)
(between Topsham Quay riverside and Topsham Lock canalside)
Exeter City Council, Canals and Rivers Department
01392 265791 (office); 07801 203338 (ferryman).
This service is tide dependent - please check tide times. Ferry operates Easter-September 09:30-17:00 daily except Tuesdays (tide dependent but may also be available outside these times weather and tide permitting). October-March ferry operates 11:00-17:00 or sunset on weekends and Bank Holidays (tide dependent). Wave or phone ferryman for service (on above number).

Weymouth Harbour
Weymouth and Portland Borough Council, Harbour Master's Office,
13 Custom House Quay, Weymouth DT4 8BG
01305 838423
www.harbour.weymouth.gov.uk
From April, Ferries operate (rowing boats), but are weather dependant.

South Haven Point to Sandbanks, Poole
See end of Walk 70, page 130.

South Haven Point/Sandbanks
Shell Bay/Sandbanks (Mouth of Poole Harbour)
Bournemouth - Swanage Motor Road & Ferry Company, Shell Bay, Studland BH19 3BA
01929 450203
Fax: 01929 450498
www.sandbanksferry.co.uk
All year round. Daily every 20 mins.
Sandbanks 07:00 to 23:00 hrs
Shell Bay 07:10 to 23:10 hrs
Christmas Day every half hour.

If you are relying on a ferry service we urge you to contact the ferry operator direct, particularly if you anticpate a fairly late finish and need to confirm the time of its last run.

Tide Times

The tide tables included in this edition refer to the times of low water at Devonport.

These tables will act as a guide for those wishing to paddle across the Gannel (Newquay) or the Erme. Please be sure to read the warnings given under the relevant section in the Guide. Coast Path walkers are advised not to try to wade any of the other estuaries around the route, but for tide times at such locations walkers should consult the local tide tables, which are usually easily available.

Those crossing the Gannel or Erme should note that there can be considerable differences in tide heights between springs and neaps; and the information below should be used for general timing guidance only. Again, details are available in tide tables locally.

• Newquay (The Gannel) deduct 30 minutes

• River Erme as at Devonport

The tidal information for the port of Devonport is reproduced by permission of the Controller of Her Majesty's Stationery Office and the UK Hydrographic Office (www.ukho.gov.uk)
© British Crown copyright. All rights reserved.

2016 Tide Timetable

Add 1 hour for British Summer Time from 27th March 2016 to 30th October 2016.

JANUARY		Low Tide		Low Tide	
		Time	Height	Time	Height
1	Friday	0345	1.8	1612	1.9
2	Saturday	04 26	2.1	1657	2.1
3	Sunday	0519	2.3	1755	2.2
4	Monday	0625	2.4	1902	2.2
5	Tuesday	0735	2.3	2008	2.1
6	Wednesday	0839	2.1	2107	1.9
7	Thursday	0937	1.8	2200	1.6
8	Friday	1028	1.5	2249	1.3
9	Saturday	1115	1.2	2335	1.1
10	Sunday			1200	1.0
11	Monday	0019	1.0	1245	0.9
12	Tuesday	0102	0.9	1327	0.8
13	Wednesday	0143	0.9	1409	0.8
14	Thursday	0223	1.0	1450	0.9
15	Friday	0305	1.1	1533	1.1
16	Saturday	0349	1.3	1619	1.4
17	Sunday	0439	1.6	1715	1.6
18	Monday	0542	1.8	1824	1.8
19	Tuesday	0704	2.0	1948	1.9
20	Wednesday	0830	1.9	2106	1.7
21	Thursday	0941	1.6	2208	1.4
22	Friday	1039	1.3	2301	1.1
23	Saturday	1128	1.0	2348	0.9
24	Sunday	1214	0.8	1813	5.3
25	Monday	0031	0.8	1255	0.7
26	Tuesday	0110	0.8	1333	0.8
27	Wednesday	0144	0.9	1406	0.9
28	Thursday	0215	1.1	1436	1.1
29	Friday	0243	1.3	1502	1.4
30	Saturday	0309	1.5	1528	1.6
31	Sunday	0336	1.8	1557	1.9

FEBRUARY		Low Tide		Low Tide	
		Time	Height	Time	Height
1	Monday	0411	2.0	1638	2.1
2	Tuesday	0509	2.3	1751	2.3
3	Wednesday	0636	2.3	1915	2.3
4	Thursday	0754	2.2	2026	2.0
5	Friday	0901	1.9	2129	1.7
6	Saturday	1001	1.5	2226	1.4
7	Sunday	1055	1.2	2317	1.0
8	Monday	1145	0.8	1753	5.3
9	Tuesday	0005	0.8	1232	0.6
10	Wednesday	0051	0.6	1316	0.5
11	Thursday	0133	0.5	1358	0.4
12	Friday	0214	0.5	1439	0.5
13	Saturday	0253	0.7	1518	0.8
14	Sunday	0334	1.0	1600	1.1
15	Monday	0418	1.3	1647	1.5
16	Tuesday	0513	1.7	1748	1.9
17	Wednesday	0627	2.0	1914	2.1
18	Thursday	0810	2.0	2050	1.9
19	Friday	0929	1.7	2156	1.6
20	Saturday	1027	1.3	2248	1.2
21	Sunday	1114	1.0	2333	0.9
22	Monday	1157	0.8		
23	Tuesday	0014	0.8	1237	0.7
24	Wednesday	0051	0.7	1312	0.7
25	Thursday	0123	0.8	1342	0.8
26	Friday	0150	0.9	1408	1.0
27	Saturday	0214	1.1	1429	1.2
28	Sunday	0235	1.3	1449	1.4
29	Monday	0257	1.5	1512	1.6

Tide Times

MARCH		Low Tide		Low Tide	
		Time	Height	Time	Height
1	Tuesday	0327	1.8	1546	1.9
2	Wednesday	0410	2.0	1639	2.2
3	Thursday	0528	2.3	1819	2.3
4	Friday	0712	2.2	1949	2.1
5	Saturday	0829	1.9	2100	1.8
6	Sunday	0935	1.5	2202	1.4
7	Monday	1033	1.0	2257	0.9
8	Tuesday	1125	0.6	2347	0.6
9	Wednesday			1213	0.4
10	Thursday	0034	0.3	1259	0.2
11	Friday	0117	0.2	1341	0.2
12	Saturday	0159	0.3	1421	0.3
13	Sunday	0238	0.5	1500	0.6
14	Monday	0317	0.8	1540	1.0
15	Tuesday	0400	1.2	1625	1.5
16	Wednesday	0451	1.7	1721	1.9
17	Thursday	0600	2.0	1842	2.2
18	Friday	0748	2.1	2029	2.1
19	Saturday	0911	1.8	2136	1.7
20	Sunday	1007	1.4	2227	1.3
21	Monday	1053	1.0	2311	1.0
22	Tuesday	1134	0.8	2350	0.8
23	Wednesday			1211	0.7
24	Thursday	0025	0.7	1245	0.7
25	Friday	0057	0.8	1314	0.8
26	Saturday	0123	0.9	1338	0.9
27	Sunday	0146	1.0	1358	1.1
28	Monday	0207	1.2	1419	1.3
29	Tuesday	0230	1.4	1443	1.5
30	Wednesday	0259	1.6	1517	1.7
31	Thursday	0341	1.8	1605	2.0

APRIL		Low Tide		Low Tide	
		Time	Height	Time	Height
1	Friday	0447	2.1	1729	2.2
2	Saturday	0634	2.1	1914	2.1
3	Sunday	0758	1.8	2031	1.8
4	Monday	0907	1.4	2137	1.3
5	Tuesday	1008	1.0	2234	0.9
6	Wednesday	1102	0.6	2325	0.5
7	Thursday	1151	0.3	1755	5.6
8	Friday	0013	0.3	1238	0.1
9	Saturday	0058	0.1	1321	0.1
10	Sunday	0140	0.2	1402	0.3
11	Monday	0221	0.4	1442	0.6
12	Tuesday	0302	0.7	1522	1.0
13	Wednesday	0344	1.2	1607	1.5
14	Thursday	0434	1.6	1700	1.9
15	Friday	0538	2.0	1810	2.2
16	Saturday	0709	2.1	1948	2.1
17	Sunday	0838	1.8	2103	1.8
18	Monday	0935	1.5	2155	1.5
19	Tuesday	1022	1.2	2240	1.2
20	Wednesday	1103	1.0	2319	1.0
21	Thursday	1140	0.9	2355	0.9
22	Friday			1213	0.9
23	Saturday	0026	0.9	1243	0.9
24	Sunday	0054	0.9	1308	1.0
25	Monday	0120	1.0	1332	1.1
26	Tuesday	0145	1.2	1357	1.3
27	Wednesday	0212	1.3	1425	1.4
28	Thursday	0244	1.5	1501	1.7
29	Friday	0327	1.7	1550	1.9
30	Saturday	0430	1.9	1703	2.1

MAY		Low Tide		Low Tide	
		Time	Height	Time	Height
1	Sunday	0601	1.9	1840	2.0
2	Monday	0726	1.7	2000	1.8
3	Tuesday	0838	1.4	2108	1.4
4	Wednesday	0940	1.0	2208	1.0
5	Thursday	1036	0.6	2301	0.6
6	Friday	1127	0.4	2351	0.4
7	Saturday			1215	0.3
8	Sunday	0037	0.2	1301	0.3
9	Monday	0122	0.3	1344	0.4
10	Tuesday	0205	0.5	1425	0.7
11	Wednesday	0247	0.8	1506	1.1
12	Thursday	0330	1.1	1550	1.5
13	Friday	0417	1.5	1639	1.8
14	Saturday	0512	1.8	1737	2.1
15	Sunday	0620	2.0	1849	2.1
16	Monday	0740	1.9	2008	2.0
17	Tuesday	0848	1.7	2110	1.8
18	Wednesday	0940	1.5	2159	1.5
19	Thursday	1024	1.3	2242	1.3
20	Friday	1103	1.1	2320	1.1
21	Saturday	1138	1.1	2354	1.1
22	Sunday			1211	1.1
23	Monday	0027	1.1	1242	1.1
24	Tuesday	0058	1.1	1312	1.2
25	Wednesday	0129	1.1	1343	1.2
26	Thursday	0202	1.2	1416	1.4
27	Friday	0239	1.2	1455	1.5
28	Saturday	0323	1.5	1544	1.7
29	Sunday	0420	1.7	1647	1.9
30	Monday	0532	1.7	1806	1.9
31	Tuesday	0652	1.7	1926	1.7

JUNE		Low Tide		Low Tide	
		Time	Height	Time	Height
1	Wednesday	0806	1.4	2038	1.5
2	Thursday	0912	1.1	2141	1.1
3	Friday	1011	0.9	2238	0.8
4	Saturday	1105	0.6	2331	0.6
5	Sunday	1155	0.5	1757	5.6
6	Monday	0020	0.5	1243	0.5
7	Tuesday	0106	0.5	1327	0.6
8	Wednesday	0150	0.6	1410	0.8
9	Thursday	0233	0.8	1450	1.0
10	Friday	0314	1.1	1531	1.4
11	Saturday	0356	1.4	1613	1.7
12	Sunday	0442	1.7	1701	1.9
13	Monday	0534	1.9	1758	2.1
14	Tuesday	0634	2.0	1901	2.1
15	Wednesday	0739	2.0	2007	2.0
16	Thursday	0841	1.8	2106	1.8
17	Friday	0934	1.6	2157	1.6
18	Saturday	1021	1.4	2242	1.4
19	Sunday	1103	1.3	2324	1.2
20	Monday	1142	1.2	1751	5.2
21	Tuesday	0003	1.1	1220	1.1
22	Wednesday	0041	1.1	1257	1.1
23	Thursday	0118	1.0	1334	1.1
24	Friday	0156	1.1	1412	1.2
25	Saturday	0236	1.1	1452	1.3
26	Sunday	0319	1.2	1537	1.4
27	Monday	0408	1.4	1630	1.6
28	Tuesday	0506	1.5	1735	1.7
29	Wednesday	0617	1.6	1852	1.8
30	Thursday	0734	1.6	2009	1.6

JULY

		Low Tide Time	Low Tide Height	Low Tide Time	Low Tide Height
1	Friday	0846	1.4	2119	1.4
2	Saturday	0950	1.2	2220	1.1
3	Sunday	1048	0.9	2315	0.8
4	Monday	1140	0.8	1740	5.5
5	Tuesday	0006	0.7	1228	0.7
6	Wednesday	0053	0.6	1312	0.7
7	Thursday	0136	0.6	1353	0.8
8	Friday	0216	0.8	1432	1.0
9	Saturday	0254	1.0	1507	1.2
10	Sunday	0329	1.3	1543	1.5
11	Monday	0405	1.6	1621	1.8
12	Tuesday	0446	1.8	1707	2.0
13	Wednesday	0537	2.0	1804	2.2
14	Thursday	0638	2.1	1910	2.2
15	Friday	0743	2.1	2014	2.0
16	Saturday	0845	1.9	2114	1.8
17	Sunday	0941	1.6	2207	1.5
18	Monday	1031	1.4	2256	1.3
19	Tuesday	1118	1.2	2342	1.1
20	Wednesday	1202	1.1	1810	5.4
21	Thursday	0025	0.9	1244	1.0
22	Friday	0107	0.8	1325	0.9
23	Saturday	0148	0.8	1405	0.9
24	Sunday	0228	0.8	1444	1.0
25	Monday	0308	1.0	1525	1.2
26	Tuesday	0352	1.2	1611	1.4
27	Wednesday	0442	1.4	1707	1.6
28	Thursday	0544	1.7	1819	1.8
29	Friday	0703	1.8	1945	1.8
30	Saturday	0826	1.7	2104	1.6
31	Sunday	0937	1.5	2209	1.3

AUGUST

		Low Tide Time	Low Tide Height	Low Tide Time	Low Tide Height
1	Monday	1036	1.2	2304	1.0
2	Tuesday	1127	0.9	2353	0.7
3	Wednesday			1213	0.7
4	Thursday	0037	0.6	1256	0.7
5	Friday	0118	0.6	1334	0.7
6	Saturday	0155	0.7	1408	0.9
7	Sunday	0228	0.9	1439	1.1
8	Monday	0257	1.2	1508	1.4
9	Tuesday	0324	1.5	1536	1.7
10	Wednesday	0352	1.8	1608	2.0
11	Thursday	0428	2.0	1658	2.2
12	Friday	0532	2.2	1816	2.3
13	Saturday	0652	2.3	1931	2.2
14	Sunday	0804	2.1	2038	2.0
15	Monday	0907	1.8	2138	1.6
16	Tuesday	1004	1.5	2232	1.3
17	Wednesday	1055	1.2	2321	1.0
18	Thursday	1143	0.9		
19	Friday	0008	0.7	1229	0.7
20	Saturday	0052	0.6	1311	0.6
21	Sunday	0134	0.5	1352	0.6
22	Monday	0214	0.6	1431	0.7
23	Tuesday	0253	0.8	1510	1.0
24	Wednesday	0333	1.1	1553	1.3
25	Thursday	0419	1.4	1644	1.6
26	Friday	0516	1.8	1753	2.0
27	Saturday	0637	2.0	1929	2.0
28	Sunday	0814	2.0	2056	1.8
29	Monday	0928	1.7	2159	1.4
30	Tuesday	1024	1.3	2251	1.2
31	Wednesday	1112	1.0	2336	0.8

SEPTEMBER

		Low Tide Time	Low Tide Height	Low Tide Time	Low Tide Height
1	Thursday	1155	0.8	1748	5.5
2	Friday	0017	0.6	1235	0.7
3	Saturday	0056	0.6	1310	0.7
4	Sunday	0129	0.7	1341	0.9
5	Monday	0157	0.9	1408	1.1
6	Tuesday	0221	1.2	1431	1.3
7	Wednesday	0241	1.4	1451	1.6
8	Thursday	0300	1.7	1515	1.9
9	Friday	0328	2.0	1552	2.1
10	Saturday	0414	2.2	1704	2.4
11	Sunday	0555	2.4	1852	2.4
12	Monday	0728	2.3	2007	2.1
13	Tuesday	0838	2.0	2111	1.7
14	Wednesday	0939	1.6	2207	1.3
15	Thursday	1032	1.2	2259	0.9
16	Friday	1122	0.8	2346	0.6
17	Saturday	1208	0.6	1811	5.8
18	Sunday	0031	0.4	1252	0.5
19	Monday	0115	0.4	1334	0.5
20	Tuesday	0155	0.5	1414	0.6
21	Wednesday	0235	0.7	1454	0.9
22	Thursday	0315	1.1	1536	1.3
23	Friday	0359	1.5	1626	1.7
24	Saturday	0454	1.9	1734	2.1
25	Sunday	0614	2.2	1915	2.2
26	Monday	0801	2.2	2043	1.9
27	Tuesday	0912	1.8	2142	1.5
28	Wednesday	1005	1.4	2230	1.1
29	Thursday	1050	1.1	2313	0.9
30	Friday	1131	0.9	2352	0.8

OCTOBER

		Low Tide Time	Low Tide Height	Low Tide Time	Low Tide Height
1	Saturday			1209	0.8
2	Sunday	0027	0.8	1242	0.8
3	Monday	0059	0.9	1311	1.0
4	Tuesday	0124	1.0	1336	1.1
5	Wednesday	0146	1.2	1357	1.3
6	Thursday	0205	1.4	1418	1.6
7	Friday	0225	1.7	1442	1.8
8	Saturday	0254	1.9	1518	2.0
9	Sunday	0336	2.2	1615	2.3
10	Monday	0448	2.4	1809	2.4
11	Tuesday	0650	2.4	1934	2.1
12	Wednesday	0808	2.1	2042	1.7
13	Thursday	0911	1.6	2140	1.3
14	Friday	1007	1.2	2233	0.9
15	Saturday	1058	0.8	2323	0.6
16	Sunday	1146	0.6		
17	Monday	0009	0.4	1232	0.4
18	Tuesday	0054	0.4	1315	0.4
19	Wednesday	0136	0.5	1357	0.6
20	Thursday	0217	0.8	1439	0.9
21	Friday	0258	1.2	1522	1.3
22	Saturday	0342	1.6	1612	1.7
23	Sunday	0436	2.0	1716	2.1
24	Monday	0549	2.3	1847	2.2
25	Tuesday	0728	2.2	2014	2.0
26	Wednesday	0843	2.0	2114	1.7
27	Thursday	0936	1.6	2201	1.4
28	Friday	1021	1.3	2244	1.1
29	Saturday	1102	1.1	2322	1.0
30	Sunday	1139	1.0	2357	1.0
31	Monday	1212	1.0	1804	5.4

Tide Times

NOVEMBER		Low Tide		Low Tide	
		Time	Height	Time	Height
1	Tuesday	0027	1.0	1242	1.1
2	Wednesday	0053	1.1	1308	1.2
3	Thursday	0117	1.3	1332	1.4
4	Friday	0139	1.5	1356	1.5
5	Saturday	0204	1.6	1425	1.7
6	Sunday	0236	1.8	1502	1.9
7	Monday	0318	2.1	1555	2.1
8	Tuesday	0421	2.3	1723	2.3
9	Wednesday	0603	2.4	1857	2.1
10	Thursday	0731	2.1	2009	1.8
11	Friday	0840	1.7	2111	1.4
12	Saturday	0939	1.3	2207	1.0
13	Sunday	1033	0.9	2258	0.7
14	Monday	1124	0.7	2347	0.5
15	Tuesday	1212	0.5	1816	5.8
16	Wednesday	0033	0.5	1258	0.5
17	Thursday	0118	0.6	1342	0.6
18	Friday	0201	0.8	1426	0.9
19	Saturday	0244	1.1	1510	1.2
20	Sunday	0328	1.5	1558	1.6
21	Monday	0417	1.9	1652	1.9
22	Tuesday	0516	2.2	1800	2.1
23	Wednesday	0630	2.3	1921	2.1
24	Thursday	0752	2.2	2030	1.9
25	Friday	0855	1.9	2123	1.7
26	Saturday	0945	1.7	2208	1.5
27	Sunday	1028	1.4	2248	1.3
28	Monday	1107	1.3	2324	1.2
29	Tuesday	1143	1.2	2357	1.2
30	Wednesday	1215	1.2	1817	5.3

DECEMBER		Low Tide		Low Tide	
		Time	Height	Time	Height
1	Thursday	0027	1.2	1246	1.3
2	Friday	0056	1.3	1315	1.3
3	Saturday	0124	1.4	1345	1.4
4	Sunday	0155	1.5	1418	1.6
5	Monday	0229	1.7	1457	1.7
6	Tuesday	0311	1.9	1546	1.9
7	Wednesday	0405	2.0	1650	2.0
8	Thursday	0518	2.2	1811	2.0
9	Friday	0646	2.1	1931	1.8
10	Saturday	0805	1.8	2040	1.5
11	Sunday	0911	1.5	2141	1.2
12	Monday	1011	1.1	2237	0.9
13	Tuesday	1105	0.9	2329	0.7
14	Wednesday	1155	0.7		
15	Thursday	0017	0.6	1244	0.6
16	Friday	0104	0.6	1330	0.6
17	Saturday	0148	0.8	1414	0.8
18	Sunday	0230	1.0	1457	1.0
19	Monday	0311	1.3	1539	1.4
20	Tuesday	0354	1.6	1623	1.7
21	Wednesday	0440	1.9	1713	2.0
22	Thursday	0534	2.2	1812	2.1
23	Friday	0639	2.3	1920	2.2
24	Saturday	0751	2.2	2028	2.0
25	Sunday	0856	2.0	2124	1.8
26	Monday	0949	1.8	2211	1.6
27	Tuesday	1034	1.6	2252	1.4
28	Wednesday	1115	1.4	2330	1.3
29	Thursday	1152	1.3		
30	Friday	0006	1.2	1229	1.2
31	Saturday	0041	1.2	1304	1.2

2017 Tide Timetable

Add 1 hour for British Summer Time from 26th March 2017 to 29th October 2017

JANUARY		Low Tide		Low Tide	
		Time	Height	Time	Height
1	Sunday	0114	1.2	1339	1.2
2	Monday	0149	1.3	1414	1.3
3	Tuesday	0225	1.4	1452	1.4
4	Wednesday	0304	1.5	1534	1.5
5	Thursday	0349	1.7	1624	1.7
6	Friday	0445	1.8	1728	1.8
7	Saturday	0558	2	1847	1.9
8	Sunday	0725	1.9	2007	1.7
9	Monday	0845	1.7	2118	1.5
10	Tuesday	0952	1.4	2220	1.2
11	Wednesday	1051	1	2315	0.9
12	Thursday	1143	0.8		
13	Friday	0005	0.7	1232	0.6
14	Saturday	0051	0.6	1318	0.5
15	Sunday	0134	0.7	1400	0.6
16	Monday	0214	0.8	1439	0.8
17	Tuesday	0251	1	1515	1.1
18	Wednesday	0327	1.3	1551	1.4
19	Thursday	0403	1.7	1628	1.8
20	Friday	0445	2	1713	2.1
21	Saturday	0538	2.2	1811	2.2
22	Sunday	0643	2.3	1918	2.3
23	Monday	0754	2.3	2028	2.1
24	Tuesday	0901	2	2129	1.9
25	Wednesday	0958	1.7	2221	1.6
26	Thursday	1047	1.5	2306	1.4
27	Friday	1131	1.2	2348	1.2
28	Saturday			1212	1.1
29	Sunday	0027	1	1251	0.9
30	Monday	0106	1	1329	0.9
31	Tuesday	0142	0.9	1406	0.9

FEBRUARY		Low Tide		Low Tide	
		Time	Height	Time	Height
1	Wednesday	0218	1	1442	1
2	Thursday	0254	1.1	1520	1.1
3	Friday	0334	1.3	1603	1.4
4	Saturday	0422	1.6	1656	1.7
5	Sunday	0524	1.8	1807	1.9
6	Monday	0649	2	1938	1.9
7	Tuesday	0826	1.9	2103	1.7
8	Wednesday	0941	1.5	2210	1.3
9	Thursday	1041	1.1	2305	1
10	Friday	1133	0.8	2353	0.7
11	Saturday			1219	0.5
12	Sunday	0037	0.5	1302	0.4
13	Monday	0118	0.5	1341	0.5
14	Tuesday	0154	0.6	1416	0.7
15	Wednesday	0227	0.8	1448	0.9
16	Thursday	0257	1.1	1516	1.3
17	Friday	0326	1.4	1544	1.6
18	Saturday	0357	1.8	1616	1.9
19	Sunday	0437	2.1	1705	2.2
20	Monday	0545	2.3	1821	2.4
21	Tuesday	0703	2.4	1937	2.3
22	Wednesday	0816	2.2	2048	2
23	Thursday	0922	1.8	2149	1.7
24	Friday	1019	1.5	2241	1.4
25	Saturday	1107	1.1	2327	1.1
26	Sunday	1152	0.9		
27	Monday	0010	0.8	1234	0.7
28	Tuesday	0051	0.7	1314	0.6

MARCH		Low Tide		Low Tide	
		Time	Height	Time	Height
1	Wednesday	0129	0.6	1352	0.6
2	Thursday	0206	0.6	1428	0.7
3	Friday	0242	0.8	1505	0.9
4	Saturday	0321	1	1546	1.2
5	Sunday	0405	1.4	1635	1.6
6	Monday	0503	1.8	1741	1.9
7	Tuesday	0625	2	1916	2.1
8	Wednesday	0814	1.9	2053	1.8
9	Thursday	0932	1.5	2159	1.4
10	Friday	1029	1.1	2251	1
11	Saturday	1117	0.7	2337	0.7
12	Sunday	1201	0.5		
13	Monday	0018	0.5	1241	0.4
14	Tuesday	0056	0.5	1318	0.5
15	Wednesday	0130	0.6	1350	0.6
16	Thursday	0200	0.8	1417	0.9
17	Friday	0227	1	1441	1.2
18	Saturday	0251	1.3	1502	1.5
19	Sunday	0313	1.6	1525	1.8
20	Monday	0342	1.9	1559	2.1
21	Tuesday	0436	2.2	1715	2.4
22	Wednesday	0617	2.3	1854	2.4
23	Thursday	0736	2.2	2009	2.1
24	Friday	0845	1.8	2115	1.8
25	Saturday	0946	1.4	2212	1.4
26	Sunday	1039	1	2302	1
27	Monday	1127	0.7	2348	0.7
28	Tuesday			1211	0.5
29	Wednesday	0031	0.5	1254	0.4
30	Thursday	0112	0.4	1334	0.4
31	Friday	0151	0.4	1413	0.5

APRIL		Low Tide		Low Tide	
		Time	Height	Time	Height
1	Saturday	0229	0.6	1451	0.8
2	Sunday	0309	0.9	1533	1.2
3	Monday	0355	1.3	1621	1.6
4	Tuesday	0452	1.7	1725	2
5	Wednesday	0612	2	1858	2.1
6	Thursday	0759	1.9	2034	1.9
7	Friday	0913	1.5	2138	1.5
8	Saturday	1008	1.1	2229	1.1
9	Sunday	1054	0.8	2313	0.8
10	Monday	1136	0.6	2353	0.7
11	Tuesday			1215	0.6
12	Wednesday	0030	0.6	1250	0.6
13	Thursday	0103	0.7	1320	0.8
14	Friday	0132	0.8	1346	1
15	Saturday	0157	1.1	1409	1.2
16	Sunday	0220	1.3	1429	1.5
17	Monday	0242	1.5	1452	1.7
18	Tuesday	0310	1.8	1526	2
19	Wednesday	0357	2	1623	2.2
20	Thursday	0529	2.2	1808	2.3
21	Friday	0657	2.1	1930	2.1
22	Saturday	0808	1.8	2038	1.8
23	Sunday	0910	1.4	2138	1.4
24	Monday	1007	1	2232	1
25	Tuesday	1058	0.7	2322	0.7
26	Wednesday	1146	0.5		
27	Thursday	0008	0.4	1232	0.3
28	Friday	0053	0.3	1315	0.3
29	Saturday	0136	0.4	1357	0.5
30	Sunday	0218	0.5	1439	0.8

MAY		Low Tide		Low Tide	
		Time	Height	Time	Height
1	Monday	0301	0.8	1523	1.1
2	Tuesday	0348	1.2	1612	1.5
3	Wednesday	0444	1.6	1713	1.9
4	Thursday	0557	1.8	1832	2
5	Friday	0727	1.8	1959	1.9
6	Saturday	0841	1.6	2106	1.6
7	Sunday	0937	1.3	2158	1.3
8	Monday	1024	1.1	2243	1.1
9	Tuesday	1107	0.9	2324	0.9
10	Wednesday	1145	0.8		
11	Thursday	0001	0.9	1220	0.9
12	Friday	0034	0.9	1250	1
13	Saturday	0104	1	1317	1.1
14	Sunday	0131	1.1	1342	1.3
15	Monday	0157	1.3	1406	1.4
16	Tuesday	0223	1.5	1433	1.6
17	Wednesday	0255	1.7	1509	1.8
18	Thursday	0340	1.8	1601	2
19	Friday	0448	2	1720	2.2
20	Saturday	0614	2	1847	2.1
21	Sunday	0728	1.7	1959	1.8
22	Monday	0834	1.4	2103	1.4
23	Tuesday	0934	1.1	2202	1.1
24	Wednesday	1030	0.8	2256	0.8
25	Thursday	1122	0.6	2347	0.5
26	Friday			1211	0.4
27	Saturday	0035	0.4	1258	0.4
28	Sunday	0122	0.4	1344	0.5
29	Monday	0207	0.5	1428	0.7
30	Tuesday	0253	0.8	1514	1.1
31	Wednesday	0340	1.1	1601	1.4

JUNE		Low Tide		Low Tide	
		Time	Height	Time	Height
1	Thursday	0432	1.4	1654	1.7
2	Friday	0531	1.7	1756	1.9
3	Saturday	0640	1.8	1908	2
4	Sunday	0753	1.8	2019	1.9
5	Monday	0855	1.6	2118	1.6
6	Tuesday	0947	1.4	2208	1.4
7	Wednesday	1032	1.3	2251	1.3
8	Thursday	1113	1.2	2331	1.1
9	Friday	1149	1.1		
10	Saturday	0006	1.1	1222	1.1
11	Sunday	0039	1.1	1253	1.2
12	Monday	0110	1.2	1322	1.3
13	Tuesday	0140	1.3	1351	1.4
14	Wednesday	0211	1.4	1423	1.5
15	Thursday	0246	1.5	1459	1.6
16	Friday	0327	1.6	1545	1.8
17	Saturday	0420	1.7	1644	1.9
18	Sunday	0528	1.8	1759	1.9
19	Monday	0644	1.7	1918	1.8
20	Tuesday	0757	1.5	2030	1.6
21	Wednesday	0903	1.3	2135	1.2
22	Thursday	1004	1	2234	0.9
23	Friday	1101	0.8	2329	0.7
24	Saturday	1154	0.6		
25	Sunday	0020	0.5	1244	0.5
26	Monday	0110	0.4	1331	0.5
27	Tuesday	0157	0.5	1416	0.7
28	Wednesday	0242	0.6	1500	0.9
29	Thursday	0326	0.9	1543	1.2
30	Friday	0410	1.2	1628	1.5

Tide Times

JULY		Low Tide		Low Tide	
		Time	Height	Time	Height
1	Saturday	0457	1.5	1716	1.8
2	Sunday	0549	1.8	1813	2
3	Monday	0650	1.9	1917	2.1
4	Tuesday	0757	1.9	2025	2
5	Wednesday	0900	1.8	2126	1.8
6	Thursday	0953	1.6	2217	1.6
7	Friday	1039	1.4	2301	1.4
8	Saturday	1120	1.3	2340	1.2
9	Sunday	1157	1.2		
10	Monday	0017	1.2	1233	1.2
11	Tuesday	0052	1.1	1306	1.2
12	Wednesday	0127	1.1	1339	1.2
13	Thursday	0200	1.2	1413	1.3
14	Friday	0235	1.2	1448	1.4
15	Saturday	0313	1.3	1528	1.5
16	Sunday	0357	1.5	1616	1.7
17	Monday	0451	1.6	1718	1.8
18	Tuesday	0601	1.7	1837	1.9
19	Wednesday	0722	1.7	2001	1.7
20	Thursday	0838	1.5	2114	1.5
21	Friday	0946	1.3	2219	1.1
22	Saturday	1047	1	2316	0.8
23	Sunday	1141	0.7		
24	Monday	0009	0.5	1231	0.6
25	Tuesday	0058	0.4	1318	0.5
26	Wednesday	0143	0.4	1400	0.6
27	Thursday	0225	0.5	1440	0.8
28	Friday	0304	0.8	1518	1.1
29	Saturday	0341	1.1	1555	1.4
30	Sunday	0418	1.5	1635	1.7
31	Monday	0500	1.8	1722	2

AUGUST		Low Tide		Low Tide	
		Time	Height	Time	Height
1	Tuesday	0552	2.1	1822	2.2
2	Wednesday	0655	2.2	1930	2.2
3	Thursday	0805	2.1	2039	2.1
4	Friday	0911	1.9	2141	1.8
5	Saturday	1006	1.6	2232	1.5
6	Sunday	1053	1.4	2316	1.3
7	Monday	1135	1.2	2356	1.1
8	Tuesday			1213	1.1
9	Wednesday	0034	1	1250	1
10	Thursday	0111	0.9	1325	1
11	Friday	0146	0.9	1359	1
12	Saturday	0220	1	1434	1.1
13	Sunday	0256	1.1	1511	1.3
14	Monday	0335	1.3	1554	1.5
15	Tuesday	0423	1.6	1649	1.8
16	Wednesday	0526	1.8	1805	2
17	Thursday	0653	1.9	1941	1.9
18	Friday	0823	1.8	2104	1.6
19	Saturday	0937	1.5	2210	1.2
20	Sunday	1037	1.1	2306	0.8
21	Monday	1129	0.8	2355	0.5
22	Tuesday	0559	5.4	1216	0.5
23	Wednesday	0041	0.4	1300	0.5
24	Thursday	0123	0.4	1339	0.5
25	Friday	0201	0.5	1415	0.7
26	Saturday	0235	0.8	1448	1
27	Sunday	0306	1.1	1519	1.4
28	Monday	0336	1.5	1551	1.7
29	Tuesday	0408	1.9	1631	2.1
30	Wednesday	0453	2.2	1730	2.3
31	Thursday	0603	2.4	1845	2.4

SEPTEMBER		Low Tide		Low Tide	
		Time	Height	Time	Height
1	Friday	0719	2.4	1958	2.3
2	Saturday	0831	2.1	2106	1.9
3	Sunday	0934	1.8	2202	1.6
4	Monday	1025	1.5	2249	1.3
5	Tuesday	1110	1.2	2332	1
6	Wednesday	1151	1		
7	Thursday	0012	0.8	1231	0.9
8	Friday	0051	0.7	1308	0.8
9	Saturday	0128	0.7	1343	0.8
10	Sunday	0203	0.8	1418	0.9
11	Monday	0238	1	1454	1.1
12	Tuesday	0316	1.3	1536	1.4
13	Wednesday	0402	1.6	1629	1.8
14	Thursday	0503	2	1746	2.1
15	Friday	0635	2.2	1933	2.1
16	Saturday	0817	2	2059	1.7
17	Sunday	0929	1.6	2200	1.3
18	Monday	1024	1.2	2251	0.9
19	Tuesday	1113	0.8	2337	0.6
20	Wednesday	1156	0.6		
21	Thursday	0019	0.4	1237	0.5
22	Friday	0058	0.5	1314	0.6
23	Saturday	0133	0.6	1347	0.8
24	Sunday	0203	0.9	1416	1.1
25	Monday	0230	1.2	1442	1.4
26	Tuesday	0253	1.6	1508	1.7
27	Wednesday	0315	1.9	1535	2.1
28	Thursday	0343	2.2	1626	2.4
29	Friday	0456	2.5	1800	2.5
30	Saturday	0637	2.6	1920	2.4

OCTOBER		Low Tide		Low Tide	
		Time	Height	Time	Height
1	Sunday	0753	2.3	2029	2.1
2	Monday	0859	2	2128	1.6
3	Tuesday	0953	1.6	2218	1.3
4	Wednesday	1041	1.2	2303	1
5	Thursday	1125	0.9	2346	0.7
6	Friday			1207	0.8
7	Saturday	0027	0.6	1247	0.7
8	Sunday	0107	0.6	1325	0.7
9	Monday	0145	0.7	1403	0.8
10	Tuesday	0222	0.9	1442	1.1
11	Wednesday	0302	1.3	1526	1.4
12	Thursday	0349	1.7	1620	1.8
13	Friday	0451	2.1	1738	2.1
14	Saturday	0622	2.3	1924	2.1
15	Sunday	0803	2.1	2044	1.7
16	Monday	0911	1.7	2141	1.3
17	Tuesday	1004	1.3	2230	1
18	Wednesday	1050	1	2313	0.7
19	Thursday	1132	0.8	2353	0.7
20	Friday			1211	0.7
21	Saturday	0030	0.7	1246	0.8
22	Sunday	0103	0.8	1317	0.9
23	Monday	0131	1.1	1345	1.2
24	Tuesday	0155	1.3	1410	1.4
25	Wednesday	0216	1.6	1433	1.7
26	Thursday	0236	1.9	1458	2
27	Friday	0305	2.2	1537	2.3
28	Saturday	0353	2.4	1706	2.5
29	Sunday	0544	2.6	1837	2.4
30	Monday	0710	2.4	1949	2.1
31	Tuesday	0819	2.1	2050	1.7

NOVEMBER		Low Tide		Low Tide	
		Time	Height	Time	Height
1	Wednesday	0917	1.7	2143	1.3
2	Thursday	1009	1.3	2233	1
3	Friday	1057	1	2319	0.8
4	Saturday	1142	0.8		
5	Sunday	0004	0.6	1227	0.6
6	Monday	0047	0.6	1309	0.6
7	Tuesday	0129	0.7	1351	0.8
8	Wednesday	0210	0.9	1434	1
9	Thursday	0254	1.3	1521	1.4
10	Friday	0342	1.6	1616	1.7
11	Saturday	0442	2	1727	2
12	Sunday	0600	2.2	1856	2
13	Monday	0732	2.1	2014	1.8
14	Tuesday	0841	1.8	2113	1.5
15	Wednesday	0936	1.5	2202	1.3
16	Thursday	1023	1.2	2246	1.1
17	Friday	1105	1.1	2326	1
18	Saturday	1144	1		
19	Sunday	0002	1	1219	1
20	Monday	0035	1.1	1251	1.1
21	Tuesday	0103	1.2	1319	1.3
22	Wednesday	0128	1.4	1346	1.5
23	Thursday	0152	1.6	1412	1.7
24	Friday	0217	1.8	1441	1.9
25	Saturday	0248	2	1518	2.1
26	Sunday	0331	2.2	1616	2.2
27	Monday	0439	2.4	1743	2.3
28	Tuesday	0615	2.4	1902	2.1
29	Wednesday	0733	2.2	2008	1.8
30	Thursday	0838	1.8	2108	1.5

DECEMBER		Low Tide		Low Tide	
		Time	Height	Time	Height
1	Friday	0936	1.5	2203	1.1
2	Saturday	1030	1.1	2254	0.9
3	Sunday	1120	0.8	2343	0.7
4	Monday			1209	0.7
5	Tuesday	0030	0.6	1257	0.6
6	Wednesday	0117	0.7	1343	0.7
7	Thursday	0202	0.9	1429	0.9
8	Friday	0247	1.1	1516	1.1
9	Saturday	0335	1.4	1607	1.5
10	Sunday	0427	1.8	1704	1.8
11	Monday	0527	2	1811	1.9
12	Tuesday	0640	2.1	1926	2
13	Wednesday	0756	2	2033	1.8
14	Thursday	0859	1.8	2128	1.6
15	Friday	0951	1.6	2215	1.4
16	Saturday	1037	1.4	2257	1.3
17	Sunday	1118	1.3	2335	1.2
18	Monday	1155	1.2		
19	Tuesday	0010	1.2	1229	1.2
20	Wednesday	0041	1.3	1300	1.3
21	Thursday	0110	1.4	1330	1.4
22	Friday	0138	1.5	1400	1.5
23	Saturday	0206	1.6	1431	1.6
24	Sunday	0238	1.7	1506	1.7
25	Monday	0316	1.9	1549	1.9
26	Tuesday	0406	2	1647	2
27	Wednesday	0512	2.2	1803	2
28	Thursday	0636	2.1	1922	1.9
29	Friday	0756	1.9	2032	1.7
30	Saturday	0905	1.6	2135	1.4
31	Sunday	1007	1.3	2233	1.1

A rest at Torbay

Beach at Beer

Kit Transfer

Coast Path walking can be arduous in places but some of the hard work can be eliminated. One of the harder tasks can be having to carry a heavy pack from one B&B to the next. There are, however, potential ways around this.

Luggage Transfers South West

Luggage Transfers Ltd, started in 2008 by two Association members, moves up to 10,000 bags a month for walkers on the Coast Path, and is the only comprehensive service covering the entire Path.

The large volume of deliveries means that they can combine and "daisy chain" transfers which has kept the cost of the service low at an average of £8 for each bag movement. The effect of volume delivery also saves an estimated 200 tons of carbon emissions each season.

For information on their service and to book transfers, go to their web site at www.luggagetransfers.co.uk

Walking Holiday Companies

For those who require a Coast Path walk without carrying rucksacks and have their accommodation fixed in advance there are several businesses that will arrange everything. Also there are some excellent organisations that run walking holidays with guides.

Other Suggestions

You could send items ahead to your accommodation or to a Poste Restante address. Send maps, guides, books etc home once you have finished with them.

Coast Path Safety Advice

Your safety is your responsibility – please look after yourself and other members of your group. Keep to the path and stay away from cliff edges – please follow advisory signs and waymarks. Supervise children and dogs – please look out for your children and pets at all times. Be prepared and well equipped – wear suitable clothing and footwear and be ready for possible changes in the weather.

Stay within your capabilities – some sections of the Coast Path can be strenuous and/or remote. In an emergency dial 999 and ask for the coastguard.

Weather

The South West Coast Path is more exposed to wind than any other long distance trail, so please pay attention to gale forecasts as well as rain. Along some sections, strong winds can be dangerous, especially when rounding exposed headlands and crossing bridges; a high backpack can act like a sail.

Always use sun protection especially on bright cloudy or breezy days when the risk of sunburn seems lower.

Military Ranges

Two lengths of the Coast Path may be affected by the use or otherwise of military ranges. The use of one, at Tregantle in south east Cornwall, only means that a more inland and less pleasant route must be used for a length of some 1.25 miles/2km in Section 35, Portwrinkle-Cremyll (Plymouth Ferry). However, if there is military use of the other, east of Lulworth Cove in Dorset, this means the whole of Section 51 between Lulworth Cove and Kimmeridge Bay will be impossible. Generally the Lulworth ranges are closed to walkers Monday to Friday during school term time and also up to six times a year at weekends. Try to arrange your walk so as not to miss this superb but tough section.

Information details for the ranges are included in the relevant Section descriptions.

Telephones

Mobile phones sometimes will not work in remote places and it's reassuring to see a public telephone box just when you need it. However, many of these remote telephones have recently been converted to only take debit cards. You can use the following cards in these boxes - Switch; Maestro; Delta; Solo; Visa Debit but not Electron. There are still some telephone boxes which will accept BT Phonecards and all boxes will accept BT Chargecards (these are only available to BT landline customers). Mobile phones are always useful to have whilst on the Coast Path. However, do not rely on them as coverage is not always good in the South West. You may also have difficulty in obtaining top-up in some areas.

Banks

There are small Post Offices in most villages. Overseas visitors, we suggest, will find their cashpoint cards very useful. ATM machines are widely available along the Coast Path and can be sourced at www.link.co.uk/atmlocator

Dogs

Beaches

Most district councils and unitary authorities have implemented dog bans on beaches generally from 1st May to 31st October. Our Association and most of the general public regard this as a sensible measure.

There are several sections of the South West Coast Path that cross beaches and are officially marked as such. These beaches are Croyde Bay in Devon, Harlyn Bay, Constantine, Treyarnon, Perranporth and Penberth slipway in Cornwall, and Studland in Dorset. The routing of the Coast Path (with its designation as a National Trail) across these beaches means that they are public rights of way. A public right of way does carry precedence over seasonal regulations banning dogs, and ultimately any walker in the process of walking along, but not stopping on, these sections of the path may be accompanied by a dog under total control.

However we strongly recommend the following:

a) If an alternative route is provided and signposted, that you use it.

b) That residents near to dog ban beaches use other walks and do not use the beach path during the ban period.

c) Total control means that the dog should be on a short (not extendable) lead.

d) That your progress should be as unobtrusive as possible to other beach users. To aid this, close attention should be paid to the actual route marked on the map.

e) Lastly, but most importantly, should the worst happen, any dog mess MUST be removed from the beach.

Along the Coast Path

Many walk the Coast Path with their dogs and all have an enjoyable time and we receive many reports of dogs completing the whole path.

However we do urge caution because the Coast Path is very high along many sections, and it takes only an excited dog to go chasing after a rabbit, to cause much grief if it goes over the edge. If your dog is well-trained and you can trust it, then please enjoy your Coast Path walk with your four-legged friend. If it is not and you cannot, then do take care.

Many sections along the South West Coast Path will have farm livestock grazing. Again, walkers should maintain proper control of their dogs.

Important – Please Note

Information included or available through The Association is given in good faith and is believed to be accurate and correct at the time of going to print – however it cannot be guaranteed not to include inaccuracies or typographical errors.

Advice received via the The Association should not be relied upon for personal decisions and you should take into account the weather and your own capabilities before following the walks set out in this Guide. It is for the individual concerned to weigh up the risks of each of the walks described in this book.

The Association makes no representations about the suitability of walks to any one person and will accept no liability for any loss or damage suffered as a result of relying on this book; it should be used for guidance only.

In no event shall The Association be liable for any personal injury or any loss suffered as a result of using this publication.

Week 1 (Seven days)

Day	Distance		From - to
1	10mi	15km	**Minehead – Porlock Weir** *Take National Rail main line to Taunton; bus Taunton - Minehead; or National Express coach to Minehead*
2	12mi	20km	**Porlock Weir – Lynton**
3	13mi	21km	**Lynton – Combe Martin**
4	13mi	20km	**Combe Martin – Woolacombe**
5	16mi	27km	**Woolacombe – Braunton**
6	12mi	20km	**Braunton – Instow**
7	11mi	18km	**Instow – Westward Ho!**
Total	87mi	141km	*Take bus Westward Ho! - Barnstaple; train Barnstaple - Exeter; National Rail main line from Exeter; or National Express coach from Westward Ho!*

Week 2 (Seven days)

Day	Distance		From - to
1	11mi	18km	**Westward Ho! – Clovelly** *National Rail main line to Exeter; train Exeter - Barnstaple; bus Barnstaple - Westward Ho!; or National Express coach to Westward Ho!*
2	10mi	16km	**Clovelly – Hartland Quay**
3	15mi	25km	**Hartland Quay – Bude**
4	10mi	16km	**Bude – Crackington Haven**
5	11mi	18km	**Crackington Haven – Tintagel**
6	9mi	15km	**Tintagel – Port Isaac**
7	12mi	19km	**Port Isaac - Padstow**
Total	78mi	127km	*Bus to Bodmin Parkway; National Rail main line from Bodmin Parkway*

Week 3 (Six days)

Day	Distance		From - to
1	14mi	22km	Padstow – Porthcothan *National Rail main line to Bodmin Parkway; bus Bodmin Parkway - Padstow*
2	11mi	18km	Porthcothan – Newquay
3	11mi	18km	Newquay – Perranporth
4	12mi	20km	Perranporth – Portreath
5	12mi	20km	Portreath – Hayle
6	6mi	9km	Hayle – St Ives
Total	66mi	107km	*Train St Ives-St Erth; National Rail main line from St Erth; or National Express coach from St Ives.*

Week 4 (Six days)

Day	Distance		From - to
1	14mi	22km	**St Ives – Pendeen Watch** *National Rail main line to St Erth; train St Erth - St Ives; or National Express coach to St Ives*
2	9mi	15km	**Pendeen Watch – Sennen Cove**
3	12mi	19km	**Sennen Cove – Lamorna Cove**
4	9mi	15km	**Lamorna Cove – Marazion**
5	11mi	17km	**Marazion – Porthleven**
6	13mi	22km	**Porthleven – Lizard**
Total	68mi	110km	*Bus Lizard Town - Helston; bus Helston - Redruth; National Rail main line from Redruth*

It is possible to use one accommodation base in summer between St Ives and Marazion as summer bus service 300 travels in a circuit both ways around the Land's End peninsula. See page 15 Local Transport.

www.southwestcoastpath.org.uk

Week 5 (Six days)

Day	Distance		From - to
1	11mi	17km	**Lizard – Coverack** *National Rail main line to Redruth; bus Redruth-Helston; bus Helston - Lizard Town*
2	13mi	21km	**Coverack – Helford**
3	10mi	16km	**Helford – Falmouth**
4	14mi	22km	**Falmouth – Portloe**
5	12mi	20km	**Portloe – Mevagissey**
6	12mi	19km	**Mevagissey – Par**
Total	72mi	115km	*National Rail main line from Par*

Week 6 (Seven days)

Day	Distance		From - to
1	13mi	21km	**Par – Polperro** *National Rail main line to Par*
2	12mi	20km	**Polperro – Portwrinkle**
3	13mi	21km	**Portwrinkle – Plymouth**
4	15mi	24km	**Plymouth – Wembury (ferry crossing)**
5	14mi	22km	**Wembury (ferry crossing) – Bigbury on Sea**
6	14mi	22km	**Bigbury on Sea – Salcombe**
7	13mi	21km	**Salcombe – Torcross**
Total	94mi	151km	*Bus Torcross - Plymouth; National Rail main line or National Express coach from Plymouth*

Week 7 (Six days)

Day	Distance		From - to
1	10mi	16km	**Torcross – Dartmouth** *National rail main line or National Express coach to Plymouth; bus Plymouth - Torcross*
2	11mi	17km	**Dartmouth – Brixham**
3	11mi	17km	**Brixham – Babbacombe**
4	16mi	27km	**Babbacombe – Exmouth**
5	13mi	21km	**Exmouth – Sidmouth**
6	11mi	17km	**Sidmouth – Seaton (Devon)**
Total	72mi	115km	*Bus Seaton - Exeter; National Rail main line or National Express Coach from Exeter*

Week 8 (Seven days)

Day	Distance		From - to
1	14mi	23km	**Seaton (Devon) – Seatown (Dorset)** *National Rail main line or National Express coach to Exeter; bus Exeter - Seaton.*
2	12mi	19km	**Seatown (Dorset) – Abbotsbury**
3	11mi	17km	**Abbotsbury – Ferry Bridge (Wyke Regis)**
4	13mi	21km	**Isle of Portland**
5	14mi	23km	**Ferry Bridge (Wyke Regis) – Lulworth Cove**
6	14mi	23km	**Lulworth Cove – Worth Matravers**
7	14mi	22km	**Worth Matravers – South Haven Point (Poole Harbour)**
Total	92	148km	*Ferry South Haven Point-Sandbanks; bus Sandbanks-Poole or Bournemouth; National Rail main line or National Express coach from Poole or Bournemouth.*

An alternative to the suggested itinerary with direct nationwide public transport access at both ends of each stage is:

Stage 1	Minehead to Barnstaple	68 miles/110 km
Stage 2	Barnstaple to Bude	56 miles/90 km
Stage 3	Bude to St Ives	108 miles/174 km
Stage 4	St Ives to Falmouth	103 miles/165 km
Stage 5	Falmouth to Plymouth	81 miles/131 km
Stage 6	Plymouth to Exmouth	98 miles/158 km
Stage 7	Exmouth to Weymouth	60 miles/97 km
Stage 8	Weymouth to Poole (via Portland)	56 miles/90 km

If you're interested in creating your own itinerary national network train stations are at:

Barnstaple	branch line from Exeter
Newquay	branch line from Par
St Ives	branch line from St Erth
Penzance	
Falmouth	branch line from Truro
Par	
Looe	branch line from Liskeard
Plymouth	
Paignton	
Torquay	
Teignmouth	
Dawlish	
Exmouth	branch line from Exeter
Weymouth	
Poole	

Other stations are accessible in the summer months by private railways; usually steam trains:

Minehead	West Somerset Railway
Kingswear & Paignton	Dartmouth Steam Railway
Swanage	Swanage Railway

Report a Problem

Be our Eyes, Ears as well as Feet on the ground!

If you spot a problem on the Path please let us know. Council and National Trust Rangers and Wardens work really hard to keep the Path well looked after and it really helps to have problems reported promptly. So if you find a broken signpost, or one that's missing, stiles or gates in need of repair or have any real difficulties with the Path surface, please use the Report a Problem form on the website, contact us on 01752 876237 or email us at hello@southwestcoastpath.org.uk and we'll make sure your report gets to the right person.

Standing on a Giant Mushroom south of Hartland

www.southwestcoastpath.org.uk

Follow the Acorn

The South West Coast Path is one of the "family" of National Trails. It is generally well signposted and waymarked, using the National Trail symbol of the acorn. In some parts of the Coast Path waymarking relates to the local environment, for example the use of granite waymarks in parts of West Cornwall and Purbeck stone signs in Dorset. Be sure when walking the route to follow any such directions on the ground rather than relying on literature – things change over time, even including the route of the South West Coast Path, literature can become out-of-date.

Those who set out to walk all or any of this beautiful trail should remember that much of it is a cliff-top Path – in places a very high cliff top. Those who manage the Coast Path want to keep it safe, but walkers should be reminded that it is unwise to leave the Path at any point on the seaward side. Sometimes the edges of cliff tops away from the path can be unstable and unsafe.

Now and again the descriptions suggest an alternative path away from the officially designated route. These alternatives will themselves follow rights of way or, occasionally, "permitted routes" maintained by the landowner for use by the public. They are suggested for a more scenic and enjoyable experience than the formal route.

Once again, the Association stresses that ANYONE USING THE PATH SHOULD NOT WANDER OFF IT, ESPECIALLY ON THE SEAWARD SIDE. TO DO SO WOULD BE PUTTING YOURSELF AND POSSIBLY OTHERS IN DANGER OF SEVERE PERSONAL INJURY, OR EVEN DEATH.

 Always follow the National Trail Waymark.

That said, the South West Coast Path is a wonderful environment enjoyed by millions. Choose a length, long or short, and undertake one of the greatest walking experiences the country has to offer.

The Environment of the South West Coast Path

The South West Coast Path is one of the country's National Trails; it is, indeed, the longest of them at 630 miles/1,105km.

In common with all National Trails, the Coast Path passes through an outstanding environment. In the Coast Path's case, this outstanding environment is recognised by the large number of formal designations throughout its length. These include both international and national designations.

International Designations

i. North Devon Biosphere Reserve

Biosphere Reserves are places with world-class environments designated by UNESCO to promote and demonstrate a balanced relationship between nature and people. They are places where conservation and sustainable development go hand in hand. North Devon is a UNESCO Biosphere Reserve because of its blend of special landscapes and wildlife areas, rich cultural heritage and communities that care about it and want to sustain it into the future. The core area of the Biosphere Reserve is at Braunton Burrows (Section 5 of the Trail Descriptions following), but including the outer areas the Reserve covers the Coast Path between Lynmouth and Marsland Mouth (Sections 3-10).

ii. Cornwall and West Devon Mining Landscape World Heritage Site

World Heritage Sites are designated by UNESCO for their "Outstanding Universal Value". This World Heritage Site is defined by the mining landscape which was formed by the cultural tradition of non-ferrous hard-rock mining. It contributed to developing the Industrial Revolution in Britain and pioneered its transfer overseas. The designation covers ten distinct areas, of which five relate to the Coast Path. These are the St Agnes Mining District (Section 18), the Port of Hayle (Sections 19 and 20), the St Just Mining District (Sections 21 and 22), the Tregonning and Gwinear Mining District with Trewavas (Section 325) and the Luxulyan Valley and Charlestown (Section 32).

iii. Jurassic Coast World Heritage Site

This was England's first World Heritage Site designated for its natural properties. Is it designated as it clearly depicts a geological "walk through time" of 185 million years of Earth's history in 95 miles/152km. Geological history of the Triassic, Jurassic and Cretaceous periods are successively exposed and are accessible over the length of the Site, which stretches between Exmouth and Swanage (Sections 44-52).

National Designations

Most of the South West Coast Path is covered by the national landscape designations of National Park or Area of Outstanding Natural Beauty (AONB). In landscape terms these designations are regarded as equal, representing the country's finest landscapes.

Exmoor National Park
Minehead - Combe Martin (Sections 1-3).

North Devon AONB
Combe Martin - Marsland Mouth, excluding Ilfracombe, the Taw-Torridge Estuary and Westward Ho! (Sections 4-6 and 8-9).

Cornwall AONB
The entire coast of Cornwall, excluding Bude and its environs, Polzeath and Rock, Carnewas - Newquay, Gwithian - St Ives, Newlyn - Marazion, Charlestown - Par and Looe - Rame Head (Sections 10-19 and 21-34).

South Devon AONB
Plymouth - Brixham (Sections 36-41).

East Devon AONB
Exmouth - Lyme Regis, excluding Sidmouth and Beer - Seaton (Sections 44-46).

Dorset AONB
The entire coast of Dorset, excluding Weymouth - Portland (Sections 46-48 and 50-53). The South Dorset Ridgeway (Section 53) also falls within this designation.

The Landscape of the South West Coast Path

The wealth of landscape and environmental designations outlined above gives some idea of the quality of the landscape through which the South West Coast Path passes. However, this hides the fact there is a wide range of landscape types to be experienced. For those not over familiar with the south west, we have divided the Coast Path into eight areas, shown on the map on page 2, and noted on each of the Section descriptions. This will help to pinpoint geographically the various Path Sections, but can also be used to describe the Path's landscapes.

The various areas are identified by using a colour coding system as shown on the map

on page 2 and set out in the Contents page 5. The colour code is used on the corner tabs of the Walk Sections, the title information and the page numbers.

Exmoor

Minehead - Combe Martin (Sections 1-3)

The Exmoor length is characterised by two main landscape types. The first is the meeting of the rolling expanse of high moorland and the sea. The coastline itself is one of high cliffs, some of them among the highest sea cliffs in England, but this height is sometimes disguised by the cliffs' convex shape, usually referred to as "hog's back". Views are often extensive inland, over the undulating moorland, while seaward in good visibility the coast of Wales may be seen across the Bristol Channel. In contrast, substantial lengths of the Exmoor coast comprise deep and steep valleys cutting across the high land. These valleys, locally known as "combes", are typically wooded, often with ancient oak woodland. Often this woodland spreads along the adjacent cliff faces, also convex in shape. Views from the Coast Path here are inevitably less extensive, and sometimes quite limited by the woodland, but the nature of the ancient woodland makes for an environment of considerable ecological interest. The combes and the height of the cliffs in this length result in some notable gradients in places.

North Devon

Combe Martin - Marsland Mouth (Sections 4-10)

Most of the North Devon coast faces north over the Bristol Channel. Much of this length comprises cliffs of moderate height with, in the east, some prominent headlands like Morte Point and Baggy Point which offer fine coastal vistas. In the centre of this length is the large joint estuary of the Taw and Torridge Rivers, flanked by areas of sand dunes and marshland. Adjacent to the estuary and just east of it are extensive sandy beaches, popular with surfers and families. Seascapes typically have the coast of Wales beyond the Bristol Channel as the backdrop in the east of this length. In the centre and west the offshore island of Lundy, at the "mouth" of the Bristol Channel, is the focal point. At the west end of this length is Hartland Point, one of the Coast Path's major headlands (referred to as the Point of Hercules in a Roman geography). It marks an abrupt change in direction from the east-west typical of most of North Devon (and Exmoor) to the north-south length beyond. This north-south length is very dramatic, with high cliffs fronted by jagged fingers of rock stretching into the Atlantic. Deep and steep valleys cut into this coastline, but there are no bays or harbours – an historic attempt to make a harbour at Hartland Quay was foiled by the elements. This is a section of great atmosphere.

North Cornwall

Marsland Mouth - Portreath (Sections 10-18)

This section of coast trends either north-south or north east-south west. As such, it faces the prevailing Atlantic westerlies, making for a sometimes exposed landscape. This is exacerbated by the fact that much of the length comprises high cliffs, often quite sheer, with prominent headlands giving excellent coastal vistas. In places the feet of these cliffs are fronted by extensive sandy beaches, as north of Bude or at Watergate and Perran Beaches, north and south of Newquay. The cliff line is also punctuated by numerous sandy coves. There are also two main breaches in the cliff where river estuaries reach the sea, the Camel at Padstow and the Gannel at Newquay. These estuaries are also flanked by extensive sandy beaches. The uncompromising nature of the cliffs means there are few ports or harbours. Padstow, sheltered within the Camel estuary, is an ancient port and Newquay has a medieval origin, sheltered behind the promontory of Towan Head. Newquay has now, of course, expanded into a major holiday centre. Smaller 19th century harbours at the north-east end at Bude, originally largely based on its canal, and at the south-west end at Portreath, originally based on exporting mineral ores, have also expanded into tourism centres. These are very much exceptional settlements on this coast.

West Cornwall

Portreath - Falmouth (Sections 18-29)

Most of this part of the coast is occupied by the two great peninsulas of Penwith, the westernmost part of England, and the Lizard, the southernmost. Both are composed of hard, resistant rocks making for a rugged cliff coastline, but their characters differ. Penwith is largely granite and inland of its impressive cliffs, frequently marked by rock pinnacles and solid jointed slabs, is a rough semi-moorland landscape. The Lizard has a much smoother profile, with its inland landscape an unusual flat-topped plateau. The exposed locations of these two peninsulas result in harsh, weather-beaten coastlines with a lack of large-scale tree cover, though both are magnificently dramatic. Only on the eastern, lee side of the Lizard does the coastline become a little more lush. Flanking these two peninsulas are lower, more sheltered lengths – St Ives Bay on the north-east side of Penwith, Mount's Bay between Penwith and the Lizard and the Helford and Fal estuaries east of the Lizard. It is in these sheltered areas the only ports and harbours of any size are found, principally Penzance and Falmouth.

South Cornwall

Falmouth - The Tamar (Sections 29-35)

The South Cornwall stretch of coast is relatively sheltered being either south-east or south-facing and being largely in the lee of the large peninsula of the Lizard. Cliffs of moderate height are found along most of the length, and there are numerous intimate little bays and some quite prominent headlands. In the eastern half of the length the coast is cut by wooded river valleys, at Fowey, Looe and Seaton. In the centre is the major feature of St Austell Bay, the only part that lacks the otherwise ubiquitous cliffs. This bay also has the only major length of coastal development in South Cornwall, based on the town of St Austell and its extensions. Elsewhere, small ancient fishing ports such as Mevagissey, Fowey and Looe are scattered along the coast, all of them very picturesque. Major estuaries, of the Fal and Tamar, mark the two ends, each of them of great historic maritime importance.

South Devon

Plymouth - Lyme Regis (Sections 35-46)

This section of coast may be conveniently subdivided into three landscape types. In the west, between the Rivers Tamar and Dart, is an area of largely slate cliffs, sometimes quite rugged, these being cut by the drowned mouths of wooded river valleys. This area is usually referred to as the South Hams and extends south to the major headland of Prawle Point, west of this headland being relatively exposed and the east of it much more sheltered. To the east, between the Dart and the Exe, is an area of low, mostly red sandstone cliffs. This length, the "Riviera", is largely occupied by towns based on tourism such as Paignton, Torquay, Teignmouth and Dawlish, and being east-facing is mainly sheltered. Much of this length presents an almost continuously developed coastline. Further east still, between the Exe and the Dorset border at Lyme Regis, the cliffs rise again. This section, East Devon, has a slightly different character to the rest of the south coast of Devon. The red sandstone cliffs continue across the Exe for a while. Then, halfway along the East Devon coast, chalk and greensand make for a change in the landscape, to a mixture of white cliffs and extensive undercliffs and landslips. South Devon has many holiday resorts, some of the earliest in the country such as Exmouth and Teignmouth, some famed for their elegance such as Torquay, and some based on historic towns and villages such as Dartmouth and Beer. The biggest urban area of all on the South West Coast Path is Plymouth. Its historic importance is, of course, largely based on the Royal Navy.

Dorset

Lyme Regis - South Haven Point (Poole Harbour) (Sections 46-52)
South Dorset Ridgeway (Section 53)

Geology is both the curse and the boon of the Dorset part of the South West Coast Path. As a curse, the geology means the Dorset cliffs are vulnerable to slippage, especially at the western end. This has meant that several diversions, necessary but hardly ideal, have had to be put in place for the Coast Path. The Marine and Coastal Act of 2010 will help address some of these issues, as once implemented on a stretch of coast it will enable the authorities to quickly reinstate the Coast Path in most locations following cliff falls. Implementation is well underway in West Dorset, and in July 2105, Natural England published its detailed proposals for the stretch from Lyme Regis to Portland. Their proposals include route improvements from Lyme Regis through Charmouth to Stonebarrow, and from Abbotsbury eastwards towards the Fleet. Consultations on these have been completed and the next stage is for the Secretary of State to decide whether to approve or amend the proposals, and it is hoped that work will start on the new paths in the latter part of 2016. However, as a boon, Dorset's exposed and accessible layers of geological history have made it a textbook example for a wide range of coastal features. These features are also landscape highlights – the great shingle bar of Chesil Beach backed by the semi-freshwater lagoon of the Fleet; the fortress-like monolith of the Isle of Portland, jutting into the English Channel; the textbook arch of Durdle Door; the erosion of soft rock once the harder limestone has been broken through forming hollowed-out bays, as at Lulworth Cove; the offshore Purbeck stone stacks at Handfast Point. Inland, the rolling green hills evoke the spirit and landscape of Thomas Hardy, a worthy addition to the range of South West Coast Path landscapes.

Key to Walk Descriptions

Based on the Suggested Itinerary on page 31, the South West Coast Path has been divided into 52 Sections. Each Section represents a day's or half-day's walk of the Itinerary. However, it must be emphasised that these Sections should not be confined to use by those walking long stretches of the Coast Path. Each Section is designed to be used on its own as a one-off if so wished, as well as by those planning long walks of several days. The Sections are arranged in anti-clockwise order, from Minehead to Poole, with an additional Section 53 for the alternative inland South Dorset Ridgeway.

Each Section entry follows in the following format:

Distance – length of the Section in miles and kilometres;

Cumulative distance – total length of the Coast Path from Minehead to the end of the Section in miles and kilometres;

Ascent – height climbed during the Section in feet and metres;

Cumulative ascent – total height climbed on the Coast Path from Minehead to the end of the Section in feet and metres;

Grading – each Section is graded as Easy, Moderate, Strenuous or Severe. Inevitably, such grading is subjective to an extent, and not all of any Section will be identical throughout, but the grading will give an idea of the effort required;

Timing – this is an estimated fair average for completing the Section. Times will vary depending on weather, number in party, gear carried, number of refreshment or photograph stops. The estimate should be an aide in planning;

OS Maps – the reference numbers of the OS Maps needed to walk the Section are given. Both Landranger (1:50,000) and Explorer (1:25,000) maps are given;

Area – for those not geographically acquainted with the South West, the Coast Path has been sub-divided into eight areas for ease of identification of each Section's location; see map on page 2 and area descriptions on pages 35-37;

Walking Guides – the Association has published a series of Walking Guide booklets which give detailed walking directions as well as pointing out items of interest along the route; see page 10. The relevant Walking Guide booklet title for the Section is given.

There is then an overview of each Section. This covers the landscape, its general character and some of its highlights.

Next, there is a short description of how the Section can be undertaken as a day or part-day walk with public transport or a local circular walk. For more details about local public transport see pages 15-20.

Finally, the main body of the Section description contains simplified instructions for walking in a Minehead – Poole direction, generally only highlighting those locations where it is possible to go astray.

At the end of each section are places to Sleep, places to Eat & Drink and things to Do in that area. Please support these businesses as they are all members and supporters of the Path, you can identify them by looking for the blue South West Coast Path Association window sticker.

Remember, as a National Trail, the South West Coast Path is usually well signed and waymarked throughout its length, using the National Trail acorn symbol. Bear in mind that things change over the years, including the actual route of the Coast Path, so using out-of-date literature can be misleading. If in doubt, follow the signs and waymarks on the ground.

The various areas are identified by using a colour coding system as shown on the map on page 2 and set out in the Contents page 5. The colour code is used on the corner tabs of the Walk Sections, the title information and the page numbers.

Week 1 - Day 1

OS Maps: Landranger 181; Explorer OL9

	This Walk	Cumulative	This Walk	Cumulative	Grading	Timing
Ascent	1,824ft	1,824ft	556m	556m	Official: Moderate Alternative: Strenuous	4.5 hours
Distance	9.5mi	9.5mi	15.3km	15.3km		

For detailed directions see our Minehead to Porlock Weir Path description booklet.

This is a classic example of where moorland meets the sea. Inland, the high expanse of Exmoor rolls away, broken by deep wooded valleys; where it meets the Bristol Channel there are high, convex cliffs, cut by deep and narrow "coombes". This is a lonely, remote length, away from main roads and settlements, with often the only evidence of modern life being development far away on the opposite shore of the Bristol Channel on the South Wales coast. At the western end is the contrasting landscape of Porlock Vale, a flat-floored area of farmland and marshland behind its shingle ridge, quite different in character from the rest of this Section.

Directions

There is no bus service between Porlock Weir and Lynton since the company running it ceased trading in 2014.

The South West Coast Path starts from the celebratory marker on the sea front, approximately 100 yards/91m beyond the Quay Inn. The current route, which may not be shown on older maps, proceeds along the sea front, past the quay. Just before Greenaleigh Farm it turns left on ascending zigzags to North Hill.

At the summit of North Hill follow the acorn sign towards Selworthy and Bossington. At the next Coast Path sign there is a fork, the route to the right being marked "Rugged Cliff Top Path", and either option can be taken. Do not be put off by the description of the seaward path as "rugged" – it is a splendid alternative and not difficult, and gives much better sea views than the inland "official" path. It is well waymarked, and dogs are permitted but must be under very close control. There is likely to be cattle grazing.

On the "rugged" path, at the stile, take the left fork towards a bench, then continue downhill to take the lower path by a "Rugged Path" signpost. From Grexy Combe (GR 937 481) take the well-defined diagonal path up the hill to a wall, which is then followed first towards the sea then parallel to it to Western Brockholes. Here it turns inland to re-join the inland "official" path behind Hurlstone Point. (This seaward path will add about an hour to the estimated time.)

The inland route, meanwhile, follows good tracks parallel to the sea. Joining the "rugged" path on Bossington Hill, the now-combined route descends Hurlstone Combe. There is an optional diversion out to Hurlstone Point which gives a superb view. From Hurlstone, take care not to follow the obvious path to the left which contours round Bossington Hill.

Porlock Bay

The Path descends and goes inland to Bossington village and then just past the car park out towards the sea again. The route now crosses the marsh to Porlock Weir, easy to follow the whole way. At high spring tides it can become impassable, and signs to Porlock village should be followed. (For tidal information contact Minehead TIC - see page 155.) If the diversion via Porlock village is taken, leave the village on the Toll Road then bear right on a footpath that goes behind West Porlock to Porlock Weir.

Week 1 - Day 2

OS Maps: Landranger 181 (eastern half); Landranger 180 (western half); Explorer OL9

	This Walk	Cumulative	This Walk	Cumulative	Grading	Timing
Ascent	3,156ft	4,980ft	962m	1,518m	Moderate, strenuous in parts	5.5 hours
Distance	12.3mi	21.8mi	19.8km	35.1km		

For detailed directions see our Porlock Weir to Lynmouth Path Description booklet.

This is a Section of two halves. In the east, approximately between Porlock Weir and the Devon/Somerset border, Exmoor meets the sea at a run of high, convex but well-wooded cliffs. The Coast Path here is a woodland walk with frequent glimpses of the sea, quiet and remote in character. To the west the cliffs become more open and steeper and the area around The Foreland and Countisbury is a spectacular viewpoint with panoramas over the double-decker towns of Lynton and Lynmouth.

Directions

The bus service which linked Porlock Weir and Lynton ended in September 2014 after the bus company which operated it ceased trading. At the time of writing, it is not yet known if another company will fill this gap in bus provision. For up to date details, it is recommended you visit www.travelinesw.com, or telephone 0871 200 2233.

The official route is signposted left of the Anchor Hotel at Porlock Weir but it is possible to go in front of the hotel, past the shops then left signposted to Culbone.

Reaching Culbone turn right to visit the charming tiny church, which is recommended. From the church retrace steps and turn right uphill on the Coast Path. After about 300 yards/275m bear right into Culbone, Embelle and Yenworthy Woods. This route may not be shown on some older maps. Unfortunately, recent land slippages towards the end of Yenworthy Wood have forced an inland diversion via Yenworthy Combe.

Continue to Sister's Fountain, where the access path to the bus route at County Gate on the A39 leaves the Coast Path. Go uphill through a pair of wild boar head gateposts, then take care not to miss the narrow signposted path 300 yards/275m past the cottage as the drive bears left. An alternative waymarked route may be taken between Culbone and Yenworthy Wood. Although slightly more inland, it offers better views than the mainly woodland more coastal route.

At Coddow Combe, the route is signposted left off the lighthouse track "Countisbury 1.5 miles". From Countisbury the now spectacular path continues down the seaward side of the A39 road. Lower down it joins the road for a short way before descending on zigzags to the foreshore. Walk into Lynmouth, crossing the footbridge, then turn right to the sea front. Lynton is vertically above Lynmouth and is reached by turning left up the steps before the cliff railway (which can be taken as an interesting alternative). A new route is also available past the Esplanade car park at the end of the sea front, where a pleasant path, signposted to Lynton, goes left up the steep wooded hillside to emerge on the Coast Path west of Lynton. Both Lynmouth and Lynton have all facilities.

It is interesting to know that from Lynmouth it is possible to walk Devon's Coast to Coast route using the Two Moors Way and its southern extension to the south coast at Wembury. Guide books are available from Lynton TIC.

www.southwestcoastpath.org.uk

Week 1 - Day 3

OS Maps: Landranger 180; Explorer OL9

	This Walk	Cumulative	This Walk	Cumulative	Grading	Timing
Ascent	3,766ft	8,746ft	1,148m	2,666m	Strenuous	7 hours
Distance	13.3mi	35.1mi	21.4km	56.5km		

For detailed directions, see our Lynmouth to Ilfracombe Path Description booklet.

This generally quiet and remote Section passes through a series of spectacular coastal landscapes: the Valley of Rocks with its rocky crags and pinnacles; the steep wooded cliffs at Woody Bay; the breathtaking scenery of the deep and steep crevice carved through the cliffs at Heddon's Mouth; the wide open spaces of Holdstone Down; and the heights of the Great Hangman, the highest point on the entire Coast Path and one of the highest coastal locations in the country.

Directions

Lynton and Combe Martin are connected by a summer bus service (year-round at weekends). Heddon's Mouth (6.5 miles/10.5km from Lynton) makes a good break in this length (though not on the bus route). It has refreshment facilities at Hunter's Inn and as there is a parallel higher path between here and Woody Bay there is scope for a scenic circular walk.

The Coast Path out of Lynton is on North Walk, and this path leads to Castle Rock in the Valley of Rocks. The next section follows a minor but sometimes busy road, but a diversion to the right from the turning circle at the end of the Valley avoids its first length. Continue past the Toll House and up the hill. A permissive path on the right to Crock Point then avoids another length, and also gives stunning views.

The Coast Path leaves the road just before the Woody Bay Hotel opposite the Red House. Arriving at another road turn left uphill. Follow the next Coast Path sign ahead. When this superb stretch reaches the dramatic Heddon's Mouth valley follow it down to the valley floor. On reaching the stone bridge over the Heddon River turn right, over the river, and at the next path turn hard left. Continue for 100 yards/91m to the signpost on the right to Combe Martin. (Inland on either side of the river the path leads to the pub and shop at Hunter's Inn.)

Climb steeply away from the valley floor, keeping right at the top where the path levels off. Continue round the headland (take care in windy conditions) then the path heads inland to reach a stone wall; this is followed parallel to the sea. The wall ends and the signed path continues across the heathland of Holdstone Down. At Sherrycombe the route follows the grass track along the top of the combe to the inland end and then down. Ascending Great Hangman from Sherrycombe bear away from the wall on the left and ignore the many paths going to the right, meeting the wall higher up. From Great Hangman the path is obvious to Little Hangman and beyond to Combe Martin.

Woody Bay looking towards Lynton

Week 1 - Day 4 (half day)

OS Maps: Landranger 180; Explorer 139 or OL9

	This Walk	Cumulative	This Walk	Cumulative	Grading	Timing
Ascent	1,280ft	10,026ft	390m	3,056m	Moderate, strenuous in parts	2.5 hours
Distance	5.3mi	40.4mi	8.6km	65.1km		

For detailed directions see our Lynmouth to Ilfracombe Path description booklet.

This is a Section of rocky inlets, one of which, Watermouth, is spacious enough for boats to be moored. These bays are divided by rugged headlands. The cliffs here are grey and slatey, making for a forbidding looking coastline, notwithstanding the little bays. At the western end the site of a prehistoric hill fort gives a panoramic view over Ilfracombe. This Section is never far from the A399 coast road and various tourist facilities, so despite the impressive cliffs it is not a lonely length.

Near Combe Martin

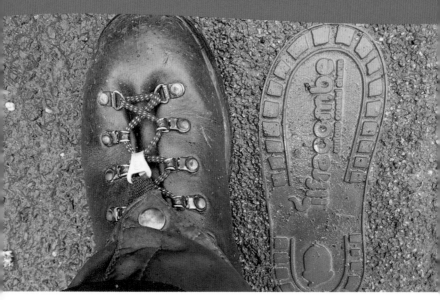

SWCP Marker

Directions

Combe Martin and Ilfracombe are linked by a regular bus service, allowing a bus-walk to be easily undertaken on this Section.

The Coast Path leaves the Lime Kiln car park in Combe Martin, passing the TIC, then forks right to join the A399 road. Turn right (Seaside Hill Road) above the beach. Turn right onto a narrow tarmac lane which climbs steeply to re-join the A399 road. Walk on the slightly raised path along the roadside through two gates. Go along a path beside a field to a flight of steps, then turn left up the slip road back to the main road and on to the brow, passing the bus shelter. Turn right to follow the road down to the old main road, with a bus shelter, now used as an Information Point, over to the right. Here turn left beside the entrance to the Sandy Cove Hotel to follow a track towards Watermouth Cove.

At Watermouth it is possible to cross the foreshore for some 110 yards/100m to a flight of steps at most states of the tide; take care, as the rocks can be slippery. However, if the tide is high, use the route running parallel to the main road. (Check the Watermouth tide timings by contacting Ilfracombe or Combe Martin TICs - see page 155.)

This roadside path is a great improvement as it avoids the need to walk in the road carriageway. It was completed in late 2013 following the Association's offer of £50,000 from our reserves towards its cost, because of our safety concerns. The offer enabled the remainder of the funding to be secured from the Rural Development Fund for England and Devon County Council, a successful conclusion to a decade of pressure.

The next pleasant section of path passes the western side of Watermouth Cove and on around Widmouth Head and then Rillage Point. There is then a roadside section into Hele. Turn right here then climb some steps on the far left of the beach. The path zigzags up past Beacon Point to the top of Hillsborough. Follow the waymarks down the hill to Ilfracombe Harbour.

Week 1 - Day 4 (half day)

OS Maps: Landranger 180; Explorer 139

	This Walk	Cumulative	This Walk	Cumulative	Grading	Timing
Ascent	2,037ft	12,063ft	621m	3,677m	Easy to moderate; strenuous west of Lee Bay	3.5 hours
Distance	7.3mi	47.7mi	11.7km	76.8km		

For detailed directions see our Ilfracombe to Croyde Bay Path Description booklet.

Most of this Section is characterised by grass-topped cliffs fronting numerous small coves and a foreshore of rock ledges. Half-way along is the focal point of Bull Point lighthouse. At Morte Point the character of the coastline changes abruptly as the enormous beach of Woolacombe Sands in its vast bay comes into view, often dotted with surfers. The dark jagged rocks of Morte Point give this headland a superb brooding atmosphere.

Directions

Ilfracombe and Woolacombe are linked by a regular bus service, allowing a bus-walk to be easily undertaken on this Section.

From Ilfracombe Harbour pass the Sandpiper Inn into Capstone Road. After some 170 yards/150m turn right to pass around Capstone Point. At the far end take a flight of steps that goes up behind the back of the Landmark Theatre. Follow this path to the top of the gardens and through a gate by a shelter. Bear right along Granville Road then right again onto an unmetalled road which leads to the Torrs Walk on the right; the Torrs Walk is well waymarked.

At the top of the Torrs Walk bear right and follow the path down the field to the stile in the corner. Continue ahead around the hill to another stile then cross the field to meet the old coach road ahead. Bear right on this track, which later becomes a minor road into Lee Bay. Refreshments are available year-round at the Grampus Inn in Lee village, a short way inland.

The next length from Lee Bay is quite strenuous. Proceed up the road from Lee, turning right at the top of the hill through a brick-pillared gate. Two steep valleys are crossed before Bull Point and its lighthouse are reached. The path continues on and out around Morte Point, a spectacular jagged slate ridge like a dinosaur's back emerging from the sea. The path leaves Morte Point and continues beneath the cliffs past small sandy bays to arrive at Woolacombe.

On the SWCP from Lee Bay to Woolacombe

Week 1 - Day 5 (half day)

OS Maps: Landranger 180; Explorer 139

	This Walk	Cumulative	This Walk	Cumulative	Grading	Timing
Ascent	725ft	12,788ft	221m	3,898m	Moderate	3 hours
Distance	6.3mi	54.0mi	10.2km	87.0km		

For detailed directions see our Ilfracombe to Croyde Bay Path Description booklet.

The main feature of this Section is the vast sandy beach of Woolacombe Sands, backed by a substantial line of dunes. Busy with families and surfers close to the town, it becomes surprisingly empty away from the facilities. Beyond the beach is the superb headland of Baggy Point, a contrast to the beach with its steep cliffs and broad, grassy top. Rounding the headland another, smaller sandy bay comes into view, Croyde Bay, with the wider vista of Bideford Bay beyond.

Directions

Croyde Bay is an excellent centre for a circular walk using the Coast Path, around Baggy Point to Putsborough, giving views over Woolacombe Sands while experiencing the superb character of the headland.

At Woolacombe the Coast Path leaves the Watersmeet Hotel parallel to the Esplanade road, then turns up Challacombe Road. It leaves this road on the right at approximately the National Trust sign – there may be no waymark here. The path continues through the enormous dunes of Woolacombe Warren – the waymarking means that going astray is unlikely. An alternative is to follow Marine Drive and the track beyond, which gives better views. If the tide is low many walk the length of Woolacombe Sands but this should not be attempted on a high or rising tide.

The official path leaves the Warren by a set of steep steps, joining the extension to Marine Drive and the alternative route. It continues along the track then a road, leaving it to the right after the caravan site. As an alternative, take the earlier path on the right to the car park at Putsborough, where there are seasonal refreshments and toilets (the beach route joins here). Go left of the caravan site to a stile and up the cliff slope to re-join the official path.

The excellent high level path continues to the end of Baggy Point, giving superb views. At the end of the headland, bear right to join the lower path towards Croyde. Follow the road, partly on a parallel path. Do not leave the road at the first slipway. The official path leaves the road a little further on to cross the beach, but many will continue on to visit Croyde and its facilities.

Week 1 - Day 5 (half day)

OS Maps: Landranger 181 (eastern half); Landranger 180 (western half); Explorer OL9

	This Walk	Cumulative	This Walk	Cumulative	Grading	Timing
Ascent	506ft	13,294ft	154m	4,052m	Easy	3.25 hours
Distance	8.8mi	62.8mi	14.0km	101.0km		

For detailed description see our Croyde Bay to Barnstaple Path Description booklet.

The length immediately adjacent to Croyde Bay follows a low cliff and gives stunning views over the truly enormous length of Saunton Sands with the dune complex of Braunton Burrows behind. Beyond is the sweep of Bideford Bay, with the possibility of seeing as far as Hartland Point lighthouse, many miles away. Offshore on the horizon is the isle of Lundy. The remainder of this Section is low and level, through a huge range of dunes (the official route) or along the seemingly endless Saunton Sands. Then comes the twin estuary of the Rivers Taw and Torridge, with mudbanks and reclaimed marshes making for a birdwatcher's delight. This is a length displaying a relatively rare aspect of the South West coast.

Directions

Croyde Bay and Braunton are linked by a regular year-round bus service, making this a good bus-walk possibility.

The Coast Path leaves Croyde Bay via the beach (no dogs May-September) and on to the low cliffs at Down End. Turn left at the old coastguard lookout to the B3231 road. Cross the road with care here, turn left then climb some stone steps. The path now contours round Saunton Down, parallel to and above the road. This ends opposite the large white building of the Saunton Sands Hotel.

From here there are optional routes. The first option is to cross the road and pass around the hotel to the Saunton Sands car park, where there are toilets and seasonal refreshments. Leave the car park by the entrance road and after 55 yards/50m bear right along a stony lane to the B3231. Continue carefully along the road for some 400 yards/365m, past the Golf Club driveway, turning right at a red brick partially rendered house.

If there is no need for the toilets or refreshments, a better option is to turn left uphill opposite the hotel, away from the road. Follow the path as it bears round to the right until it arrives at the B3231 opposite the red brick house described above. Cross the road to continue on the same route as above.

This route now enters the Braunton Burrows nature reserve, designated a UNESCO Biosphere Reserve for its nature conservation importance. The route through the Burrows is well waymarked; first follow a clear track through patchy woodland along the edge of the golf course with the military training area on the right. After the Sandy Lane car park follow the signing for nearly two miles along a rough, traffic-free, military dirt road known as the American Road to arrive at Broad Sands car park by the estuary of the Taw and Torridge rivers. Follow another dirt road, approximately eastwards, to arrive at the White House, a well-known local landmark.

Many walkers prefer to miss the Burrows and walk from Saunton Sands car park the length of the beach, for some 3.5 miles/5.5km. Near the end of the beach, just after a wooden groyne, look out for a slatted wooden catwalk entering the dunes to the left. Follow this to arrive at the Broad Sands car park. This beach route keeps the sea in sight, not the case with the Burrows route.

From the White House follow the estuary side on top of the Great Sea Bank. This is followed, between estuary and reclaimed marshes, to the old quay at Velator on the edge of Braunton. To visit Braunton and its facilities, turn left at Velator along the footpath and cycleway, following the former railway track.

Local taxi firm, Saunton Taxis, are happy to do bag transfer as well as walkers. They have a 6 seater taxi and their web site is at www.sauntontaxis.co.uk

Saunton Sands and Braunton Burrows

Week 1 - Day 6 (half day)

OS Maps: **Landranger 180; Explorer 139**

	This Walk	Cumulative	This Walk	Cumulative	Grading	Timing
Ascent	16ft	13,310ft	5m	4,057m	Easy	2 hours
Distance	5.6mi	68.4mi	9.1km	110.1km		

For detailed directions, see our Croyde Bay to Barnstaple Path Description booklet.

This is a flat, low-level Section, following the line of the former railway track once used by the Atlantic Coast Express. As well as the Coast Path, it is also used by Devon's Coast to Coast Cycle Route. At the Braunton end, the main item of interest is the Royal Marines air base at Chivenor, next to the path, but further on the path runs alongside the estuary of the River Taw, with its interplay of water and sand and mud banks. This makes for a pleasant environment; in character, however, this length is semi-urban.

Directions

There is a regular and year-round bus service between Braunton and Barnstaple, which can also be accessed at Chivenor and at the Braunton Inn, approximately mid-way along the route, giving various short walks options.

From Braunton's main car park the signed route to Barnstaple leads to the Coast Path at Velator and from here the path follows the former railway past Chivenor Royal Marines base and then alongside the Taw Estuary all the way to Barnstaple.

The new high level bridge across the River Taw is now signed as the Coast Path, and offers a superb view down the river. However, most will prefer to continue on the riverside path into Barnstaple, an attractive town with many facilities for walkers.

Approaching Barnstaple on the former railway (signed as Tarka Trail), the path crosses a bridge over the tributary River Yeo and then passes the old railway station to a riverside embankment. Leave this at steps climbing to Barnstaple's historic Long Bridge. Barnstaple, North Devon's major centre, is a pleasant and interesting historic town well worth exploring, as well as offering a range of facilities, including a branch line railway to the main line at Exeter.

Barnstaple Bridge

Week 1 - Day 6 (half day)

OS Maps: Landranger 180; Explorer 139

	This Walk	Cumulative	This Walk	Cumulative	Grading	Timing
Ascent	36ft	13,346ft	11m	4,068m	Easy	2.5 hours
Distance	7.4mi	75.8mi	11.9km	122.0km		

For detailed directions see our Barnstaple to Westward Ho! Path Description booklet.

This is a flat, low-level Section, much of it following a former railway line on the south side of the Taw Estuary. It passes through a landscape of marshland and pastures, with the tidal expanses and sand banks of the river never far away. This is an area of great value for birdlife. Approaching Instow the estuary opens out as the Taw's sister river, the Torridge, joins and there are wide areas of sand bars and dunes. This Section, despite its proximity to "civilisation" and the use of the former railway as part of the Devon Coast to Coast Cycle Route, is nevertheless one of much interest and character.

Directions

There is a regular and frequent all-year bus service between Barnstaple and Instow, which can also be accessed at Fremington, approximately mid-way along the route. A variety of short walk options is therefore available.

Cross Barnstaple's historic Long Bridge then keep to the right of the large roundabout, following Tarka Trail signing, then cross a mini-roundabout to a path which curves around to a subway under the approach road for the high-level bridge. A link path to the railway station goes off to the left here. In addition, this link path gives access to the Station Master's Cafe, which usefully also carries a range of local walking information. The main path, signed Coast Path and Tarka Trail, then links to the former railway line. The direct Coast Path route across the high-level bridge joins here.

The former railway continues past the delightfully restored Fremington Quay, with its all-year cafe and Information Point. At Yelland look out for the path leaving the railway to the right which takes the Coast Path behind the site of an old power station. After passing inland of the cricket ground the route then crosses an area of dunes to arrive at the estuary-side road through Instow, which has all facilities.

Old Appledore Irsha Street

Week 1 - Day 7

OS Maps: Landranger 180; Explorer 139

	This Walk	Cumulative	This Walk	Cumulative	Grading	Timing
Ascent	528ft	13,871ft	160m	4, 228 m	Easy	4.5 hours
Distance	11.7mi	87.5mi	18.8km	140.8km		

For detailed directions see our Barnstaple to Westward Ho! Path Description booklet.

Much of this Section follows the estuary of the River Torridge, first on its east bank then turning back on its west. The estuary is largely enclosed by green hills, but houses and roads are ever-present and a high-level road bridge over the estuary is a major feature. The Coast Path crosses the river at the charming old port of Bideford. Passing beyond the estuary and through the characterful old fishing town of Appledore, the path crosses the open spaces of Northam Burrows and its surrounding marshlands and then alongside an enormous pebble ridge as it arrives again at the open sea. As an alternative option, missing out Bideford, a ferry service is now operating from April to October between Instow and Appledore, for details see page 18.

Directions

A regular bus service links Instow and Westward Ho! and another connects Instow to Appledore, both via Bideford. These services allow for a range of Coast Path-based walk options.

From Instow go through the old railway station and follow the former railway, passing underneath the high-level bridge, to the restored Bideford station. Leave the station to cross Bideford Long Bridge, then turn right along the bustling quay. Bideford has all facilities. Keep alongside the river past the car park then next to the rugby club to a lane which passes under the high-level bridge. Follow the waymarked tracks to a riverside lane then, after the old tank traps, fork right to a small woodland area.

Descend to a boardwalk then, if the tide is low, continue on the old sea wall. At high tide a well waymarked route circles the marshy area. Follow the waymarked route round Appledore shipyard and at the road turn right into Appledore via Myrtle Street. Continue along the quay and on into the charming old part of the town, along Irsha Street and past the lifeboat station. Here the route follows a path along the edge of low cliffs and across a field to a slipway, where the route joins a road. (A cliff fall may mean the route follows the road from the lifeboat station to here.) Follow the road for approximately 0.3 mile/0.5km to a crossroads and here turn right.

Follow the track ahead alongside the marshes then on the seaward side of the dunes to the pebble ridge. Continue ahead on the landward side of the ridge to Westward Ho! (At most states of the tide it is possible to walk along the beach next to the ridge.)

If you enjoy sleeping, eating or drinking at any business on the Path please suggest they join us as Business Members so that we can share their brilliance!

The businesses listed here are all supporters of the South West Coast Path, they have joined as Business Members and it would be great if you could show your support for them too. Additional Businesses are listed on **www.southwestcoastpath.org.uk** with links to their own sites for more information.

DO	
Lena **Minehead Visitor Centre** The Beach Hotel, The Avenue, Minehead, TA24 5AP	minehead.visitor@hotmail.com www.visitminehead.org 01643 702624

EAT & DRINK	
Rocky Lethaby **Lee Meadow Farm Shop**, Lee Meadow Farm, Lee, Woolacombe, EX34 8FF	sales@glampig.co.uk www.leemeadowfarmshop.co.uk 01271 879825

SLEEP	
Jenny Richards **Ash Farm B&B,** Porlock Hill, Minehead, TA24 8JN	jenniferwren@jenniferwren.plus.com 01643 862414
J Bakker **Beverleigh B&B**, Beacon Road, Minehead, TA24 5SE	beverleighminehead@gmail.com www.beverleigh.co.uk 01643 708450
Antony Brunt **Yarn Market Hotel**, 25 - 31 High Street, Dunster, TA24 6SF	enquiries@yarnmarkethotel.co.uk www.yarnmarkethotel.co.uk 01643 821425
Steve Thompson **Exmoor Country House**, Minehead Road, Porlock, TA24 8EY	info@exmoor-house.co.uk www.exmoor-house.co.uk 01643 863599
Gill Kenyon **Sea View B&B**, High Bank, Porlock, TA24 8NP	seaview.porlock@btconnect.com www.seaviewporlock.co.uk 01643 863456
Nigel & Janet Southwood **Myrtle Cottage**, High Street, Porlock, TA24 8PU	enquiries@myrtleporlock.co.uk www.myrtleporlock.co.uk 01643 862978
Chris & Clare Gladstone **The Cottage B&B**, High Street, Porlock, TA24 8PU	cottageporlock@gmail.com www.cottageporlock.co.uk 01643 862996
Yvonne Fagan **Orchard House Hotel**, 12 Watersmeet Road, Lynmouth, EX35 6ET	yvonne.fagan@tesco.net www.lynmouthhotel.co.uk 01598 753247
Clifford Parker **The Old Sea Captain's House**, Tors Road, Lynmouth, EX35 6ET	thecaptainshouse@btinternet.com www.thecaptainshouseinlynmouth.co.uk 01598 753369
Jeremy Batch **Bonnicott House**, 10 Watersmeet Road, Lynmouth, EX35 6AP	stay@bonnicott.com www.bonnicott.com 01598 753346
Ann Wilford **Gable Lodge**, 35 Lee Road, Lynton, EX35 6BS	gablelodge@btconnect.com www.gablelodgelynton.co.uk 01598 752367
Richard & Caroline Walsh **Fernleigh**, Park Street, Lynton, EX35 6BY	hello@fernleigh.net www.fernleigh.net 01598 753575
Lauren Tongue **Longmead House**, 9 Longmead, Lynton, EX35 6DQ	info@longmeadhouse.co.uk www.longmeadhouse.co.uk 01598 752523
John Tuck **The Denes Guest House**, 15 Longmead, Lynton, EX35 6DQ	enquiries@thedenes.com www.thedenes.com 01598 753573
David Orton **The Hunters Inn**, Heddon Valley, Parracombe, EX31 4PY	info@thehuntersinn.net www.thehuntersinnexmoor.co.uk 01598 763230

Mrs Heather Deville **Martinhoe Cleave Cottages**, Martinhoe, Parracombe, Barnstaple, EX31 4PZ	info@exmoorhideaway.co.uk www.exmoorhideaway.co.uk 01598 763313
Frances Dallyn **Mannacott Farm**, Hunters Inn, Martinhoe, EX31 4QS	francesdallyn@gmail.com 01598 763227
John James **Mellstock House**, Woodlands, Combe Martin, EX34 0AR	enquiries@mellstockhouse.co.uk www.mellstockhouse.co.uk 01271 882592
Linda Leyland **Channel Vista Guest House**, 4 Woodlands, Combe Martin, EX34 0AT	channelvista@btconnect.com www.channelvista.co.uk 01271 883514
Sarah Davey **Fontenay B&B**, Woodlands, Combe Martin, EX34 0AT	sarah@visitfontenay.co.uk www.visitfontenay.co.uk 01271 889368
Rachel & Nick Brown **Blair Lodge**, Moory Meadow, Combe Martin, EX34 0DG	info@blairlodge.co.uk www.blairlodge.co.uk 01271 882294
Katherine Armitage **Cranleigh House B&B**, High Street, Combe Martin, EX34 0EP	cranleighhouse1@btinternet.com www.cranleighhousehealing.co.uk 01271 889325 • 07985928461
Abby Tappenden **Ocean Backpackers**, 29 St James Place, Ilfracombe, EX34 9BJ	info@oceanbackpackers.co.uk www.oceanbackpackers.co.uk 01271 867835
P Connors **The Olive Branch Guest House**, 56 Fore Street, Ilfracombe, EX34 9DJ	enquiries@olivebranchguesthouse.co.uk www.olivebranchguesthouse.co.uk 01271 879005
Trudy Nunney **Lee Meadow Campsite**, Shaftsborough Lane, Lee, Woolacombe, EX34 8FF	info@leemeadowcamping.co.uk www.leemeadowcamping.co.uk 01271 879825
Tim Cole **Lundy House**, Chapel Hill, Mortehoe, Woolacombe, EX34 7DZ	info@lundyhousehotel.co.uk www.lundyhousehotel.co.uk 01271 870372 • 07969723811
Andy Heal **Marine House**, South Street, Woolacombe, EX34 7BB	info@marinehouse.co.uk www.marinehouse.co.uk 01271 870972
Wendy & Martin Lambert **The Rocks Hotel**, Beach Road, Woolacombe, EX34 7BT	woolacomberocks@gmail.com www.therockshotel.co.uk 01271 870361
Gwen Adams **Combas Farm**, Putsborough, Croyde, EX33 1PH	info@combasfarm.co.uk www.combasfarm.co.uk 01271 890398
Jean Watkins **North Cottage**, 14 North Street, Braunton, EX33 1AJ	north_cottage@hotmail.com www.northcottagebraunton.co.uk 01271 812703
Sue Rayner **The Whiteleaf**, Croyde, Braunton, North Devon, EX33 1PN	bookings@thewhiteleaf.co.uk www.thewhiteleaf.co.uk 01271 890266
Sophie Holker **Silver Cottage B&B**, 14 Silver Street, Braunton, EX33 2EN	silvercottage.braunton@gmail.com www.silvercottagebraunton.co.uk 01271 814165 • 0778 9063539
Mrs A Benning **Bennings B&B**, The Firs, Higher Park Road, Braunton, EX33 2LG	alisonbenning@btinternet.com 01271 814358
Mrs J Manning **Herton Guest House**, Lake Hill, Barnstaple, EX31 3HS	janice@janicemanning93.wanadoo.co.uk www.herton-guesthouse.co.uk 01271 323302
Maggie Cumiskey **The Poplars**, Rumsam Road, Barnstaple, EX32 9EW	info@thepoplarsbarnstaple.co.uk www.barnstaplebedandbreakfast.co.uk 01271 378773
Mark & Marcelline Thomson **Culloden House**, Fosketh Hill, Westward Ho! Bideford, EX39 1UL	cullodenhouse@gmail.com www.culloden-house.co.uk 01237 479421

Week 2 - Day 1

OS Maps: Landranger 180 (eastern half) ; Explorer 139 (eastern half); Landranger 190 (western half); Explorer 126 (western half)

	This Walk	Cumulative	This Walk	Cumulative	Grading	Timing
Ascent	2,995ft	16,866ft	913m	5,141m	Strenuous	6 hours
Distance	11.2mi	98.7mi	18.0km	158.8km		

For detailed directions see our Westward Ho! to Clovelly Path Description booklet.

This Section is one of cliffs and woods. The eastern half is an area of undulating cliffs, cut in places by substantial valleys, though in the length closest to Westward Ho!, where the line of an old railway is used, the path is generally level. The western half passes through lengthy wooded stretches, much of it along the old carriage road known as the Hobby Drive. At the western end, Clovelly is probably one of the most picturesque villages in England.

Directions

There is no direct bus route between Westward Ho! and Clovelly. However, there is one between Bideford and Clovelly, as well as a frequent link to Bideford from Westward Ho! Buck's Mills, about two thirds of the way along this length towards Clovelly, is on the Bideford-Clovelly bus route, giving a possible bus-walk at this end.

At Westward Ho! walk along the path above the beach. After passing the last of the holiday chalets, the path follows the track of the long-disused Bideford to Westward Ho! railway. This makes a fine easy scenic walk. Where the railway turns inland, the path continues along the cliffs, rising and falling to cross a short pebble beach before climbing again. At Peppercombe turn inland to cross the stream and then continue through woodland. Note that some old maps may not show the correct route at Worthygate Wood. The path drops to Buck's Mills, a picturesque little spot, then climbs again into more woods. On leaving Barton Wood, keep to the bottom edge of the field until crossing a bridge to the Hobby Drive at the end of a second field. The Hobby Drive section is nearly 3 miles/5km long, and although very pleasant offers sea glimpses rather than sea views. The path arrives at Clovelly at the top of the steep village street. Clovelly is very picturesque and has most facilities, though perhaps limited in range.

Bucks Mills Waterfall

Week 2 - Day 2

OS Maps: Landranger 190; Explorer 126

	This Walk	Cumulative	This Walk	Cumulative	Grading	Timing
Ascent	2,382ft	19,248ft	726m	5,867m	Moderate to strenuous	5 hours
Distance	10.3mi	109.0mi	16.6km	175.4km		

For detailed directions see our Clovelly to Hartland Quay Path Description booklet.

There is a great contrast in this Section between east and west. In the east the landscape is one of parkland, the domesticated and partly ornamental landscape of the grounds of Clovelly Court. After leaving the parkland a run of high cliffs culminates at Hartland Point, one of the great defining headlands of the Coast Path. Here the coast turns from east-west to north-south and its character changes into one of the Coast Path's most breathtaking stretches, with dark brooding cliffs behind jagged fingers of rock stretching into the Atlantic Ocean. Experiencing its magnificent scenery is well worth the effort of crossing the spectacular deep valleys which cut the coast. The Section ends at the pub and hotel at Hartland Quay, which has a wonderful remote atmosphere.

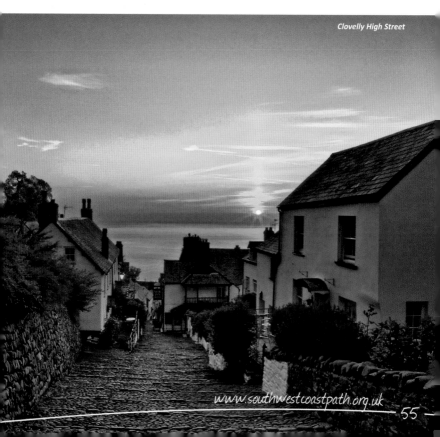

Clovelly High Street

www.southwestcoastpath.org.uk

Directions

Hartland Quay has no public transport. However, there are numerous walking links from the Coast Path to Hartland village, 2.5 miles/4km inland, which is on the bus route to Clovelly.

If using Clovelly as a base, it is requested that walkers use the main car park. If you are only walking the Path and not visiting the village, car parking is £7.50. If you are on your own however, it is cheaper to pay for the village visit which is £6.75. Enquire at the Visitor Centre.

From the main car park walk out of the entrance and turn right down the road for some 220 yards/200m to a black gate on the left. Go through and follow the track first right and through a gap in the wall, then leave the track and follow the marked path down to the right. After a while go through a kissing-gate then follow the fence on the right to another gate into shrubbery. Continue through the shrubbery through more gates. Turn right at a T-junction and right again at the next fork. Soon the path arrives at an unusual seat known as the "Angel's Wings". At the track, turn hard right – not along the track. After passing a superb viewpoint the path descends steeply into a valley to another track. Go right here. The signed detour to the viewpoint is well worth the effort.

The Coast Path goes down the valley to the shore at Mouth Mill. Cross the stream then follow the grass track inland past the lime kiln. At times of storm, high water or heavy rain the stepping stones across the stream do get washed away, making it difficult to cross.   A bridge is planned to help with this problem.

Shortly, turn right and climb the valley side. Half-way up, follow the steps to the right. On reaching the top pass through fields to a stile on the right leading to some descending zigzags. Cross the bridge at the bottom, turn left then take the first right.

After the prehistoric earthwork of Windbury Castle the path continues on the cliff-top to Shipload Bay and then on to Hartland Point, where there are seasonal refreshments. The Coast Path turns sharp left off the lighthouse track towards the coastguard lookout before the lighthouse gate. A short diversion gives a good view of a wreck on the rocks below.

At Hartland Point, there is a café open from April to October and some days in winter too. From Hartland Point the path descends into an unusual valley, almost parallel to the coast, at Smoothlands, before climbing again. Descending then to the valley at the Abbey River the path goes inland to cross at a stone bridge. At the next cliff top, past an old folly tower, the path arrives at a road by the old Rocket House. Bear right to follow the path downhill to Hartland Quay, a lonely outpost with car park, toilets and refreshments, as well as a hotel.

Week 2 - Day 3

OS Maps: Landranger 190; Explorer 126 (most of length); Explorer 111 (Bude)

	This Walk	Cumulative	This Walk	Cumulative	Grading	Timing
Ascent	4,170ft	23,418ft	1,271m	7,138m	Severe	8.5 hours
Distance	15.4mi	124.4mi	24.8km	200.2km		

For detailed directions see our Hartland Quay to Bude Path Description booklet.

This is an awe-inspiring and dramatic coastline. Great jagged ridges of rock stretch out into the Atlantic Ocean, backed by high, surf-fringed cliffs. The coast is punctuated by jutting headlands and tiny, often inaccessible beaches. In the south, towards Bude, the coast softens a little and, at low tide, long sandy beaches appear. This is a spectacular Section.

Directions

Hartland Quay has no public transport connections. There is, however, an infrequent bus service between Bude and Morwenstow, half-way along, which could be used for a bus-walk on the southern half of this Section.

Note that this is probably the most arduous of all the days in the suggested itinerary. It is necessary to cross ten river valleys to complete the length, all of them steep and deep. Because of this, many may prefer to split the length at Morwenstow.

From Hartland Quay a track then a grassy path passes behind St Catherine's Tor. There is a climb then the cliff path reaches the dramatic waterfall at Speke's Mill Mouth. Keep to the eastern side of the stream here for some 150 yards/135m then cross by the wooden footbridge. Follow the signs up the valley inland of Swansford Hill. Take care at Sandhole Cliff, after joining the metalled road, to look out for the signpost after about 0.3 mile/0.5km indicating the turn right back to the coast. (It is hoped this length of road may be eliminated in the near future.) After Welcombe Mouth, Marsland Mouth marks the Cornish border, indicated by a wooden sign. The ascents and descents continue, and a diversion to Morwenstow might be worth considering. The church is picturesque and interesting and there are seasonal refreshments nearby. At the radio dishes do not

miss the sign directing right towards the cliff edge. Descending to Duckpool, cross the stream by a footbridge. There are toilets here. Continue on to Sandy Mouth where there are more toilets and seasonal refreshments. The going now eases at last and after passing over the open cliffs at Maer Down the path arrives at Crooklets Beach at Bude. Follow the path along the low cliffs behind the beaches into the town, which has all facilities.

The 'Summer House' near Mouthmill

Week 2 - Day 4

OS Maps: Landranger 190; Explorer 111

	This Walk	Cumulative	This Walk	Cumulative	Grading	Timing
Ascent	2,494ft	25,912ft	760m	7,898m	Easy then strenuous	4.75 hours
Distance	10.2mi	134.6mi	16.4km	216.6km		

For detailed directions see our Bude to Crackington Haven Path Description booklet.

Low grassy cliffs and surfing beaches south of Bude give way to an ever higher and more rugged coastline fronted by rough rock ledges and cut by deep and steep valleys. There are some superb viewpoints along this later quiet and remote-feeling length which reward the effort. Crackington Haven is a pleasant spot and on the cliffs above, St Gennys Church is a superb spot for contemplation.

Directions

A regular bus service links Bude with Crackington Haven, and also serves Widemouth Bay, about 3 miles/7km from Bude, thus offering a number of bus-walk options.

The path south from Bude starts at the sea lock on the historic Bude Canal, then climbs to the cliff top at Compass Point and on to Efford Beacon. There are excellent views from here. The path over Efford Down to Upton and on to Widemouth Bay is easy to follow. Widemouth has toilets and refreshments, the last before Crackington Haven. (There are further refreshment facilities a little inland at Whalesborough, reached by a scenic footpath from Widemouth.)

South of Widemouth the path follows the low cliff for a short distance then diverts inland slightly at Wanson Mouth to join the coast road in the stream valley. Turn right and follow the road as it climbs steeply to Penhalt Cliff. There are more magnificent views from the cliff-top car park.

From the southern end of the car park the Coast Path crosses a field and descends steeply to Millook Haven. Now follow the steep road uphill for a short distance then turn right onto the cliff top at Raven's Beak. From here the path climbs steadily past the stunted oak woodland at Dizzard Point and on to Chipman Point. Two further deep and steep valleys are crossed, then a ridge walk leads to Castle Point, which gives tremendous views. Another steep valley crossing leads on to Pencannow Point and views over Crackington Haven. The path descends easily into the cove, where there are toilets, refreshments, buses and accommodation.

Bude

Week 2 - Day 5 (half day)

OS Maps: Landranger 190; Explorer 111

	This Walk	Cumulative	This Walk	Cumulative	Grading	Timing
Ascent	2,264ft	28,176ft	690m	8,588m	Strenuous	3.75 hours
Distance	6.8mi	141.4mi	10.9km	227.5km		

For detailed directions see our Crackington Haven to Tintagel Path Description booklet.

This is a Section of high cliffs, the highest, indeed in Cornwall. Not only are they high, but they also present an appearance of bulk, of being literally massive, and the walker will often feel dwarfed by them, especially on a climb or descent or perhaps on a headland. Much of this Section is also quite lonely, and this combination makes this a coast with an imposing character.

Directions

Crackington Haven and Boscastle are linked by a regular bus service, making this an option for a bus-walk.

There are toilets and seasonal shops, cafes and a pub at Crackington Haven. Leave behind the beach near the toilets and head out for the headland of Cambeak. Rounding the headland, keep away from its high and sheer cliff edges. Beyond Cambeak the path is relatively level, passing above the landslip zone at Strangles Beach. Ahead looms High Cliff, the appropriately-named highest cliff in Cornwall. There is a steady ascent but the descent on the south side is very steep. The path then climbs through a landfall at Rusey Cliff, twisting and turning to the top. A cliff top section through fields follows to the sheer black cliff at Buckator. The path then dips slightly before continuing at high level to Fire Beacon Point. Here the descent is steep, but helped by attractive slate steps. The path then follows the cliff face into the inlet of Pentargon, with its impressive waterfall. This is best seen from the southern side – do not be tempted to leave the path for a better view.

Shortly afterwards the path passes refreshment facilities at Boscastle Farm Shop (call 01840 250827 for details).

The now easy path continues on to Boscastle. Aim for the white mast on Penally Hill, then follow the path alongside the beautiful harbour inlet into Boscastle, now happily restored after its 2004 experiences.

Boscastle Harbour

Week 2 - Day 5 (half day)

OS Maps: Landranger 190 (eastern half); Landranger 200 (western half); Explorer 111

	This Walk	Cumulative	This Walk	Cumulative	Grading	Timing
Ascent	1,230ft	29,406ft	375m	8,963m	Moderate	2.25 hours
Distance	4.6mi	146.0mi	7.4km	234.9km		

For detailed directions see our Crackington Haven to Tintagel Path Description booklet.

This fairly short Section is a great local favourite, as it combines all the best of the Coast Path – headlands, sandy bays, historic features and, yes, steep valleys, all in a manageable but picturesque length which is not too taxing. In addition, although popular, it never seems crowded and is, indeed, a "real" walk. With all this and its convenient bus links it is a perfect Coast Path taster.

Directions

Boscastle and Tintagel are linked by a regular bus service. It also serves Rocky Valley, half-way between the two, enabling a variety of bus-walks to be undertaken.

Boscastle has been attractively rebuilt after the floods of 2004, and has all facilities.

The Coast Path leaves the south side of the harbour over the new stone bridge and climbs towards the headland of Willapark, with its prominent white watch tower. The path cuts across the neck of the headland, but a diversion to the end is worthwhile.

After a steep descent and climb at Grower Gut the path continues easily, turning seaward of the Manor House at Trevalga. The headland beyond gives views over the rocky offshore islands important for breeding seabirds. The path continues past Firebeacon Hill – look out for the Ladies Window rock arch in the gully to the right – then passes seaward of a cliff-top caravan and camping site. There is then a des cent into the exquisite Rocky Valley. There is a path up the valley to a bus stop on the coast road, passing prehistoric carvings in the cliff wall.

From the footbridge in the valley the path climbs again, round the edge of the grassy Bossiney Common and above the sandy bay at Bossiney Haven. Another climb then leads to another headland also, confusingly, called Willapark. Again the Coast Path cuts across the neck of the headland and, again, a diversion to the end is worthwhile.

The path now continues to Barras Nose headland, from where it descends to Tintagel Haven below the castle ruins. Here are toilets, cafe and English Heritage gift shop. A good but steep path leads inland to the village.

Tintagel coastline

Week 2 - Day 6

OS Maps: Landranger 200; Explorer 111 (eastern half); Explorer 106 (western half)

	This Walk	Cumulative	This Walk	Cumulative	Grading	Timing
Ascent	2,589ft	31,995ft	789m	9,752m	Severe	4.75 hours
Distance	9.1mi	155.1mi	14.7km	249.6km		

For detailed directions see our Tintagel to Port Isaac Path Description booklet.

Both ends of this Section are relatively popular and accessible. At Tintagel the Coast Path passes the remains of the medieval castle perched on its isolated headland then the atmospherically located cliff-top church and the now picturesque evidence of coastal slate quarrying. At the other end is the beautifully quaint village of Port Isaac in its scenic bay. The long central length, though, comprises high cliffs cut by sometimes precipitously steep valleys. It is remote, lonely and often tough, and will be especially appreciated by those who relish an empty, arduous and dramatic coastline.

Trebarwith Strand

Directions

It is possible to take a bus between Tintagel and Port Isaac although it is usually necessary to change at Camelford. A bus-walk is therefore possible, particularly using Camelford as a base.

Tintagel has all necessary facilities. Surprisingly, however, little in the village is very old other than the Old Post Office, once a local manor house.

From the village walk down the path to Tintagel Haven. From here the Coast Path climbs past the entrance to the Castle and gives excellent views over the headland which forms the castle site. A good path continues seaward of the church and on beyond past the Youth Hostel in its former quarry building and round Penhallic Point with its superb views.

The path drops steeply to Trebarwith Strand, where there are toilets, refreshments and pub, the last facilities before Port Isaac. The next part is particularly tough as it climbs steeply out of the Trebarwith valley then almost immediately drops down to sea level and up again at Backways Cove. There follows a level stretch of about a mile/1.5km to the stream valley behind Tregardock Beach. Descend on the inland side of the detached

piece of cliff known as The Mountain, then climb again to Tregardock Cliff. Another level length follows, before the deepest and steepest valley yet at Jacket's Point. At the top yet another deep valley almost immediately follows. Then comes a further valley, at Barrett's Zawn. This is an area of massive rock falls. The next valley follows, this one with exceptionally steep and stony sides.

At last the path levels out again through cliff-top meadows, with just a small valley to cross at St Illickswell Gug. Eventually, the path reaches the road at Cartway Cove. Take the path on the right and round the headland to Port Gaverne, a charming spot. Follow the road uphill to the car park at the edge of Port Isaac. Go through this and follow the well-signed path above the attractive harbour inlet into the village.

Port Isaac is a very picturesque village clustered round the little harbour at the head of a sheltered bay. It has all facilities.

The path to Port Isaac

Week 2 - Day 7

OS Maps: Landranger 200; Explorer 106

	This Walk	Cumulative	This Walk	Cumulative	Grading	Timing
Ascent	2,923ft	34,918ft	891m	10,643m	Strenuous then easy	5.5 hours
Distance	11.7mi	166.8mi	18.9km	268.5km		

For detailed directions see our Port Isaac to Padstow Path Description booklet.

This Section can be divided into three distinct characters. From Port Isaac to Port Quin is a rollercoaster of a path, closely following the ups and downs and ins and outs of the quiet, scenic but energy-sapping coast. From Port Quin to Polzeath the character becomes rather more open, if still very scenic, including the broad headland of The Rumps and Pentire Point, a wonderful airy lookout. From Polzeath to the Padstow ferry the landscape is tamer, more domesticated, often with housing or tourist development and more estuarine than maritime as it reaches the mouth of the River Camel.

Directions

There is a regular bus service between Port Isaac and Rock, the ferry point for Padstow. This service also passes through Polzeath at the mouth of the Camel estuary, giving several scenic bus-walk options, including an almost level estuary-side one. There is a popular circuit using the Coast Path between Port Isaac and Port Quin and others from Polzeath around Pentire Point.

Port Isaac has all necessary facilities, and is a scenic gem. To leave the village, take the road to the right behind the fish market. Climbing, it bears right and becomes a cliff path, soon dropping into Pine Haven. From here to Port Quin the path is magnificent and clear, but tough as it follows the cliff edge next to a fence line. There is an optional diversion to the end of Varley Head.

The path enters the beautiful Port Quin inlet, descending to what was once a busy pilchard port, though there are no facilities here now. Follow the road westbound up the steep hill and a little way up the Coast Path leaves to the right, towards Doyden Point. The path follows above the cove, keeping seaward of and below the large house. Head to a prominent stone cairn, then continue ahead on a grassy path and past some old mineshafts. From the cairn a diversion to the right goes to the folly of Doyden Castle and to Doyden Point, where there is a superb view back to Port Quin.

Kellan Head, Port Quin

Towards the Rumps

There is a sharp descent to Epphaven Cove then the path passes through a delightful little wooded valley before climbing past the impressive Lundy Hole. The clear cliff path now heads for the Iron Age fortress on The Rumps headland. A detour to the end is well worthwhile.

From The Rumps the path climbs through a little former quarry area then continues at high level round Pentire Point, giving spectacular views. An easy descent follows to Polzeath, all well marked. Polzeath has all necessary facilities, including now an all-year café, "Tubestation", open Wednesday-Saturday during the winter. The path follows the road past the beach car park then goes right by the cottages, where the road bends sharp left on the steep hill. It now follows a low cliff to Daymer Bay, where there are toilets and a seasonal cafe, then down steps to the beach. At the far end of the beach it leaves through dunes and over a footbridge below Brea Hill. It is possible to detour to visit the little St Enodoc Church from here.

To continue on the Coast Path follow the path clinging to the side of Brea Hill, though it is possible to go over the top or, at low tide, along the beach. On the far, south, side of Brea Hill the well-signed path continues through dunes to arrive at Rock car park. A water taxi service operates between Rock and Padstow all year but much less frequently in low season. See page 18 for details.

A water taxi service operates between Rock and Padstow between 19:00 and midnight from Easter to 31st October, weather and tides permitting. For further details see page 18.

Note that it is possible to walk Coast to Coast across Cornwall between Padstow and Fowey on the south coast, using the Saints' Way. A guidebook is available from Padstow TIC.

The businesses listed here are all supporters of the South West Coast Path, they have joined as Business Members and it would be great if you could show your support for them too. Additional Businesses are listed on **www.southwestcoastpath.org.uk** with links to their own sites for more information.

EAT & DRINK

Jill Savage **Rectory Tearooms**, Rectory Farm, Crosstown, Morwenstow, EX23 9SR	jill@rectory-tearooms.co.uk www.rectory-tearooms.co.uk 01288 331251
Andrea Tippett **The Cabin Café**, Crackington Haven, St Gennys, Bude, EX23 0JG	thecabincafe@gmail.com www.cabincafecrackington.co.uk 01288 361098

SLEEP

Toni-Louise Newell **Hartland Holiday Barns**, Higher Huddisford, Woolsery, Bideford, EX39 5QX	info@hartlandholidaybarns.co.uk www.hartlandholidaybarns.co.uk 01237 432118 07814899281 • 027854156007
Susan Curtis **Fuchsia Cottage B&B**, Burscott, Higher Clovelly, Bideford, EX39 5RR	tom@clovelly-holidays.co.uk www.clovelly-holidays.co.uk 01237 431398
Chris & Sylvia West **Pillowery Park**, Burscott, Higher Clovelly, Bideford, EX39 5RR	info@clovellyaccommodation.co.uk www.clovellyaccommodation.com 01237 431668
Greta Sanders **The Old Police House**, Burscott, Higher Clovelly, Bideford, EX39 5RR	enquiries@clovellybandb.co.uk www.clovellybandb.co.uk 01237 431256
Mary McColl **Southdown B&B**, Higher Clovelly, EX39 5SA	maryfmcoll@hotmail.com 01237 431504
Annie Shillito **Cheristow Farm Cottages**, Cheristow, Hartland, Bideford, EX39 6DA	stay@cheristow-cottages.co.uk www.cheristow-cottages.co.uk 01273 441522
Jill George **Gawlish Farm**, Gawlish, near Hartland, EX39 6AT	01237 441320
Merlyn Chesterman **2 Harton Manor,** Hartland, EX39 6BL	merlyn@twohartonmanor.co.uk www.twohartonmanor.co.uk 01237 441670 07789 756789
Zoe Allin **Hartland Caravan Holidays**, South Lane, Hartland, EX39 6DG	info@hartlandcaravanholidays.co.uk www.hartlandcaravanholidays.co.uk 01237 441664
Alex Wilkinson **Little Barton**, Hartland, Bideford, EX39 6DY	enquiries@littlebartonhartland.co.uk www.littlebartonhartland.co.uk 01237 441259
Anna Dart **1 Coastguard Cottages**, Stoke, Hartland, EX39 6DU	annajon@btinternet.com www.coastguardcottagestoke.com 01237 441011
Paul & Claire Summers **Clouds B&B, Stoke**, Hartland, Bideford, EX39 6DU	paul-summers1@hotmail.co.uk www.cloudatstoke.com 01237 440236

Colin & Helen Davey **Stoke Barton Farm Campsite**, Stoke, Hartland, Bideford, EX39 6DU	helen@stokebartonfarm.co.uk www.westcountry-camping.co.uk 01237 441238
Mrs T Goaman **Elmscott Youth Hostel**, Elmscott, Hartland, Bideford, EX39 6ES	john.goa@virgin.net www.elmscott.org.uk 01237 441367 (hostel) • 01237 441276 (owner)
Mrs T Goaman **Elmscott Farm Bed and Breakfast**, Hartland, Elmscott, Hartland, Bideford, EX39 6ES	john.goa@virgin.net www.elmscott.org.uk 01238 441367 (hostel) • 01238 441276 (owner)
Joanne Steadman **Tee Side Guest House**, 2 Burn View, Bude, EX23 8BY	teeside.bude@gmail.com www.tee-side.co.uk 01288 352351
Mohammed & Ann Safdar-Wallace **Sea Jade Guest House**, 15 Burn View, Bude, EX23 8BZ	seajadeguesthouse@yahoo.co.uk www.seajadeguesthouse.co.uk 01288 353404
Elizabeth White **The Grosvenor**, 10 Summerleaze Crescent, Bude, EX23 8HH	enquiries@thegrosvenor-bude.co.uk www.thegrosvenor-bude.co.uk 01288 352062
Paul & Tina Collins **Mordros B&B**, Maer Down Road, Bude, EX23 8NE	paul@collinsbude.plus.com www.mordrosbude.com 01288 356340 • 0780 0780039
Beth Lewitt **Beach House**, Marine Drive, Widemouth, EX23 0AW	enquiries@beachhousewidemouth.co.uk www.beachhousewidemouth.co.uk 01288 361256
Stephen Cullie **Hannah's Cottage**, Hallagather Farm, Crackington Haven, Bude, EX23 0LA	hannahscottage1@gmail.com www.hannahscottage.com 01840 230955
Brigitte Mussell **Trewartha By Chy**, Crackington Haven, EX23 0NN	trewarthabychy@gmail.com 01840 230420
Jon Scott **The Wellington Hotel**, The Harbour, Boscastle, PL35 0AQ	info@wellingtonhotelboscastle.com www.wellingtonhotelboscastle.com 01840 250202
Mrs Tinney **Bossinney Cottage**, Tintagel, PL34 0AY	paulinetinney@btinternet.com 01840 770327
Julie & Keith Walker **Bosayne**, Atlantic Road, Tintagel, PL34 0DE	enquiries@bosayne.co.uk www.bosayne.co.uk 01840 770514
Joan Liddle **Pendrin Guest House**, Pendrin House, Atlantic Road, Tintagel, PL34 0DE	info@pendrintintagel.co.uk www.pendrintintagel.co.uk 01840 770560
Cyril Monk **Lane End Farm**, Pendoggett, Port Isaac, PL30 3HH	nabmonk@tiscali.co.uk www.laneendcornwall.co.uk 01208 880013 • 07724 133820
Sophie Rapson **Cornish Traditional Cottages**, Trewardale, Blisland, Bodmin, PL30 4HS	bookings@corncott.com www.corncott.com 01208 821666

Week 3 - Day 1 (half day)

OS Maps: Landranger 200: Explorer 106

	This Walk	Cumulative	This Walk	Cumulative	Grading	Timing
Ascent	744ft	35,662ft	227m	10,870m	Easy	2.5 hours
Distance	5.7mi	172.5mi	9.1km	277.6km		

For detailed directions see our Padstow to Porthcothan Path Description booklet.

The length from Padstow to Stepper Point, at the mouth of the Camel, is a scenic length of ever-changing estuarine views with sandy stretches, especially at low tide. Beyond, the coast is an easy but picturesque length of cliffs, which include occasional views right across the headland at the mouth of the estuary and up the Camel as well as west to Trevose Head. The two elements of this Section combine to form a popular local walk.

Directions

A regular bus service links Padstow with the inland end of Trevone, about one mile/1.5 km from the Coast Path. This allows for a possible bus-walk. There are also a number of possible circular walks from Padstow using the Coast Path which take in the Stepper Point headland.

Padstow is a charming and bustling little harbour town a short way up the Camel Estuary. If arriving from Rock, notice that normally this arrives in Padstow at the harbour, but at low tide it lands a short distance downstream at St Saviour's Point. In either event, it is well worthwhile taking time to explore the town.

The Coast Path leaves the north end of the harbour past the TIC and proceeds on low cliffs alongside the estuary. After passing a wooded little stream valley at St George's Cove the path heads inland of a marshy area before going back to the cliffs and on to Hawker's Cove. Refreshments (including gluten free cream teas) are available at Hawker's Cove at the "Rest a While" tea garden. The tea garden is normally open 10.30am to 4.30pm Easter until late October, weather permitting. Only outside seating is available and it may be best to telephone 01841 532919 to check opening times. Pass behind the old pilots' houses here then fork right to climb to Stepper Point, with its Daymark tower. From here there are remarkable views, inland to Bodmin Moor as well as along the coast.

The path is now on the exposed Atlantic coast. Go round the precipitous inlet of Butter Hole Cove, looking out for the small Pepper Hole to the right of the path just before. An easy length to Gunver Head follows, with excellent sea views. Approaching Trevone the path skirts the impressive Round Hole collapsed cave – approach this with caution as the sides are sheer. Follow the cliffs round into the bay at Trevone, which has toilets, cafe and pub, as well as a car park.

Between Padstow and Stepper Point

Week 3 - Day 1 (half day)

OS Maps: Landranger 200; Explorer 106

	This Walk	Cumulative	This Walk	Cumulative	Grading	Timing
Ascent	817ft	36,479ft	249m	11,119m	Easy	3.5 hours
Distance	7.9mi	180.4mi	12.7km	290.3km		

For detailed directions see our Padstow to Porthcothan Path description booklet.

This is a popular Section, never far from a variety of holiday accommodation. It is perhaps most associated with a range of scenic sandy surfing beaches, some of them quite extensive. As a contrast, around the middle of the length is the great landmark of Trevose Head and its lighthouse, visible from great swathes of the North Cornwall coast and an atmospheric location.

Directions

A regular bus service passes the inland end of Trevone, about one mile/1.6km from the Coast Path, and links to Porthcothan. The same route serves Constantine Bay, about two-thirds of the way along the coast from Trevone, giving a potential for a variety of bus-walks.

Trevone has all necessary facilities. The path crosses the rear of the beach and leaves behind the little headland on the south-west side of the bay, following the cliff edge round rocky Newtrain Bay. Reaching Harlyn there are refreshments and toilets. Cross the stream on the road bridge then follow the beach below the low cliff for some 330 yards/300m before climbing left onto the cliff and then continuing to the headland at Cataclews Point.

The path passes inland of Padstow's lifeboat station, accessible by a cul-de-sac path, and then goes on to Trevose Head, passing the lighthouse. On a clear day the coastal views are incredibly extensive, ranging from the satellite dishes north of Bude to the granite hills of West Penwith behind St Ives. This is an atmospheric headland.

After an old quarry the path passes a Round Hole collapsed cave and descends to the partly rocky Booby's Bay. Continue on to the rear of Constantine Bay, a very attractive and extensive beach at low tide. Walk the length of the beach. There are toilets and seasonal refreshments at the far end and a bus stop a little way inland. Beyond the dunes the path rounds Treyarnon Head to cross another attractive beach at Treyarnon Bay, with seasonal toilets and refreshments.

An unusually indented coastline follows, with sheer-sided headlands and impressive coves. Near Pepper Cove the ramparts of an Iron Age cliff fort may be seen, and the whole coastline is quite spectacular. The path then turns into another sandy cove, at Porthcothan Bay, which has toilets and refreshments and also has a pub, the Tredrea Inn, about 500 yards/458m inland up the road.

Trevose Head Lighthouse

Week 3 - Day 2

OS Maps: Landranger 200; Explorer 106

	This Walk	Cumulative	This Walk	Cumulative	Grading	Timing
Ascent	1,447ft	37,926ft	441m	11,560m	Moderate	5 hours
Distance	11.1mi	191.5mi	17.9km	308.2km		

For detailed directions see our Porthcothan to Newquay Path Description booklet.

**This is a relatively well-walked Section, particularly around Newquay.
It shows the interplay of high cliffs and sandy beaches particularly well. Almost the whole length is characterised by high, flat-topped cliffs, sometimes with prominent headlands, which for long stretches form the back of extensive attractive sandy beaches, many of them popular with surfers. While never a lonely Section, its cliffs and bays make it one well worth exploring, helped by the relatively easy terrain.**

Directions

Porthcothan and Newquay are linked by a regular bus service. This route follows a road parallel and close to the coast, meaning that there are a number of possible links to the Coast Path from this bus, allowing for quite a range of possible bus-walks.

Porthcothan has all facilities that may be needed. The Coast Path leaves past the shop and keeps in front of the houses and on around the headland. After a short steep descent and climb, an easy level walk leads to Park Head, an excellent viewpoint. There have been numerous landslips here so keep to the path inland of the white posts. The whole headland is worth wandering over and exploring. Ahead now is the National Trust's Carnewas property, with its spectacular beach. The Trust's cafe and Information Centre are open through the summer. On the beach below are the massive stacks forming Bedruthan Steps.

The Bedruthan Steps area can be busy, but the steps to the beach are closed in the winter months. A quieter length follows to Trenance Point and into the sandy bay of Mawgan Porth, where there are toilets, refreshments and a pub as well as a bus stop. Surprisingly, this was once the site of an unfinished canal project.

Cross the stream using the road then leave it to the right on the sharp bend on the hill out of Mawgan Porth. There then follows a long high level length to Watergate Bay on airy flat-topped cliffs, cut by a couple of minor descents. The path passes Iron Age remains here while inland is the contrast of Newquay Airport. The path continues on the cliff top behind the magnificent Watergate Beach, much used for surfing and other activities. The path then descends to the road by the Watergate Bay Hotel, and here there are toilets, refreshments and another bus stop.

Cross the stream using the road then leave it to the right on the sharp bend on the hill out of Mawgan Porth. There then follows a long high level length to Watergate Bay on airy flat-topped cliffs, cut by a couple of minor descents. The path passes Iron Age remains here while inland is the contrast of Newquay Airport. The path continues on the cliff top behind the magnificent Watergate Beach, much used for surfing and other activities. The path then descends to the road by the Watergate Bay Hotel, and here there are toilets, refreshments and another bus stop.

Fistral Beach

Cross the stream at the road then turn right by the car park and climb back to the cliffs, which are now followed to the outskirts of Newquay. The coastal view ahead to the town and its headlands is excellent. The Coast Path leaves the road to pass round the headland of Trevelgue Head, an important prehistoric location. Although the path bypasses the island at the very end, this can be visited via the footbridge, and is worth the diversion for the views. The path returns to the road by Porth Beach before leaving it at steps down on the left, to pass underneath the main road and cross the next little headland to emerge above Lusty Glaze beach – look for the information board here relating to the canal previously encountered at Mawgan Porth.

The path continues into the park at Barrowfields, skirting its seaward side, to reach the main road into Newquay town centre. Follow this just past the railway station then take the old tramway road on the right. Follow the waymarked route along the footpath above Towan Beach.

At the corner go down the steps on the right then from the car park cross Beach Road and follow the tarmac path ahead. At the end follow the steps on the left to pass a bowling green and public toilets to Fore Street. Turn right here as far as the Red Lion and here turn right again to the harbour down North Quay Hill.

As well as all facilities, Newquay has a branch line railway station linking to the main line to Penzance and is the centre of a network of local bus routes.

Week 3 - Day 3 (half day)

OS Maps: Landranger 200; Explorer 104

	This Walk	Cumulative	This Walk	Cumulative	Grading	Timing
Ascent	1,145ft	39,071ft	349m	11,909m	Moderate	3.5 hours
Distance	6.3mi	197.8mi	10.2km	318.4km		

For detailed directions see our Newquay to Perranporth Path Description booklet.

This Section includes some superb viewpoints from headlands in and around Newquay, the panoramas quite unspoiled by the proximity of the large town. Beyond Newquay a range of landscapes is experienced, from wide sandy beaches to exposed cliff tops to small sandy bays to dune systems. In addition, unexpectedly, the wooded estuary valley of the river known as The Gannel is crossed at the edge of Newquay. This variety, and the proximity to a range of facilities and accommodation, make this a popular, well-used length.

Directions

A regular bus service links Newquay with Holywell Bay, and also serves Crantock, between the two. This gives a number of bus-walk possibilities.

Newquay is the biggest town on Cornwall's north coast. Although usually busy, being especially popular with surfers and also with groups of young holidaymakers, it is in a very attractive setting of beaches and headlands. All the facilities are here, and there is a branch railway linking to the main line to Penzance.

From Newquay Harbour the Coast Path climbs past the old Huer's Hut to Towan Head. This is a good lookout spot, and is excellent for seabird watching. From Towan Head the path then follows the back of Fistral Beach. This is probably the country's most popular surfing beach and international competitions are held here. The path climbs to the cliffs at the southern end and then crosses the road to go along Pentire Crescent which leads into Penmere Drive. The path then arrives above the Gannel Estuary. However, this misses the major headland of Pentire Point East, which is well worth the diversion to the end. (If following the diversion round the headland, on returning from the end aim for the far bottom of the car park at the neck of the headland. From here head along the suburban road parallel to the Gannel. Follow this to the Fern Pit Cafe.)

There are four options from here for crossing the Gannel, depending on the tide and time of year.

OPTION 1: FERN PIT FERRY (deduct 2 miles/3km from total mileage)

The first option is to use the Fern Pit Ferry from behind the cafe. The cafe is approximately 0.7 mile/1.1km west of Penmere Drive. The ferry operates continuously, 7 days a week, 10.00-18.00 mid May until mid September weather dependent – telephone 01637 873181. For further details see page 18.

OPTION 2: PENPOL CROSSING (official route)

Go along Penmere Drive then turn right into Trevean Way. Follow the waymarks right and go downhill across a grassy area. At the foot of the grass bank turn right along the footpath then take the steps on the left down to the tidal Penpol Footbridge across the Gannel Estuary. This can be used 3-4 hours either side of low water. Cross the Gannel here. (If coming from the headland circuit, continue past the Fern Pit Cafe and on along Riverside Avenue, then ahead and right. At a junction where there is a footpath to the right keep ahead, ignoring the footpath. Bear right into Penmere Drive, again ignoring another footpath on the right. Go along Penmere Drive and re-join the route detailed in Option 1.)

OPTION 3: TRENANCE FOOTBRIDGE (add 3 miles/4.8km to total mileage)

This route is usable at most states of the tide. From the Newquay side of the Penpol crossing continue upstream on the path parallel to the river until it arrives at the A392 Gannel Road. There is a footbridge on the right just before the junction with the A3058 Trevemper Road. Cross the bridge and continue ahead. Do not follow the creekside path to Penpol but instead take the bridleway on the left towards Trevemper. Turn right just before reaching the tarmac and follow the footpath through Treringey to arrive at the south side of the Penpol tidal footbridge.

OPTION 4: MAIN ROAD ROUTE (add 4.5 miles/7.2km to total mileage)

Continue past the Trenance footbridge and along the A392 Trevemper Road from the roundabout. At the next roundabout turn right and after about 100 yards/90m take the little unsigned lane on the right. This leads to Trevemper, going forward and right as the lane goes left. After the gate turn left on the route described under Option 3 through Treringey.

Options 2, 3 and 4 come together at Penpol. At the ford turn right to follow the lane then take the signed path on the right above the estuary. After passing the ferry landing for Option 1 this path leads to Crantock Beach car park. Crantock village with its facilities and bus stop is a little way inland. Cross the car park to the dunes; bear left at the junction of grassy paths on entering the dune area and follow this inland of the main dune area to re-emerge at a coastal path which leads to the cliffs of Pentire Point West

where the Bowgie Inn and C-Bay Café provide meals and refreshments. The path goes round Porth Joke (known locally as Polly Joke), then on around Kelsey Head to Holywell Bay, descending across more dunes either into the village or to cross the river on a seaward footbridge. There are facilities, some seasonal, here.

Penpol tidal bridge across the Gannel

Week 3 - Day 3 (half day)

OS Maps: Landranger 200; Explorer 104

	This Walk	Cumulative	This Walk	Cumulative	Grading	Timing
Ascent	755ft	39,826ft	230m	12,139m	Moderate	2 hours
Distance	4.5mi	202.3mi	7.3km	325.7km		

For detailed directions see our Newquay to Perranporth Path Description booklet.

The theme of this Section is sand, in the form of both dunes and beaches, although it begins by rounding headlands at Penhale and Ligger Points. However, even at Penhale the inland vista is dominated by dunes, although the adjacent former Army Camp is also prominent. For the bulk of this Section sand is everywhere around, on the seemingly endless length of Perran Beach and the dunes which back it. Both ends, Holywell and Perranporth, are busy holiday settlements but the more remote areas of Perran Beach can be surprisingly quiet.

Directions

Holywell Bay and Perranporth are linked by a regular bus service, making a bus-walk a feasible option here.

Holywell Bay has all facilities, some seasonal. From Holywell Bay the path rounds Penhale Point, skirting the seaward edge of the somewhat unattractive former Penhale army camp. It then goes on out to Ligger Point, where there is a panoramic view of the length of Perran Beach. The path heads towards the dunes then descends behind the cliff quarry to the beach. It now follows the back of the beach for some 1.5 miles/2.5km. This is possible even at high tide, and usually on firm sand. At Cotty's Point the tide often makes it necessary to climb the steps leading to Perran Sands holiday park. At the top of the steps turn right following the slate Coast Path waymarks. The path descends back to the beach on the south side and then crosses the stream by the footbridge when nearly at Perranporth, where there are again all needed facilities.

Porth Joke

Week 3 - Day 4

OS Maps: Landranger 200 (Perranporth); Landranger 203 (remainder); Explorer 104

	This Walk	Cumulative	This Walk	Cumulative	Grading	Timing
Ascent	2,250ft	42,076ft	686m	12,825m	Moderate then strenuous	5.75 hours
Distance	12.2mi	214.5mi	19.7km	345.4km		

For detailed directions see our Perranporth to Portreath Path Description booklet.

This Section is one in which Cornwall's coastal mining heritage is paramount. There is much evidence of former mining activity, this including somewhat stark areas of spoil and sometimes slightly sad building relics, but also some grand and imposing engine houses and chimneys. In some locations, the large-scale level of the activity is difficult to imagine now. Nevertheless, the scale and grandeur of the cliffs, the beaches and the surf mean that nature always re-asserts itself.

Directions

A regular bus service links Perranporth to St Agnes. A skeletal summer service links Perranporth to Portreath, also passing St Agnes and Porthtowan along the way, giving numerous bus-walk options.

Perranporth is a busy holiday centre with all facilities. The Coast Path goes west from the main car park and follows the hill up Cliff Road. Keep left of the castellated building then along Tregundy Lane. Go half left at the entrance to the Youth Hostel and on to the cliffs, the path clinging to the cliff face out to Cligga Head. Here the path enters quarry and mine workings, but is well signposted. There is then a level stretch alongside Perranporth Aerodrome before the steep descent to Trevellas Porth, a valley marked by many relics of the mining industry. Go upstream to cross at the road bridge, then back to the cliffs and back down again into Trevaunance Cove, where there are toilets and refreshments. The bus stop at St Agnes is a little way inland.

On reaching the road at Trevaunance Cove go straight across passing the Driftwood Spars car park and a large tall house on the right. Follow the waymarked footpath immediately right along a metalled lane then fork right along a footpath. Soon the path climbs steeply to the cliff top. A long and scenic high-level path now goes around St Agnes Head, giving superb views ahead, then past the iconic engine house at Towanroath before descending to Chapel Porth, a small and attractive cove with toilets and seasonal refreshments. Refreshments are available at the Chapel Porth Beach Café daily from 1st April (or Easter if in March) until the end of October and weather permitting at weekends and during school holidays in winter. Phone 01872 552487 to check opening times. The toilets here are only unlocked when the cafe is open. Follow the stream inland for 200 yards/185m then turn right and up to the cliffs, before it is back down again into Porthtowan. Again there are toilets and refreshments and a magnificent beach. There is a bus stop a little inland.

Follow the road inland then turn right up West Beach Road, then left up the narrow road to the cliff top. More mine workings are passed, then the path runs alongside a prominent fence next to MOD land before reaching a road which descends into Portreath. This former industrial harbour town has all facilities.

Week 3 - Day 5

OS Maps: Landranger 203; Explorer 104 (eastern half); Explorer 102 (western half)

	This Walk	Cumulative	This Walk	Cumulative	Grading	Timing
Ascent	1,362ft	43,438ft	415m	13,240m	Moderate/ easy	5.5 hours
Distance	12.4mi	226.9mi	19.9km	365.3km		

For detailed directions see our Portreath to Hayle Path Description booklet.

There are two distinct characters to the coast of this Section. Between Portreath and Godrevy it is one of high, level cliffs, the sea far below. In contrast, between Godrevy and Hayle the walk focuses on sand, either dunes or beach, on the focal view of Godrevy lighthouse and on the great colourful sweep of St Ives Bay. This is never a lonely or remote length, but it is a scenic, fascinating and rewarding one.

Directions

A skeletal summer bus service links Portreath and Hayle, and also passes Godrevy, half-way between the two. This allows for bus-walk options over the whole Section or over either of the two distinct character lengths.

Portreath has all facilities and a nice beach. Leave the town crossing the bridge next to the car park then right, up Battery Hill. Continue ahead, meandering between properties at the end, turning right just beyond them up steps to the top of Western Hill, with its excellent views. After a couple of noticeable valleys the path then embarks on a long easy cliff-top walk along Reskajeague Downs, eventually arriving at Hell's Mouth, where there is a seasonal cafe. The path then narrows and turns right at an obvious T-junction. Cross a stile next to a gate and cross the seaward side of a field before continuing easily round Navax and Godrevy Points, the lighthouse becoming a focal point offshore. Keep seaward of the car park and access road and follow the signs along the low cliffs and over the dunes to another car park, at the Godrevy Cafe. Follow the boardwalk from the car park to cross the Red River. Turn left for 30 yards/29m then go right, following the large slate waymarks through the former quarry, now a nature reserve.

Keep ahead through the dunes, following the signposts. Note it is often possible to walk along the beach here but beware the incoming tide which can mean being cut off below the cliffs. If the tide is right, leave the beach at the lifeguard hut near the foot of Black Cliff. If coming through the dunes, keep ahead above the hut. Then, with either option, turn left up some steps just before two chalets. Turn right towards a house, leaving it on the right, and walk along a line of chalets on the left. The path is slightly overgrown but then opens out at a car park. Follow the access track ahead then bear right onto the raised walkway parallel to the harbour and continue ahead on this level. Descend the steps at the far end and follow the pavement ahead then cross the old swing bridge to the road. Turn right to reach the railway viaduct in the centre of Hayle.

Ralph's Cupboard

Week 3 - Day 6

OS Maps: Landranger 203; Explorer 102

	This Walk	Cumulative	This Walk	Cumulative	Grading	Timing
Ascent	617ft	44,055ft	188m	13,428m	Easy	2.5 hours
Distance	5.6mi	232.5mi	9.0km	374.3km		

For detailed directions see our Hayle to Pendeen Watch Path Description booklet.

This Section is never far from roads and houses, so often has a suburban air. However, this is outweighed by the views over the River Hayle estuary and, particularly, by the vistas over the great sweep of St Ives Bay with its vast sandy beaches and dunes, the iconic offshore Godrevy Lighthouse as a focal point and the fabulous sea colours, turquoises, greens and blues, whenever the sun shines on this length.

Directions

A regular bus service links Hayle and St Ives, giving a bus-walk option. In addition, a branch-line railway plies between Lelant and St Ives, and this gives marvellous sea views. This makes for an unusual and especially scenic train-walk option.

Hayle has all facilities, including a railway station on the main line to Penzance. Walk to the viaduct and turn right on the path immediately before it. Go ahead to Carnsew Road and continue on the pavement, turning right on a narrow path between housing. Go left at the end then continue to arrive alongside a large lagoon. Keep on to the end then bear left to the road. Continue as the road passes alongside the River Hayle estuary on The Causeway, a birdwatchers' delight. Cross to the far side of the road then back to the riverside again before forking right at the Old Quay House – take care on the road here. Under the bridge turn right, signed to St Ives Park and Ride. At the car park attendant's kiosk turn left to a lane, then turn right here. Follow the lane next to the railway and estuary all the way to Lelant Church. Go along the path next to the church to pass under the railway. Just before the beach turn left along the seaward side of the railway through dunes. (NB this is also the route of the St Michael's Way, a cross-peninsula path from Lelant to Marazion – a guide leaflet is available at St Ives TIC.)

Follow the clear path parallel to the magnificent Porthkidney Beach. Approaching the headland of Carrack Gladden the path forks – keep right then continue ahead. Descend the road to Carbis Bay, where there are toilets and seasonal refreshments, walking inland of the cafe but seaward of the hotel. Climb over a railway bridge then continue as the path becomes a minor road. Pass the path taking St Michael's Way inland then at a little cross-

roads go straight ahead, steeply downhill. (Turning right shortly after the St Michael's Way turning down a private, pedestrians only path gives a more scenic alternative to the official route, re-joining at the little cross-roads.) Cross the railway bridge and double back right then left to arrive at Porthminster Beach, just below St Ives railway station.

Baulking House

If you enjoy sleeping, eating or drinking at any business on the Path please suggest they join us as Business Members so that we can share their brilliance!

Padstow to St Ives

The businesses listed here are all supporters of the South West Coast Path, they have joined as Business Members and it would be great if you could show your support for them too. Additional Businesses are listed on **www.southwestcoastpath.org.uk** with links to their own sites for more information.

SLEEP

Anthea Crowley **Trealaw**, 22 Duke Street, Padstow, PL28 8AB	anthea.crowley@btinternet.com 01841 533161
Peter Cullinan **South Quay B&B,** 4 Riverside, Padstow, PL28 8BY	cullinan@madasafish.com www.southquaybedandbreakfastpadstow.co.uk 01841 532383
Mark Hixon **Coswarth House**, 12 Dennis Road, Padstow, PL28 8DD	coswarth@cawlimited.co.uk www.coswarthhouse.com 07907626084
Mary Neale **Penlan B&B**, Portcothan Bay, PL28 8LP	mary@idenna.com www.porthcothanbay.co.uk 01841 520440
Michelle Woodhead **Old MacDonald's Farm**, Porthcathan Bay, PL28 8LT	info@oldmacdonalds.co.uk www.oldmacdonalds.co.uk 01841 540826
Mrs Bridie Watts **Tir Chonaill Lodge**, 106 Mount Wise, Newquay, TR7 1QP	tirchonaillhotel@talk21.com www.tirchonaill.co.uk 01637 876492
Christine Stringer **Cornish Coastal Accommodation**, Long Trail, Rawley Lane, Newquay, TR7 2EU	christine.stringer@icloud.com 01637 859136 • 07891205595
Meryl Dewolfrey **Dewolf Guesthouse,** 100 Henver Close, Newquay, TR8 5DD	holidays@dewolfguesthouse.com www.dewolfguesthouse.com 01637 874746
Ulrica & Brad Harris **St George's Country House Hotel,** St George's Hill, Perranporth, TR6 0ED	info@stgeorgescountryhotel.co.uk www.stgeorgescountryhotel.co.uk 01872 572184
Mr R Fitton **Cambrose Touring Park,** Portreath Road, Redruth, TR16 4HT	cambrosetouringpark@gmail.com www.cambrosetouringpark.co.uk 01209 890747
David Ilett **Portreath Arms,** The Square, Portreath, TR16 4LA	email@theportreatharms.co.uk www.theportreatharms.co.uk 01209 8442259
Gillian Barnett **Cliff House,** Cliff Terrace, Portreath, TR16 4LE	cliffhousebookinginfo@gmail.com www.cliffhouseportreath.co.uk 01209 843847
Linda Davies **Nanterrow Farm,** near Gwithian, Hayle, TR27 5BP	nanterrow@hotmail.com www.nanterrowfarm.co.uk 01209 712282
Lee Strickland **Cohort Hostel,** The Stennack, St Ives, TR26 1FF	hello@stayatcohort.co.uk www.stayatcohort.co.uk 01736 791664
Lynne Bowden **Carlill,** 9 Porthminster Terrace, St Ives, TR26 2DQ	carlillguesthouse@hotmail.co.uk www.carlillguesthouse.co.uk 01736 796738

Week 4 - Day 1

OS Maps: Landranger 203; Explorer 102

	This Walk	Cumulative	This Walk	Cumulative	Grading	Timing
Ascent	3,428ft	47,483ft	1,045m	14,473m	Severe	7 hours
Distance	13.9mi	246.4mi	22.3km	396.6km		

For detailed directions see our Hayle to Pendeen Watch Path Description booklet.

There are no settlements on this Section and the character is lonely and remote. It is also tough going, with rocky scrambles and boggy lengths. But it can only be described as a magnificent length. Stark cliffs, rock pinnacles, tiny scenic coves with translucent water, rugged exposed headlands – all are here. Inland the view is often of empty moorland. This is the Coast Path at its most awe-inspiring. Prepare for its rigours, then enjoy the wonderful experience.

Directions

A regular summer bus service links St Ives and Pendeen village, a little inland of the Coast Path. It also passes through other inland settlements linked by footpath to the Coast Path, principally Zennor, Treen (Gurnard's Head) and Morvah, allowing for various bus-walks options.

A warning: this is a tough and deserted length of the Coast Path. There are no settlements or refreshment facilities, though there are some path links inland to small settlements. The terrain is often rough and rocky and in places can be boggy. But a compensation: this is a length of wonderfully dramatic coastal scenery.

From the path below St Ives railway station keep along as close as possible to the sea and harbour. The official route goes round the green St Ives Head, usually known as The Island. This is reached by following signs to the museum from the far end of the harbour and on through a small car park. From The Island go through the old "Downlong" quarter to Porthmeor Beach and the Tate. There are also short cuts direct to here – follow signs to the Tate.

Clodgy Point

Zennor Head

Go along the rear of Porthmeor Beach then bear off right along the path next to the putting green. The Coast Path now leads out to the rugged Clodgy Point and then on round Hor Point to Pen Enys Point, where it cuts across the neck of the headland. Pass the trig point on Carn Naun, where there are extensive views forward and back, then descend to cross the stream at River Cove. Just beyond the path passes the offshore Carracks, where seals are regularly seen. Approaching Zennor Head the path forks – keep right to follow the seaward path round the headland. From Zennor Head the path heads inland – look out for the signed Coast Path descending steeply to the right. If in need of refreshments, or for the bus, continue along the path inland to Zennor, where there is a pub and seasonal cafe.

On the Coast Path, more ups and downs lead to the distinctive headland of Gurnard's Head. The path cuts across its neck, but a diversion onto the headland, an Iron Age fortified site, is worth the effort. There are also diversions inland here to Treen, where refreshments are available at the Gurnard's Head Inn and there is a bus stop.

The Coast Path continues, generally easy to follow if not always an easy walk. Approaching Bosigran, another Iron Age fortification, head for the high point of the ridge, following Coast Path signs and keeping on the landward side of a low wall. At the crest of the ridge head inland and downhill aiming for a stream and building. Cross the stream on a small bridge near a ruined building then follow the path uphill, just seaward of an obvious stone wall. There is a diversion path inland here to a bus stop at Rosemergy. After heavy rain the path round here can be boggy.

Further on the Coast Path, look out for a path inland to Morvah for another bus stop if needed. Otherwise keep on the obvious Coast Path round the back of Portheras Cove and on to the lighthouse at Pendeen Watch. Pendeen village, with its pubs, cafe, shop, toilets and bus stop, is about 1 mile/1.5km inland.

Week 4 - Day 2

OS Maps: Landranger 203; Explorer 102

	This Walk	Cumulative	This Walk	Cumulative	Grading	Timing
Ascent	1,683ft	49,166ft	513m	14,986m	Moderate	4.25 hours
Distance	9.0mi	255.4mi	14.6km	411.2km		

For detailed directions see our Pendeen Watch to Porthcurno Path Description booklet.

This Section offers a wide range of walking experiences. Between Pendeen Watch and Botallack the overriding experience is of Cornwall's coastal mining heritage. This ranges from unattractive early 20th century industrial relics to romantic stone-built cliff-face engine houses, all this next to sheer cliffs and often wild seas. Beyond Botallack is a superb length of scenic exposed cliffs, highlighted by the magnificent headland of Cape Cornwall. This Section has all that is best on the Cornish coast – rugged cliffs, mining relics, translucent water, turquoise coves, purple heather, rocky scrambles, the view of a lighthouse. Then, approaching Sennen Cove, there is a sweep of broad sandy beaches backed by dunes, and the length ends with a scenic harbour and a lifeboat station. A wonderful length.

Directions

A regular summer bus service links Pendeen village, a little inland of the Coast Path, with Sennen Cove. It also serves St Just, inland of Cape Cornwall, which is used as the centre of various Coast Path-based circular walks. Bus-walks are also possible from Geevor and Botallack, reached by footpath from the coast.

Towards Levant Engine House

From Pendeen Watch the path goes along the road to the end of the row of cottages, then turns right at a granite marker. (The road continues into Pendeen village, with its range of facilities.) The Coast Path is clear and leads to the old mining area at Geevor. A diversion inland leads to refreshments and toilets at the mining museum, which is itself well worth a visit if possible. Follow the signed track beyond Geevor to the National Trust's Levant Beam Engine House, open for steaming at certain times. From here the official path follows the clear track parallel to the coast, but a narrower path to seaward with better views leads from the far end of the car park. The two options come together as more mines are passed at Botallack. Look to seaward to see the famous Crowns Mine engine houses perched improbably on the cliff.

Beyond Botallack, as the mines give way, look for the signed path to the right which leads to the headland at Kenidjack Castle. A lot of the waymarking in this area uses granite stones, perfect for the landscape setting. From the old building on the headland descend left to a track, go left then bear right on a path down to another track. Go left here then turn right to cross the floor of the Kenidjack Valley. Climb to the top and turn right. Ahead now is the distinctive shape of Cape Cornwall, surmounted by its chimney. Turn right immediately before the road and then bear right across a field past the ruins of a chapel to a stone stile. Cross this, turn left and then climb right to reach the top of the headland. Savour the views, then join the path which descends over the seaward side of the Cape by zigzags and steps to reach the National Coastwatch Institution watchhouse. This recent addition to the Coast Path provides a superb experience. Go to the left of the watchhouse then down the steps and along a path past some stone buildings and through a gate to reach another set of granite steps descending to the right. In the nearby car park are seasonal refreshments and toilets. St Just is about 1 mile/1.5km up the road.

At the bottom of the steps go left then climb right on the track to a road at the top. Bear off right at the sign and follow the clear path into the Cot Valley. A new route has been established down the valley. For this, turn left at the road and almost immediately right, over a footbridge and past old mine workings, climbing to reach a path which heads to the cove at Porth Nanven. Just before reaching the cove climb left onto the cliffs. There is

a good clear cliff-face path to the beach at Gwynver, although with one rocky climb. From Gwynver the path continues through the dunes behind the sandy beaches, which can be walked at low tide, to the car park at Sennen Cove. This is a popular family and surfing spot with all facilities.

Two walkers enjoy Whitesand Bay

Week 4 - Day 3 (half day)

OS Maps: **Landranger 203; Explorer 102**

	This Walk	Cumulative	This Walk	Cumulative	Grading	Timing
Ascent	1,542ft	50,708ft	470m	15,456m	Moderate	3.25 hours
Distance	6.6mi	262.0mi	10.6km	421.8km		

For detailed directions see our Pendeen Watch to Porthcurno Path description booklet.

This is the most westerly length of coast in England. Much of it has the character of moorland meeting the sea, with great granite headlands and massive rock outcrops interspersed with isolated coves with exquisite sea colours. Towards Porthcurno the moorland is replaced by a more pastoral landscape, but the cliffs and coves continue. Much of this Section has a quiet character, interrupted only by the visitor mecca of Land's End.

Directions

Sennen Cove and Porthcurno are linked by a regular bus service, which also goes to Land's End. This allows for a choice of bus-walks and there are also numerous circuits possible based on the Land's End area.

Sennen Cove has all facilities. Leave the village passing the Round House gallery into the car park. Turn left up steps then right, towards the lookout. From here a range of parallel paths all lead to Land's End. Bear right to the First and Last House, at England's most westerly point, then keep seaward of the main complex to the outpost at Greeb Cottage. The complex has toilets and refreshments if needed. The path goes behind Greeb Cottage; then again a choice of paths all lead towards the beautiful bay of Nanjizal. At the far end of the bay head inland up the track then turn right steeply uphill on a stepped path. After passing through a gate look out for the official, unsigned, path leaving the main track to go seaward down some rocky steps. The path descends then climbs to the Coastwatch station on Gwennap Head. The main track also leads here, but less scenically.

The official path is clear from Gwennap Head down into Porthgwarra. An alternative, in good conditions only and for the sure-footed only, is to leave the main path to the right some 150 yards/140m after the Coastwatch station, then pass the hole of Tol-Pedn-Penwith ("the holed headland of Penwith") before bearing left to re-join the main path.

Porthgwarra is a charming little hamlet with toilets and seasonal refreshments and unusual passages through the cliffs. Leave along a track next to some cottages, climbing again to the cliffs. The clear path descends to Porth Chapel, passing St Levan's Holy Well. Continue straight ahead over the bridge, climbing again to arrive at the car park of the unique cliff-face Minack Theatre. Leave by the path next to the theatre entrance. The path drops very steeply, with deep steps, to Porthcurno Beach. If in doubt, because of the conditions or possible vertigo, follow the road. At the bottom of the steps keep left above the beach to Porthcurno's facilities.

Towards Sennen Cove

Week 4 - Day 3 (half day)

OS Maps: Landranger 203; Explorer 102

	This Walk	Cumulative	This Walk	Cumulative	Grading	Timing
Ascent	1,381ft	52,089ft	421m	15,877m	Strenuous	3.25 hours
Distance	5.5mi	267.5mi	8.8km	430.6km		

For detailed directions see our Porthcurno to Penzance Path Description booklet.

This is a quiet, remote and very scenic Section of cliffs and headlands, punctuated by some picturesque coves and a lighthouse. The larger coves, at each end, Porthcurno and Lamorna, are particularly attractive and are the only access points for cars, so are more popular, Otherwise, the sound of the sea and seabirds are likely to be the only disturbances in this beautiful length.

Directions

A regular bus service goes to Porthcurno and passes about 1 mile/1.5km inland of Lamorna Cove, making a bus-walk feasible. Many undertake one of a variety of circular walks between Porthcurno and Treen using the Coast Path.

Porthcurno has all facilities in summer. The Coast Path leaves at the back of the beach, climbing a steep track to Percella Point before turning to run parallel to the sea. A seaward loop gives a good view of the beautiful Pednvounder Beach, but requires a little scramble to return to the official route. The path then reaches the neck of Treen Head, or Treryn Dinas, the site of an Iron Age fortification. A cul-de-sac diversion heads for the end and the Logan Rock. Continue on the clear path over the cliff to descend into Penberth Cove, a superb little fishing hamlet with an old capstan. There are toilets but no refreshments.

After climbing away from Penberth the path continues along the cliff top, with one steep descent and climb at Porthguarnon, then starts to head inland. After passing a seaward house look out for the signed path to the right which descends into the wooded valley of St Loy and on to the boulder beach. Keep along the top of the beach for 55 yards/50m before leaving up the path.

This climbs to pass above the lighthouse of Tater-du. Approaching Lamorna Point the path crosses a length of tumbled rocks, making for slow going, until it suddenly descends to the car park at Lamorna Cove. Here are toilets and seasonal refreshments.

Looking back to Boscawen Point

Week 4 - Day 4

OS Maps: Landranger 203; Explorer 102

	This Walk	Cumulative	This Walk	Cumulative	Grading	Timing
Ascent	725ft	52,814ft	221m	16,098m	Strenuous then easy	3.5 hours
Distance	9.4mi	276.9mi	15.1km	445.7km		

For detailed directions see our Porthcurno to Penzance and Penzance to Porthleven Path Description booklets.

West of Mousehole this Section is one of lushly vegetated cliffs, but most of it is urban or semi-urban in character as it passes through Newlyn and Penzance. However, it is really defined by its views over the magnificent Mount's Bay, dominated by the iconic sight of St Michael's Mount and its castle, which give this coast a magical character.

Directions

A regular bus service passes about 1 mile/1.5km inland of Lamorna Cove and also serves Newlyn and Penzance, with links possible between Penzance and Marazion, giving a variety of possible bus-walk options.

Lamorna Cove has a seasonal cafe, toilets and, a little way inland, a pub. The Coast Path leaves the cove behind the harbour, bearing right to the cliffs. The well-marked path eventually leads to a road which descends into Mousehole. The road leads to the harbour; however, the official route turns right opposite "Lowena" then continues towards the sea, turning left along a terrace to a car park. It briefly passes along the harbour before turning left then right to reach the main harbour-side road. Mousehole has all facilities and is very picturesque.

At the far end of the harbour go through the car park, on along a concrete walkway then up some steps. Turn right along the road, then along a seaward track to arrive at Newlyn. Follow the road round the harbour and past the fish market, turning right just after the Seamen's Mission to cross a bridge. Bear right past the Tolcarne Inn then follow the promenade to Penzance. Pass the harbour then go right through the large car park to where a walkway leaves from its far right-hand end. Penzance has all facilities, is the end stop of the main-line railway and is the hub of local bus services. The train and bus stations are next to the car park.

The walkway follows the sea wall to the edge of Marazion. At the end of the walkway and cycle route either cross over and follow the road or cross the dunes to a large car park, cross this and continue behind the sea wall into Marazion.

Marazion is the centre for access to St Michael's Mount and is the southern end of the cross-peninsula St Michael's Way from Lelant. The little town of Marazion has all facilities.

Newlyn Harbour

Week 4 - Day 5

OS Maps: Landranger 203; Explorer 103 (Porthleven); Explorer 102 (remainder)

	This Walk	Cumulative	This Walk	Cumulative	Grading	Timing
Ascent	1,916ft	54,730ft	584m	16,682m	Moderate then strenuous	4.75 hours
Distance	10.6mi	287.5mi	17.1km	462.8km		

For detailed directions see our Penzance to Porthleven Path Description booklet.

Between Marazion and Cudden Point this Section is dominated by the sweep of Mount's Bay and its iconic focal point of St Michael's Mount. It is a charming length of low cliffs and small fields. East of Cudden Point the Mount is lost but the local landscape is bolder, with craggy headlands, long sandy beaches, inaccessible coves and picturesque cliff-top engine houses.

Directions

There are regular bus services which link Marazion and Porthleven and also serve Perranuthnoe and Praa Sands between the two, making a variety of bus-walks possible, Marazion is a pleasant little town with all facilities and the causeway to St Michael's Mount.

The Coast Path leaves along the main road, following it for some way to the speed restriction sign. Turn right before the cemetery, then bear left on a concrete path down steps and follow the path to the beach. Cross the top of the beach to some metal steps, climb them and continue ahead. Just after Trenow Cove the path turns inland. Look out for the signed right turn after 275 yards/250m, which goes back to the low cliffs and on to Perranuthnoe. There are toilets and seasonal refreshments here.

Take the lane on the seaward side of the car park, bearing right and then left into a field. The well-marked path leads to Cudden Point, with magnificent views over Mount's Bay. It descends past Little Cudden to Bessy's Cove, where it joins a track. Go ahead, bearing right at some granite gate posts, then through Prussia Cove on a lane between large stone buildings. Keep ahead on the path which passes above Kenneggy Sand and then descends to Praa Sands, where there are toilets and seasonal refreshments. Go down the slipway to the beach then along in front of the shop, taking the steps up beside the cafe. Keep along the top of the grassy dunes, turning left when signed at the end then right into a housing estate. At the end bear right and climb to the cliffs. The path skirts behind Rinsey Head then through a car park and down to a restored engine house. It continues to Trewavas Head, inland of more restored engine houses. Beyond there have been numerous cliff falls – be sure to follow the signed path. This then enters Porthleven on a lane – fork right entering the town to pass alongside the harbour to its head. Porthleven has all facilities.

The Bishop & The Camel

Week 4 - Day 6 (half day)

OS Maps: Landranger 203; Explorer 103

	This Walk	Cumulative	This Walk	Cumulative	Grading	Timing
Ascent	1,109ft	55,839ft	338m	17,020m	Moderate	3.25 hours
Distance	7.1mi	294.6mi	11.4km	474.2km		

For detailed directions see our Porthleven to The Lizard Path Description booklet.

This is a Section mostly of low cliffs with cliff-face paths, long stretches being above extensive beaches. It harbours a couple of unexpected features, firstly in the shape of Loe Bar, a large strip of shingle barring the freshwater Loe Pool from the sea, and secondly in the unusual position of Gunwalloe Church, hidden away in the corner of a sandy cove. Add a cliff-top monument to Marconi, a couple of picturesque coves and the rocky and atmospheric harbour at Mullion Cove and it makes for a fascinating length.

Directions

Porthleven and Mullion village, which is some 0.5 mile/1km from the Coast Path, are both served by regular but separate bus routes, which meet at Helston. The Mullion bus also serves Poldhu Cove, 1.5 miles/2.5km along the coast from Mullion Cove, allowing various bus-walks.

Porthleven has all facilities. The Coast Path goes alongside the harbour towards the clock-tower at the end near the pier. Follow the road past this building, going right at the fork and keep on out of the town to a car park. Climb the steps and continue ahead on the track to Loe Bar. Cross the bar to the far side, forking right, downhill, shortly after the memorial. After passing a renovated fishery building the path arrives at Gunwalloe Fishing Cove. Go ahead onto the National Trust's Baulk Head, then above Halzephron Cove to a road. Bear right to a small car park then go right again, away from the road, on the cliffs down to Gunwalloe Church Cove. There are toilets and seasonal refreshments here. The picturesque church is tucked away at the right-hand end of the cove.

Skirt the beach to a road, then take the signed path over a footbridge and over the rear of the beach to the path rising away. Immediately after the car park at the top turn right along the cliff top before returning to the road and dropping into Poldhu Cove, where there is a bus stop, toilets and refreshments. Cross the stream on the road and turn right up the driveway signed to the Marconi Centre, leaving this after 110 yards/100m for a path to the right. This passes the Marconi monument on the cliffs then drops into Polurrian Cove. Climb away past the Polurrian Hotel and along the slightly suburban path to the Mullion Cove Hotel. Keep to seaward and drop down to the harbour, where there are seasonal refreshments. There are toilets 110 yards/100m up the road.

Anson Memorial

Week 4 - Day 6 (half day)

OS Maps: Landranger 203; Explorer 103

	This Walk	Cumulative	This Walk	Cumulative	Grading	Timing
Ascent	1,303ft	57,142ft	397m	17,417m	Moderate	3.25 hours
Distance	6.8mi	301.4mi	10.9km	485.1km		

For detailed directions see our Porthleven to The Lizard Path Description booklet.

This is an exposed Section of high, flat-topped cliffs and spectacular coves and bays. The coastal landscape is superb throughout, but punctuated by some real scenic gems, of which Kynance Cove is probably the pick. The combination of steep cliffs, unusual geology and flora, beautiful sea colours and long stretches of easy walking make this a rewarding length. And watch out for choughs, Cornwall's iconic bird now returned to re-colonise this coast.

Directions

A regular bus service links Mullion village with Lizard Town, each settlement about 0.5 mile/1km inland from its respective end, thus giving a possible bus-walk. In addition, there are many easy local circuits based on the Coast Path in the Lizard-Kynance area.

Mullion Cove has seasonal refreshments and there are toilets a little way inland. The Coast Path leaves the quay slightly inland to the right, up the hill just after the cafe. Climb to the cliffs, keeping to the right to hug the coastline. There is an information board on the unique flora and fauna of the area here.

The easy and clear path rounds Parc Bean Cove and Lower Predannack Cliff. Approaching Vellan Head, be sure to keep close to the coast for the official route – the more obvious track misses the views. After the deep valley at Gew Graze the path rounds Rill Point and descends to Kynance Cove. The steep descent leads to a footbridge by the seasonal cafe. There are also toilets here. If the sun is shining the sea is brilliant turquoise.

From the cafe either follow the main track up towards the car park or cross the little beach (at low tide) and climb a partly stepped path to the cliffs, leaving this at a sign pointing right. This passes adjacent to the car park, where the main track arrives, and the Coast Path then continues clearly and easily above Pentreath Beach at Caerthillian and round Old Lizard Head, and on to Lizard Point, England's most southerly point, where there are cafes, gift shops and toilets. The nearby lighthouse is open to visitors at certain times. A path leads inland to Lizard Town, which has all facilities including regular bus services.

Kynance Cove

The businesses listed here are all supporters of the South West Coast Path, they have joined as Business Members and it would be great if you could show your support for them too. Additional Businesses are listed on **www.southwestcoastpath.org.uk** with links to their own sites for more information.

DO	
Doug Evans **Meneage Taxis,** 10 Cunnack Close, Station Road, Helston, TR13 8XQ	meneagetaxis@yahoo.com www.helstontaxis.com 01326 560530 • 07773 817156

SLEEP	
Olga Parish **Tamarisk,** Buthallen Road, St Ives, TR26 3AA	tamariskbb@gmail.com www.cornwall-online.co.uk/tamariskbandb-stives 01736 797201
Mrs N Mann **Trewey Farm,** Trewey, Zennor, TR26 3DA	01736 796936
Jill & Geoff Hoather **The Old Chapel,** Boscaswell Downs, Pendeen, Penzance, TR19 7DR	GEOFFGOATHERD@aol.com www.cornwallfarwest.co.uk/cfwoldchapelbb 01736 786006
Moira Keogh **St Johns House B&B,** Boscaswell Downs, Pendeen, Penzance, TR19 7DW	moriakeogh@btinternet.com www.stjohnshousebedandbreakfast.co.uk 01736 786605
Chris & Helen Buck **Gypsy Caravan B&B,** Primrose Cottage, Levant Road, Trewellard, Pendeen, TR19 7SU	holiday@gypsycaravanbandb.co.uk www.gypsycaravanbandb.co.uk 01736 787585 • 7900631628
Mrs Janet Harrison **Weavers B&B,** Trevescan, Sennen, TR19 7AQ	weaversbb@btinternet.com 01736 871565
Jeffrey Hardman **The Studio,** Treen, Porthcurno, St Leven, TR19 6LQ	jeffrey_hardman@sky.com www.sennencornwall.com 01736 810504
Rachel Hood **Castallack Farm,** Castallack, Near Mousehole, Penzance, TR19 6NL	info@castallackfarm.co.uk www.castallack.co.uk 01736 731969
Matt Martens **Cornerways Guest House,** 5 Leskinnick Street, Penzance, TR18 2HA	cornerways.penzance@yahoo.com www.cornerways-penzance.co.uk 01736 364645/800110 07582 - 722510
Frances Brint **Keigwin,** Alexandra Road, Penzance, TR18 4LZ	fran@keigwinhouse.co.uk www.keigwinhouse.co.uk 01736 363930 • 07557 057773
Christine Edwards **Tremont Guest House,** Alexandra Road, Penzance, TR18 4LZ	info@tremonthotel.co.uk www.tremonthotel.co.uk 01736 362614
Andrew & Lynsey Stott **Glencree House,** 2 Mennaye Road, Penzance, TR18 4NG	stay@glencreehouse.co.uk www.glencreehouse.co.uk 01736 362026
Mrs Marian Foy **Mzima,** Penlee Close, Praa Sands, Penzance, TR20 9SR	marianfoy@prussia-cove-holiday.com 01736 763856
Bridget Rogers **Wellmore End Cottage,** Methleigh Bottoms, Portleven, TR13 9JP	wellmoreend-bandb@tiscali.co.uk www.wellmoreend-bandb.co.uk 01326 569310
Mullion Cove Hotel Mullion, Helston, TR12 7ER	enquiries@mullion-cove.co.uk www.mullion-cove.co.uk 01326 240328

David Jeffrey **Strathallan Guest House,** 6 Monument Road, Helston, TR13 8HF	enquiries@strathallangh.co.uk www.strathallangh.co.uk 01326 573683
Jenny Lewis **Hellarcher Farm,** Penmenner Road, The Lizard, TR12 7NN	hellarcher7@btinternet.com www.hellarcherfarm.co.uk 01326 291188
Carol Barker **Stormfield,** The Lizard, TR12 7NQ	carol.annetts@hotmail.com 0754 8847512
Janet & Michale Edwards **Atlantic House B&B,** Pentreath Lane, The Lizard, TR12 7NY	atlantichse@btinternet.com www.atlantichouselizard.co.uk 01326 290399
Annie & Age Bunnetat **Treluswell B&B,** Treluswell, Lizard, Helston, TR12 7NZ	anniebunnetat@yahoo.co.uk www.treluswellbandb.co.uk 01326 290286

**If you enjoy
sleeping, eating or drinking at
any business on the Path please suggest
they join us as Business Members so that we
can share their brilliance!**

Towards Portheras Cove

Week 5 - Day 1

OS Maps: Landranger 203 (Lizard); Landranger 204 (remainder); Explorer 103

	This Walk	Cumulative	This Walk	Cumulative	Grading	Timing
Ascent	2,293ft	59,435ft	699m	18,116m	Moderate, strenuous in places	5.75 hours
Distance	10.6mi	312.0mi	17.1km	502.2km		

For detailed directions see our The Lizard to Coverack Path Description booklet.

This is a Section of cliffs and coves, punctuated by headlands giving excellent views along the coastline. Here and there are areas of sandy beach at the foot of the cliffs, but only at Kennack are they very extensive. This coast is largely sheltered from the worst of the prevailing south-westerly winds, and consequently has a lush, well-vegetated character. This being a relatively unfrequented stretch, substantial lengths are quiet and remote.

Directions

Lizard Town, about 0.5 mile/1km inland of the Coast Path, has a bus service which also passes a little inland of Cadgwith, about half-way along this length, which presents a bus-walk possibility. In addition, there are numerous easy circuits based on The Lizard using the Coast Path which are popular and attractive.

Lizard Point has cafes and toilets, while Lizard Town, inland, has all necessary facilities. Lizard Point has the distinction of being England's most southerly point and is a fine location. The Coast Path leaves the Point alongside the car parking area and on in front of the lighthouse. There is a Heritage Centre at the lighthouse and both lighthouse and Heritage Centre are open to the public at certain times (www.lizardlighthouse.co.uk). After passing the lighthouse descend to cross a footbridge then climb, passing in front of the Housel Bay Hotel and on past the Lloyds Signal Station, bearing right here. The route passes Bass Point National Coastwatch Institution lookout, the first in the country to be established. At Kilcobben Cove the path goes behind The Lizard lifeboat station with its new boathouse which was completed in 2011. It then arrives at Church Cove. Go left for a short distance then take the path through the gate on the right. There are some ups and downs to a path junction just after a stone stile at Polgwidden Cove; keep right here. A little further on the path skirts the dramatic collapsed cave of the Devil's Frying Pan. Follow the signed path past the cottages and down into the picturesque little fishing hamlet of Cadgwith.

Cadgwith has a pub, shop, refreshments and toilets. There is a superb little beach here where the fishing boats are hauled up. This is overlooked by a convenient grassy knoll with seats known as The Todn (Cornish for lawn). Walk through Cadgwith and up the hill, turning right on the signed path a little way up. The Path then descends to Poltesco, crossing a footbridge. There is a diversion to the right leading to the attractive and interesting cove, complete with old serpentine works, where the local colourful rock was made into useful items. Climbing out of Poltesco, the path then joins a road which leads to the beach at Kennack Sands. There are toilets here and seasonal refreshments.

Follow the path behind the beaches and on to the cliffs to reach the neck of the long promontory of Carrick Luz, the site of an Iron Age cliff fort. The path cuts across the neck and then negotiates the steep valley at Downas Cove. Another, shallower valley crossing leads to the end of Black Head and its lookout hut. The path now descends over the cliffs towards Chynhalls Point going amongst the natural rock outcrops which can be slippery in wet weather. Beyond the Point the path soon reaches Coverack.

An alternative inland path avoids the slippery Chynhalls Cliff. At the top of the Coast Path descent, the wide alternative path goes through gorse and passes a Sculpture Park, then the edge of a caravan park before arriving at a bungalow on a tarmac road. Turn right towards the hotel and then almost immediately bear left down a narrower path to rejoin the Coast Path at Chynhalls Point.

Reaching the road at Coverack, the path soon veers off right down some steps to arrive at a car park at the end of the village. Follow the road past the harbour. Coverack, a pretty place, has all facilities, including a regular bus service into Helston.

Lookout at Black Head

Week 5 - Day 2

OS Maps: **Landranger 204; Explorer 103**

	This Walk	Cumulative	This Walk	Cumulative	Grading	Timing
Ascent	2,192ft	61,627ft	668m	18,784m	Moderate	5.75 hours
Distance	13.1mi	325.1mi	21.1km	523.3km		

For detailed directions, see our Coverack to Helford Path Description booklet.

This is a sheltered Section of the Coast Path. It includes low cliffs facing away from the prevailing winds, but also lengths of pleasant rural field paths, a little inland, necessary to avoid inaccessible coastal working and former quarries. In addition this Section has substantial lengths which fringe a tidal creek and on wooded estuary-side paths passing pretty beaches where the Coast Path reaches the Helford River. While not as dramatic as some Sections, it is an attractive stretch with a quiet charm of its own.

Directions

Separate bus routes from Helston serve Coverack and Helford Passage, across the river via ferry (Good Friday or 1st April to October) from Helford, allowing a bus-walk based on Helston. There is an attractive local circuit using the Coast Path between Helford and Gillan Creek.

There are all necessary facilities at Coverack. The Coast Path follows the road away from the pub and past the harbour, continuing straight ahead on a narrow lane when the road goes left. Look out for the sign pointing right, just before the end of the lane. The path goes over sometimes boggy ground next to the coast to arrive at Lowland Point. Next, the old workings at Dean Quarry are passed on their seaward side. The well-signed path then arrives at the open area at Godrevy Cove. The next length of coast is inaccessible due to operating quarries, so the Coast Path heads across the open area inland to pick up a signed path going uphill between fields. This leads to the little hamlet of Rosenithon. At the T-junction, turn right on the lane, uphill, turning left into a field just after the right-hand bend. Cross three fields in the same direction, stone stiles between them, to emerge on a lane. Go left then, at a junction, right, which leads to Porthoustock, a coastal hamlet with public toilets.

The route of the next stretch, to another coastal hamlet, Porthallow, is also a rural inland walk. It leaves Porthoustock past the telephone box and up the hill. Where the road bears right go straight ahead on a narrower lane. Go past a row of thatched cottages and over a little grassy bank at the end next to a greenhouse to a kissing-gate. Just past the gate there is a fork in the path. Bear right and follow the path climbing to the far top corner of the field to cross a lifting-bar stile and a Cornish stile (a sort of stone cattle grid) into another field. Turn right in this field alongside the hedge, then bear away left at the top to cross another Cornish stile to a road.

At the road go left, passing through the tiny hamlet of Trenance. Here the route follows the road round to the right to a T-junction. At the junction go slightly right and immediately left onto an enclosed path which leads to a track between buildings. Here is the charming Fat Apples Cafe, open all year though winter hours are limited. At the road turn right to arrive at Porthallow.

Porthallow has a pub, toilets and seasonal refreshments. Fat Apples Cafe is open all year with winter opening hours between October and March. The staff at Fat Apples Cafe are happy to fill up flasks and dry clothes. They will help with lifts if they are free to do so. Look out for the marker indicating the half-way point of the Coast Path, equidistant (at 315 miles) from Minehead and Poole. Leave Porthallow along the back of the beach and up the steps. The path now follows the coastline, keeping close to the edge round Nare Point and then past a couple of pretty beaches. Moving into the mouth of the Helford River the path continues alongside its tidal tributary, Gillan Creek.

From Easter/1st April to 31st October use the signal board to request the ferry. Telephone 01326 231357 or see page 19 for ferry details.

Otherwise, the route goes left from the creekside up the hill to a sharp left-hand bend. Here go straight ahead along the field edge, then bear right over two further fields to a road. Turn right to Carne, at the head of the creek, then right again along the north side of the creek to St Anthony Church. Past the church turn left uphill then shortly right on a farm track which leads into a field. Cross diagonally left to the top of the field to a kissing-gate.

For a short, direct route from here go through the gate and turn left. However, the Coast Path includes an optional extra of a circuit of Dennis Head. For this circuit do not pass through the gate but turn right then almost immediately left over a stile. At the next junction continue straight ahead to reach the end of the headland. The path circles around the headland, re-joining the outward route to the stile and then the kissing-gate.

Go through the gate and continue along the top of the field. The route now heads up the estuary side of the Helford River through woods and past coves. Towards the end the path reaches a track – follow to the road and go right here then quickly left. The path then emerges next to the main car park at Helford. Go down the hill into the village. Helford has a pub and shop and there are toilets and a seasonal cafe at the car park.

Gillan Creek

Week 5 - Day 3

OS Maps: Landranger 204; Explorer 103

	This Walk	Cumulative	This Walk	Cumulative	Grading	Timing
Ascent	1,397ft	63,024ft	426m	19,210m	Moderate	4.5 hours
Distance	10.0mi	335.1mi	16.1km	539.4km		

For detailed directions see our Helford to Falmouth Path Description booklet.

There are two contrasting parts to this Section. Between Helford and Rosemullion Head it is a sheltered walk alongside the mouth of the beautiful Helford River, with undulating, relatively low cliffs alternating with charming little beaches. Between Rosemullion Head and Falmouth the walk flanks the sweep of Falmouth Bay, with rather larger coves overlooked by the great headland of Pendennis Point at the Falmouth end, crowned by its castle. Over the bay is St Anthony Head lighthouse. None of this is a lonely or remote walk, and the Falmouth end is decidedly urban, but it is never uninteresting and always very scenic.

Directions

Helford Passage and Falmouth are linked by a regular bus service, which also serves two of the beach coves along the route, at Maenporth and Swanpool, giving numerous bus-walk options. The short circular walk round Pendennis Head in Falmouth is a great local favourite.

Helford has pub, shop and toilets; Helford Passage, over the river, has a pub and seasonal refreshments. There is a seasonal ferry link. For ferry details see page 19.

It is possible to use local taxi services if the ferry is not operating – Autocabs, tel: 01326 573773 or Cove Cars tel. 07980 814058. Alternatively Sailaway St Anthony Ltd, tel: 01326 231357 may be able to help.

Walk around Helford River

If the ferry is not operating, a 13 mile/21km walk around the Helford River is possible. This will add another day to the itinerary. For this route, from Helford take the path up the hill in front of the Shipwright Arms to arrive at Penarvon Cove. Go round the back of the cove and turn inland up a track to a road. Turn right then left on a track to the permissive path along the atmospheric Frenchman's Creek. At the end take the path on the right signed to Withan past Frenchman's Pill Cottage, crossing a footbridge. Follow the path through the woods and aim for the far left corner of the field, taking the stile on the left. Follow the boundary on the left past Withan Farm, then head west over the fields to a lane. Here turn left to a crossroads, turning right here towards Mawgan. The lane joins a larger road; turn right past Gear then down and up into Mawgan-in-Meneage village. Turn right just after the church on the path towards Gwarth-an-drea then left behind a bungalow to a road. Turn right and at the junction bear right and continue downhill to the bridge at Gweek. There is a shop and pub here. Take the road opposite the Gweek Inn and at Tolvan Cross turn right along a bridleway to a road junction. Go straight ahead, towards Porth Navas. After crossing the stream take the footpath on the left along the field edge to the road.

Follow the road ahead to Nancenoy and Polwheveral. At the crossroads after Polwheveral turn right then after 140 yards/128m take the path on the left along the field edge then across the field corner to a road junction. Take the Porth Navas road opposite through the village to Trenarth Bridge, then turn right towards Falmouth. At the junction at Trebah turn right, then right again into Bar Road. At the end turn left on a footpath which leads to the Helford River, turning left to the Ferryboat Inn at Helford Passage, the landing place for the ferry from Helford.

Ferry users start from here

Coast Path, Helford Passage - Falmouth

From the Ferryboat Inn, facing the pub, turn right along the river and up to a grassy hill. Keep on to a concrete track and follow this, passing behind Trebah Beach at Polgwidden Cove. Continue on the riverside to Durgan, turning sharp right to enter the little village. Go up the road, ignoring one path to the right, until the road turns left and the path continues straight ahead. Follow this path, arriving at Porth Saxon Beach behind a building and then through a field to Porthallack Beach. The path then climbs round Toll Point to arrive at a wooded area. At the fork keep right and follow the path onward to Rosemullion Head, leaving the Helford River behind.

Keep seaward round the headland then descend to go through a small wood and then on, the path becoming suburban now, to reach Maenporth where there are toilets and refreshments and a bus stop. Turn right behind the cafe and continue to Swanpool, with more toilets and refreshments and another bus stop. Take the path from the far end of the beach to arrive at Gyllyngvase, then keep along Falmouth's promenade to the far end. The official path goes around the magnificent Pendennis Point – keep to the seaward road all the way to the end then at the car park descend on the signed path up the river, parallel to the road above. The path emerges from woods and passes the Leisure Centre, descending above the docks to a T-junction. Turn right then go ahead under the railway bridge, passing the Maritime Museum and along Falmouth's main shopping street to arrive at the Prince of Wales Pier at the far end. Falmouth, of course, has all facilities, including a rail link to the main line at Truro.

On the coast path at Mawnan Smith

Week 5 - Day 4 (half day)

OS Maps: Landranger 204; Explorer 105

	This Walk	Cumulative	This Walk	Cumulative	Grading	Timing
Ascent	974ft	63,998ft	297m	19,507m	Easy	2.75 hours
Distance	6.2mi	341.3mi	10.0km	549.4km		

For detailed directions see our St Mawes to Portscatho Path Description Booklet.

This Section includes a trip on the ferry across the mouth of the River Fal, a treat of scenery and interest in its own right. Beyond, the walk round St Anthony Head is one of superb estuarine and coastal views, followed by an easy but charming path on low cliffs, sheltered from the westerlies, while passing some fine sandy beaches and giving excellent views up the South Cornwall coast.

Directions

A regular bus route serves Portscatho and St Mawes from Truro, which is also linked to Falmouth by bus and train. There is also a very popular circular walk using the Coast Path in the St Anthony Head area and another from Portscatho.

Two ferries are required to cross between Falmouth and the Coast Path at Place, east of the large estuary. The first goes between Falmouth and St Mawes, across the mouth of the main Fal Estuary, sometimes referred to as Carrick Roads. The ferry operates all year from Prince of Wales Pier (year round) and Custom House Quay (summer only). Tel: 01326 741194. For ferry details see page 19.

The second leg of the crossing is the ferry between St Mawes and Place, crossing the mouth of the Fal's tributary, the Percuil River. This ferry operates 1 June – 30 September from 09:00 – 17:00 every half hour, subject to demand. Tel: 01326 741194. In winter an alternative may be offered by a water taxi service, tel: 07971 846786. For details visit www.stmaweskayaks.co.uk. For ferry details see page 19.

There is also Falmouth Water Taxi service which operates between Falmouth and St Mawes or Place, weather permitting between March and October 0900 to 1800 (2230 May to September). If needed, it is advisable to telephone 2-3 days in advance in the Summer. Tel: 07522 446659, www.falmouthwatertaxi.co.uk. Information is also available from the Fal River Visitor Information Centre at Prince of Wales Pier, or visit www.falriver.co.uk.

If arriving at St Mawes and wishing to proceed to Place when the Place ferry is not operating it is possible to take the regular bus service from St Mawes to Gerrans, walking from here to Place (2.5 miles/4km). For this option, go to Gerrans Church and pick up the walking route described below. In addition, a local taxi company, Roseland Taxis, will carry walkers around here and throughout the Roseland Peninsula, tel: 01872 501001, m: 07817 447667, website www.roselandtaxis.co.uk

St Mawes waterfront

Walk between St Mawes and Place

A walking route also exists between St Mawes and Place, via Gerrans. This adds 9 miles/14km to the overall route, effectively an extra day to the itinerary. Leaving the ferry point in St Mawes, turn left along the road. Approaching the castle, take the minor lane left, which leads to a footpath at the end. This becomes a scenic path alongside the Carrick Roads – the Fal Estuary. At a minor road go right then bear left in front of the boatyard and then on a bank above the shore. This leads to the churchyard of St Just in Roseland, a beautiful spot. Pass the church and keep to the path next to the shore. Follow the path as it bears right up the hill, signed St Just Lane, to emerge on a road. Turn left, ignoring the first footpath on the right, but take the second a little afterwards. Follow the path alongside field boundaries, first to the right, then to the left, then to the right again. Go down to the road at the end of the fourth field and turn right to the A3078 at Trethem Mill. Turn left and immediately right after the bridge up some steps and through a small wood. Out of the wood, cross the field diagonally right (bearing 110) then in the next field bear diagonally right again (bearing 140), leaving it by a wooded track. Cross the stile at the top and bear diagonally right again (bearing 137) to meet a hedge, which is followed to a road. Turn right on the road. At the next junction follow the road curving to the right past Polhendra Cottage then turn left through the second gate. Descend towards the bottom of the hedge visible on the opposite side of the valley (bearing 123). Cross the bridge and climb as close as possible with the hedge to the left. Cross the stone steps behind the gorse at the top and bear slightly left across the next two fields (bearing 125) to emerge on a road. Turn right to arrive at Gerrans Church. (Those who have taken the bus from St Mawes will join here – see above.)

At the church fork left into Treloan Lane, keeping ahead past the buildings. Go through the gate at the end of the lane, crossing an open field ahead into another enclosed track, which leads to Porth Farm. At the road turn right then go left at the sign indicating "Footpath to Place by Percuil River". Follow this very scenic path which leads to the ferry landing point then on to Place itself.

Coast Path, Place - Portscatho

At Place, walk up the lane past the gates to the grand house. Turn right into the churchyard of St Anthony Church, passing behind the church and up into a wooded area. Turn right at the track then at the creek look for the sign on the left taking the path alongside the plantation. The path now gives superb views over Carrick Roads to Falmouth. Approaching St Anthony Head keep to the coastal path to the right until passing through the gate towards the lighthouse. Just after the gate climb the steps to the left to the car parking area. There are also toilets here. Leave the car park next to the coast and the superb and easy path then leads to Portscatho, which has a shop, toilets and pubs, as well as a bus service to St Mawes and Truro.

Place House

Week 5 - Day 4 (half day)

OS Maps: Landranger 204: Explorer 105

	This Walk	Cumulative	This Walk	Cumulative	Grading	Timing
Ascent	1,674ft	65,672ft	510m	20,017m	Strenuous	3.75 hours
Distance	7.5mi	348.8mi	12.0km	561.4km		

For detailed directions see our Portscatho to Portloe Path Description Booklet.

This is a very quiet Section for the most part. Cliffs are relatively low at first, but increase in height as the great promontory of Nare Head, with its superb views, is approached. The long sandy beaches below the cliffs passed west of Nare Head are replaced by tiny isolated and inaccessible coves east of the headland. This length has a wonderfully remote atmosphere.

Directions

Portscatho and Portloe are both served by regular, but different, bus services, both linking with Truro. There are some local circular walks using the Coast Path around Nare Head, based on the inland village of Veryan.

Portscatho has a shop, pubs, toilets and bus service. The Coast Path leaves past the Harbour Club; keep right just after leaving the village at the footpath junction. The path goes round the back of Porthcurnick Beach, then up the road on the far side, turning right along the coastal edge. The path continues to undulate along the coast until it turns inland to reach a road. Turn right, past Pendower Court and down the road to its end at Pendower Beach. Cross the rear of the beach and head for the public toilets, going up the hill and turning right. The path soon diverts around the rear of the Nare Hotel to a road, descending to Carne Beach. Follow the road round the bend and up the hill for a short way, turning right to return to the cliffs. The path now heads for Nare Head, via a steep descent and ascent at Tregagle's Hole and past an old fisherman's cottage. A short diversion at the top of Nare Head reveals some stunning coastal views.

The path now goes round the seaward edge of Rosen Cliff and over the valley behind Kiberick Cove to Blouth Point. At the point enter a field and keep left for a short way before bearing right, downhill, towards some trees. The path zigzags upward to pass Broom Parc and then goes through a field to round Manare Point. After this it is downhill going over a short uneven section before joining a tarmac path which descends into Portloe. The village is very picturesque and has pubs and toilets as well as a bus service.

Pednvaden Lookout, Near Portscatho

Week 5 - Day 5

OS Maps: Landranger 204; Explorer 105

	This Walk	Cumulative	This Walk	Cumulative	Grading	Timing
Ascent	2,841ft	68,513ft	866m	20,883m	Strenuous then easy	5.75 hours
Distance	12.3mi	361.1mi	19.8km	581.2km		

For detailed directions see our Portloe to Mevagissey Path Description booklet.

This is a quiet Section of mostly high cliffs, often covered in lush vegetation. Towards Gorran Haven these cliffs reduce in height. The Section includes the great headland of Dodman Point, from where there are views to the Lizard in one direction and Devon in the other on a clear day. Below the cliffs are some sandy beaches, often all but inaccessible. This is a coastline for those preferring remoteness.

Directions

There are some excellent circular walks using the Coast Path at Dodman Point and linking to Gorran Haven, giving a variety of options here.

The scenic little harbour village of Portloe has toilets, pubs and a bus service. The Coast Path leaves behind the Lugger Hotel, leaving the road to reach a prominent converted chapel. Pass this then climb steeply to the cliffs. After a quite strenuous length the path arrives at West Portholland. Follow the road above the shore to a junction, then turn right to East Portholland. There are toilets here and a seasonal cafe and shop. Pass the cottages at the far end and climb behind them on a clear path to a field, turning right down the field edge. The path leads to a road which descends to Porthluney Cove. Here are toilets and seasonal refreshments and the picturesque setting is enhanced by the presence of Caerhayes Castle just inland. Walk behind the beach and turn right into parkland. Climb behind the field-edge trees then go to the right and follow the field edge to the woods. After crossing the rocky ridge at Greeb Point the path descends to a road behind Hemmick Beach. Cross the bridge and go right, climbing to the headland of Dodman Point ("The Dodman"), with its memorial cross and superb views. The path stays clear above the lovely sands of Bow or Vault Beach, then rounds the headland of Pen-a-maen to enter Gorran Haven. This little harbour village has a shop, pub and toilets. There is a Gorran community bus which runs 4 days a week www.gorranbus.org which walkers have recommended to us and can be hailed anywhere along its route.

Leave Gorran Haven up Church Street, turning right into Cliff Road. Turn right near the top of the hill and a stile on the left leads to the cliffs. The clear path leads to Chapel Point, where it crosses the tarmac access road to follow the path along the coast into Portmellon. Follow the road uphill and go down through the park on the right on entering Mevagissey. Steps descend to the harbour. Mevagissey is the archetypal Cornish fishing village and has all facilities.

Caerhays Castle

Week 5 - Day 6

OS Maps: Landranger 204; Explorer 105 (western half); Explorer 107 (eastern half)

	This Walk	Cumulative	This Walk	Cumulative	Grading	Timing
Ascent	2,434ft	70,947ft	742m	21,625m	Strenuous then easy	5 hours
Distance	10.5mi	371.6mi	17.1km	598.3km		

For detailed directions see our Mevagissey to Charlestown and Charlestown to Fowey Path Description booklets.

The western half of this Section has a relatively remote feel, enhanced by some quite strenuous climbs and some attractive cliffs and headlands. To the east the coastline is more urbanised but with beaches and the lovely Georgian docks of Charlestown found among the houses, golf courses and clay industry. The cliff-top path between Porthpean and Charlestown was reinstated in late 2011, avoiding two miles of road diversion.

Directions

There are bus routes from St Austell to Mevagissey, Charlestown and Par, one of these routes serving both the latter two locations, so that a range of bus-walks is possible.

The attractive fishing village of Mevagissey has all facilities. The Coast Path goes along the back of the harbour and then turns right along its eastern side before forking left steeply uphill. After crossing some playing fields, pass seaward of the houses then continue along the undulating cliffs to descend behind the ruined fish cellars at Portgiskey Cove. Continue uphill along the seaward and far field boundaries to a fenced path at the top. Turn right here, parallel to the road. At the entrance to Pentewan Sands Holiday Park follow the B3273 road pavement and turn first right before the petrol station, signposted to Pentewan. There are a few shops, toilets and a pub in the village. The official route then follows the road through Pentewan and up the hill for about 100 yards/90m, taking the first turn sharp right along The Terrace and along a narrow path at the end to arrive at the cliffs. A more interesting alternative turns right, away from the road into the harbour area just after the public toilets then, immediately after the last cottage, goes left steeply uphill, through gardens, to arrive at the official route on the cliffs.

After some 1.25 miles/2km the path descends through a wood and reaches a track. Turn right here to arrive at another track just behind the remote Hallane Mill Beach. Turn left here then quickly right, climbing back up the cliffs to arrive at Black Head. A diversion from the memorial stone goes to the tip of this atmospheric location. Continuing from

Black Head the path enters Ropehaven Woods with some confusing paths – it is important to follow the waymarking. Entering the wood turn right down a rocky and sometimes slippery path, then left. Go left again onto a walled path, ignoring descending paths on the right, to arrive beside a cottage and emerge onto a track. Go right here then

Charlestown

leave the road to the right just after a parking area and follow the cliff-top path down, up and down again to Porthpean. Walk along the promenade to the far end and climb the steps to rejoin the newly reinstated cliff-top path all the way to Charlestown.

Charlestown has a fascinating Georgian harbour, the home of a group of tall ships, and has refreshments, toilets, pubs and buses. Note that the official Coast Path does not cross the dock gate at the mouth of the harbour, though many people use that route. On the east side climb past the public toilets and on to reach a suburban road for a short way, soon forking off right over a long grassy area. Arriving at a large car park above Carlyon Bay Beach keep to seaward then cross the beach access road where a new resort is being developed and continue ahead on the low cliffs. Keep seaward of the golf course to approach the old china clay works at Par Docks. At the little beach at Spit Point turn inland and follow the narrow path past the works and then alongside a railway line to emerge on a road. Turn right along the pavement past the docks entrance and under a railway bridge. Turn right at the junction, signposted to Fowey, over a level crossing and then under another railway bridge before forking right on the road, Par Green.

To continue beyond Par on the Coast Path, walk along Par Green, looking for house no.52 and follow the path signed on the right. Par has all facilities, including a mainline railway station; for the station turn left at the far end of Par Green along Eastcliffe Road.

Descending into Mevagissey

If you enjoy sleeping, eating or drinking at any business on the Path please suggest they join us as Business Members so that we can share their brilliance!

The businesses listed here are all supporters of the South West Coast Path, they have joined as Business Members and it would be great if you could show your support for them too. Additional Businesses are listed on **www.southwestcoastpath.org.uk** with links to their own sites for more information.

SLEEP	
Kell Whittle **Silver Sands Holiday Park,** Gwendreath, Kennack Sands, Helston, TR12 7LZ	info@silversandsholidaypark.co.uk www.silversandsholidaypark.co.uk 01326 290631
Dick Powell **Penmarth House,** Coverack, Lizard Peninsula, TR12 6TQ	dick@coverack-bandb.co.uk www.coverack-bandb.co.uk 01326 280240
Christine Sanger **Tregonning Lea,** Laddenvean, St Keverne, Helston, TR12 6QD	waltersanger@aol.com 01326 280947
David Lambrick **The Five Pilchards Inn,** Porthallow, TR12 6PP	fivepilchards@btinternet.com www.thefivepilchards.co.uk 01326 280256
Pam Royall **The Sail Loft,** Helford, Point, TR12 6JY	pamroyall@btinternet.com 01326 231083
Clare Lake **Gold Martin,** Carlidnack Road, Mawnan Smith, Falmouth, TR11 5HA	gold_martin@hotmail.com www.goldmartin.co.uk 01326 250666
Melanie Williams **Trevarn B&B,** Carwinion Road, Mawnan Smith, Falmouth, TR11 5JD	enquiries@trevarn.co.uk www.trevarn.co.uk 01326 251245 • 07877 580321
Judi Goodchild **Falmouth Lodge Backpackers,** 9 Gyllyngvase Terrace, Falmouth, TR11 4DL	judi@falmouthlodge.co.uk www.falmouthbackpackers.co.uk 01326 319996
Malcolm & Lynda Cook **The Rosemary,** 22 Gyllyngvase Terrace, Falmouth, TR11 4DL	stay@therosemary.co.uk www.therosemary.co.uk 01326 314669
Krysia Moseley **Bragnaza B&B,** Grove Hill, St Mawes, TR2 5BJ	braganzak@googlemail.com www.braganza-stmawes.co.uk 01326 270281
Ian & Val Soper **Honeycombe House,** 61 Polkirt Hill, Mevagissey, PL26 6UR	enquiries@honeycombehouse.co.uk www.honeycombehouse.com 01726 843750
Andrew Knights **Portscatho Holidays Ltd,** 4 The Quay, Truro, TR2 5DG	info@portscathoholidays.co.uk www.portscathoholidays.co.uk 01326 270900
Matthew Bailey **Par Inn,** 2 Harbour Road, Par, PL24 2BD	Mattybailey1@hotmail.co.uk www.parinn.co.uk 01726 815695

Week 6 - Day 1 (half day)

OS Maps: Landranger 200 or 204; Explorer 107

	This Walk	Cumulative	This Walk	Cumulative	Grading	Timing
Ascent	1,132ft	72,079ft	345m	21,970m	Moderate	3 hours
Distance	7.0mi	378.6mi	11.1km	609.4km		

For detailed directions see our Charlestown to Fowey Path Description booklet.

This Section goes out to the prominent Gribbin Head. The west side of the headland is relatively exposed, mostly on high cliffs, with views west over St Austell Bay. The east side is more indented and sheltered, the cliffs lower, and the path passes numerous scenic little sandy coves. At its eastern end the path enters the lovely part-wooded estuary of the River Fowey, culminating in the atmospheric little town of Fowey.

Directions

Par and Fowey are linked by a bus service, making this a bus-walk option. In addition, a popular local circular walk from Fowey takes in most of Gribbin Head, using the waymarked Saints' Way path with the Coast Path.

Par has all facilities, including a mainline railway station. For the Coast Path walk along the road called Par Green and follow the path which leaves the road next to no.52. After crossing the private clay haul road, fork right along a grassy path immediately before the chalet park. Follow this path before turning left then quickly right along the road to a small car park at the western end of the sands of Par Beach. Walk along the back of the beach to another car park at the far, eastern end. This is Polmear; a pub and buses are to be found on the road outside the car park.

The Coast Path crosses the car park to a footbridge and then up the cliffs and continues on to the little harbour village of Polkerris. Here are a pub, toilets and restaurant. The path continues from the back of the beach, up a ramp to join a zigzag path through woods to the top. The path now continues to the Daymark on Gribbin Head (or "The Gribbin"). The tower is open to visitors on some summer Sundays. From the Daymark follow the path downhill to the scenic cove at Polridmouth ("Pridmouth"), said to have inspired the setting for Daphne du Maurier's "Rebecca". Cross behind the beach and go up into the woods, then on over cliff-top fields and past a couple of small coves to arrive at another woodland. Look out for the path on the right, which goes past St Catherine's Castle and gives superb views upriver to Fowey. Now follow the path down a rocky track and behind Readymoney Cove before following the lane into Fowey.

Note that it is possible to walk Coast to Coast across Cornwall between Fowey and Padstow on the north coast using the Saints' Way. A guidebook is available from Fowey TIC.

The Coast Path and Gribbin Head

Week 6 - Day 1 (half day)

OS Maps: Landranger 200 or 204 (Fowey); Landranger 201 (remainder); Explorer 107

	This Walk	Cumulative	This Walk	Cumulative	Grading	Timing
Ascent	1,939ft	74,018ft	591m	22,561m	Strenuous	3.5 hours
Distance	7.1mi	385.7mi	11.5km	620.9km		

For detailed directions see our Fowey to Polperro Path Description booklet.

This is a connoisseur's Section – it is quiet and remote; it is scenic, with beautiful large sandy bays and smaller coves plus impressive headlands; it is started and finished at superbly picturesque locations, the Fowey estuary at one end and Polperro at the other; and it is quite hard work, emphasising that nothing this good should come too easily.

Directions

Polruan and Polperro are linked by a bus service, giving a bus-walk option, though unfortunately it does not operate at weekends. There is a popular scenic circular walk taking in Fowey and Polruan and using two ferries, an estuary tributary valley and the Coast Path.

Fowey is a charming little town, well worth exploring, with all facilities.

The crossing of the river to Polruan on the opposite bank is by foot ferry. In summer it usually operates from Whitehouse Quay, along the Esplanade, and in winter from the Town Quay. The ferry operates all year except Christmas Day at 5-10 minute intervals, telephone 01726 870232. For ferry details see page 19.

At Polruan, a picturesque little place, go up the steps next to The Lugger. Turn right at the top in West Street then turn left up Battery Lane. At the grassy area keep left by the wall then through the car park parallel to the coast to a signed path on the right. After around 2 miles/3km the path passes above and behind the impressive Lantic Bay, climbing steeply at the far end. There is a higher path here, going to the top of the hill and turning right, or a lower one, turning off right 30 yards/28m before the top, dropping then climbing again to meet the higher path (ignore beach turnings to the right). The path goes out around Pencarrow Head then behind an old watch house to descend and pass behind two charming and remote coves at Lansallos West and East Coombes. After climbing past

a marker warning shipping of an offshore rock more ups and downs follow until the path approaches the almost hidden inlet of Polperro. Follow the waymarked path to arrive at a rocky outlook point – go left here then fork right to descend to the harbour. Polperro, an impossibly picturesque harbour village, figures justifiably in most picture books and calendars of Cornwall. It has all facilities.

Walking from Polperro to Fowey

Week 6 - Day 2 (half day)

OS Maps: Landranger 201; Explorer 107

	This Walk	Cumulative	This Walk	Cumulative	Grading	Timing
Ascent	774ft	74,792ft	236m	22,797m	Moderate	2.25 hours
Distance	5.0mi	390.7mi	8.0km	628.9km		

For detailed directions see our Polperro to Looe Path Description booklet.

The cliffs on this Section, never really lofty, tend to decrease in height towards the east. This is a relatively sheltered length passing around lush bays, while offshore, Looe Island is a seaward focal point from the eastern end. Here, also, extensive rocky platforms are exposed at low tide. These factors, and the popularity of Polperro and Looe, have made this a justifiably popular length of coast.

Directions

There is a bus route between Polperro and Looe, making a bus-walk a popular option here.

Polperro is a popular visitors' destination with all facilities. The Coast Path crosses the stone bridge behind the harbour then turns right along The Warren. Climb out of the village upwards along the main path to the top and turn left when way ahead fenced off, onto narrow path to second stile. Go over stile and turn left on track on field edge to highway. Turn right, walk down road, which becomes a path, to the beach at Talland Bay. There are toilets and seasonal refreshments here. Pass behind the beach, going left then right by the public toilets and behind a second beach to a small car parking area. The path climbs back to the cliffs from here – keep well back from the crumbling edge. It then continues very clearly (ignore all turnings towards the beach) eventually arriving at the end of a suburban road at Hannafore, the western end of Looe. Continue along the road, or the lower promenade; there are toilets and seasonal refreshments along here. At the end a short stretch of road with no pavement turns alongside the mouth of the Looe River. Take steps down on the right to the riverside of West Looe. There is a seasonal and tidal ferry from here to East Looe, the main part of the town, as an option. Otherwise continue along the West Looe riverside and over the bridge, turning right into East Looe's main street. Looe has buses to Plymouth and a branch to the mainline railway at Liskeard - for the station turn left after the bridge. Between them, East and West Looe have all necessary facilities.

Heading for Looe

Coast Path   Hannafore 1/4 m

www.southwestcoastpath.org.uk

Week 6 - Day 2 (half day)

OS Maps: Landranger 201; Explorer 107 (western half); Explorer 108 (eastern half)

	This Walk	Cumulative	This Walk	Cumulative	Grading	Timing
Ascent	1,965ft	76,757ft	599m	23,396m	Strenuous, moderate in places	4.5 hours
Distance	7.6mi	398.3mi	12.2km	641.1km		

For detailed directions see our Looe to Portwrinkle Path Description booklet.

Quiet and relatively remote cliff lengths in the western and eastern parts of this Section are separated by a low-level, suburban length, or by an optional route via sea wall and beach between Seaton and Downderry. The western cliffs are covered in lush vegetation, scrub and woodland, and there are stretches where the sea is only glimpsed through the trees. The eastern cliffs are more open and give some superb views along the coast in both directions, with the distinctive Rame Head a focal point.

Directions

A bus service connects Seaton, Downderry and Portwrinkle, making a bus-walk option possible over the eastern end of this section. Further bus-walk options may be possible with a change of bus from Looe at Hessenford (inland from Looe).

From East Looe's town centre, turn up Castle Street (Ship Inn on the corner) and keep climbing until it becomes a footpath above the sea. Continue, then at a road turn right, passing Plaidy Beach, and continue until just after the road veers left inland. Here go right, up a steep tarmac path then ahead at the top until the road turns left. The Coast Path descends steps between houses to Millendreath Beach. There are refreshment facilities here – for details call 01503 263651. On the far side go up the cul-de-sac road and climb the sunken lane to reach another road. After 50 yards (45m) turn right and take the signed route left through twin gates across a drive. Follow the path ahead through woods to rejoin the road. Turn right on the road and keep ahead past the Monkey Sanctuary onto a narrow lane. At the crest of this lane turn right and cross the field, going left on the far side to follow the path until it arrives at the lane again. Turn right to descend to Seaton beach. Turn right and along the road behind the beach, where there are toilets and seasonal refreshments.

Although the official path follows the narrow and busy road up the hill to Downderry, if the tide is not high it is preferable to walk along the top of the sea wall from Seaton and then the beach, taking one of the choice of footpath links into Downderry, where there are pubs, shops, toilets and seasonal refreshments. Note that the most easterly link path shown on the OS map is currently closed. Follow the road to the eastern end

of Downderry, where it turns inland, and take the signed path right, which zigzags steeply upward. A superbly scenic cliff-top path, with several ups and downs, continues until it arrives at a road just above Portwrinkle. Turn right to descend to the village and the quiet sea-front road. The Jolly Roger Cafe and Bistro is open all year in Portwrinkle or other facilities are at Crafthole, a 10 minute walk uphill inland.

Looking up the Looe River in Autumn

Week 6 - Day 3

OS Maps: Landranger 201; Explorer 108

	This Walk	Cumulative	This Walk	Cumulative	Grading	Timing
Ascent	2,169ft	78,926ft	661m	24,057m	Moderate	5.75 hours
Distance	13.3mi	411.6mi	21.4km	662.5km		

For detailed directions see our Portwrinkle to Cawsand and Cawsand to Cremyll Path Description Booklet.

This is a Section of great interest rather than spectacular drama. There is a golf course, a gunnery range, a cliff face of wooden chalets and an historic Country Park. It also includes the magnificent and atmospheric Rame Head, which is a significant landmark for many miles along the coast in both directions, the charming twin villages of Cawsand and Kingsand and some superb views, including Plymouth Sound and, indeed, the city itself.

Directions

A bus route links Cremyll to Cawsand, part-way along the section, and also runs along the coast road adjacent to the Coast Path between Rame Head and Tregantle, giving various bus-walk options. There are a number of popular circular walks using the Coast Path based on Mount Edgcumbe Country Park, next to Cremyll, and also around Rame Head.

From Portwrinkle walk up the road, past the first footpath, which is a cul-de-sac, then turn right on the signed path opposite the golf club. After climbing, the path goes along the seaward side of the golf course. After leaving the golf course the path begins to rise towards the Tregantle Firing Ranges. When firing is not taking place it is possible to walk an excellent, well-signed permissive path through the ranges. At the time of going to print non-firing weekends (Friday to Sunday inclusive) for 2015 had not been confirmed, but will normally alternate throughout the year starting with 1st – 4th January. But please note that live firing may still take place on these weekends if operational requirements demand. In addition there is no live firing on Bank Holiday weekends nor on any day in August. Other non-firing days are known up to two weeks in advance - telephone The Ranges on 01752 822516 during office hours to check. If live firing is in progress red flags will be raised and the access gates locked - do not proceed into the range. If open, keep closely to the marked path and, at the far end of the range path, emerge through another security gate onto the National Trust's cliff-top path.

If the range path is closed, continue on the official Coast Path through a field to a road, where the path initially continues inside the hedge before joining the road further along. The road is usually quite busy so take care. There is the compensation of a magnificent view up the Tamar to Plymouth from the car parking area here, where there is often a refreshment van. Follow the road (past Tregantle Fort entrance) then turn right at the first road junction and continue along the road to the cliffs (passing where the range path emerges).

Naughty sheep close to Portwrinkle

The Coast Path is then off-road, along National Trust land, before it rejoins the road for about 1.25 miles/2km. The signed path then leaves the road again to descend onto the sloping cliff face, although this cliff length had to be closed in 2013 because of subsidence, the Coast Path continuing on the road. There is a cafe just off the path down the cliff at this point. If open, the path undulates quite steeply and meanders unexpectedly among chalets and gardens – keep alert for the waymarking – climbing back to the road. The route then descends gently across the cliff slope to Polhawn Cove at the base of Rame Head. After crossing a private access road for Polhawn Fort the path climbs to reach the headland. The official Coast Path route omits the very end, with its medieval chapel, but the easy climb is worthwhile for the views and the atmosphere.

A good cliff path then goes to Penlee Point, where there are the first views of Plymouth Sound. Bear left to reach a road then fork off to the right on the signed path through woods to descend to the charming little village of Cawsand, with pubs, toilets, shops and refreshments. Go through the village square to Garrett Street and continue, turning right in front of the Post Office having, imperceptibly, crossed into Kingsand. At The Cleave turn left then first right up Heavitree Road, which leads to a gate on the right into Mount Edgcumbe Country Park. Continue through the park to a road, turning right then almost immediately left, forking uphill through woods. After a woodland drive there is a waymarked diversion to avoid a cliff fall, the route climbing left to a higher level path before continuing parallel to the coast. Once around the fallen cliff the path descends to the foreshore of Plymouth Sound. Keep on the signed path up and through a deer gate then back down towards the shore to follow into an Italianate garden, past the Orangery of Mount Edgcumbe House (refreshments), and out through the park gates to the ferry point. Cremyll has a pub and toilets, but most will use it as the staging point for the ferry across the Tamar to Plymouth, an interesting excursion in its own right.

Week 6 - Day 4 (half day)

OS Maps: Landranger 201; Explorer 108

	This Walk	Cumulative	This Walk	Cumulative	Grading	Timing
Ascent	463ft	79,389ft	141m	24,198m	Easy	3.5 hours
Distance	7.5mi	419.1mi	12.0km	674.5km		

For detailed directions see our Admiral's Hard to The Barbican and The Barbican to Mount Batten Path Description Booklet.

This is an urban walk along the waterfront of one of the country's prime historical maritime cities. It is therefore quite different to the vast majority of the Coast Path, but is nevertheless well worth doing. The view over the Sound, flanked on both sides by cliffs, is inspiring, and often referred to as the finest urban vista in the country. Elsewhere are lengths of waterside industry, historic quays and modern marinas, making this a fascinating excursion.

Directions

A range of urban bus services runs throughout Plymouth, including to and from Admiral's Hard, the ferry point for Cremyll, and Mount Batten. Though not on the same route, they link in the city centre. There is also a ferry link across the mouth of the River Plym between the historic Sutton Harbour and Mount Batten. These links make a range of public transport-walks possible.

The Coast Path from Cremyll uses the ferry across the Tamar. The ferry operates all year, weather, tide and other circumstances permitting, generally at 30 minute intervals. Telephone 01752 822105. For ferry details see page 19.

Plymouth's Waterfront Walk is enhanced by a variety of information plaques and pieces of artwork relating to the city's history. A companion guidebook "Plymouth's Waterfront Walkway" is available free of charge from us, you will just pay postage.

Most of the route is waymarked by white bands on lamp-posts, red metal marker signs and pavement signs.

From the ferry walk up the road and turn right, going round the car park into Cremyll Street and on to the gates of the Royal William Yard. Enter the Yard via the walkway to the right of the main entrance and go through the Yard following the sea wall. (There is a ferry from the Royal William Yard to the Barbican that will also stop at Mount Batten on request for those who want a short cut.) At the far corner of the Yard's sea wall climb the Eric Wallis Memorial Steps to Devil's Point Park. Follow the path around the Park, overlooking Drake's Island and Plymouth Sound to reach the Artillery Tower, now a restaurant. At this point bear inland into Durnford Street and continue past the Royal Marines Barracks, turning right immediately after them. Continue along Millbay Road then, after the entrance to Millbay Docks, turn right into West Hoe Road. Fork right off here into Great Western Road, then bear off right down a narrow path along the shoreline. The path returns to the road; here turn right to walk along the Hoe promenade all the way to The Barbican and Sutton Harbour, Plymouth's original harbour. Above on the left, away from the Coast Path but worth a visit, are the lighthouse of Smeaton's Tower, Drake's statue and other points of interest.

At The Barbican on the right are the Mayflower Steps, the site of the Pilgrim Fathers' embarkation. The large pontoon on nearby Commercial Wharf is the ferry point for Mount Batten, an unofficial short cut direct to the end of the Section.

The ferry operates all year, telephone 07930 838614. For ferry details see page 19.

Continuing on the Coast Path Waterfront Walk, walk across the lock gates at the entrance to Sutton Harbour, past the Marine Aquarium and then along Teat's Hill Road past the entrance to Queen Anne's Battery. At Breakwater Road, just after the entrance to Victoria Wharves, turn right up a narrow hill and footpath and down to the industrial Cattedown Wharf area. Continue past warehouses, then left along Shapters Way, right into Maxwell Road and along Finnigan Road to Laira Bridge. Turn right to cross the River Plym then, at the first roundabout, turn right (at the rhinoceros!) Go right, into Breakwater Road, and continue for about 500 yards/450m then turn left, still in Breakwater Road, to the entrance to Yacht Haven Quay Boatyard. To the left of a mesh fence is a path, signed as the Coast Path, which is followed to Oreston Quay. At the quay walk past the grassy area into Marine Road then left into Park Lane. Turn left at the top of the hill, and this path descends to Radford Lake. From here a Coast-to-Coast walk goes to Lynmouth on the north coast, following the Erme-Plym Trail and the Two Moors Way. Guidebooks are available at Ivybridge TIC.

Go across the causeway with its old mini castle folly and turn right. Follow the path along then left and at a junction turn right down Hexton Hill Road to Hooe Lake. Skirt the lake, going along Barton Road and then turn left on a path to Turnchapel. Go through the village, bearing left at the Clovelly Bay Inn, up the hill then turn right down steps to the marina and over the slipway and along the shoreline to Mount Batten and the Sutton Harbour ferry. There are toilets, refreshments and a pub here. The short walk along the breakwater is very popular, although not part of the Coast Path.

Week 6 - Day 4 (half day)

OS Maps: Landranger 201; Explorer OL20

	This Walk	Cumulative	This Walk	Cumulative	Grading	Timing
Ascent	1,260ft	80,649ft	384m	24,582m	Easy	3 hours
Distance	7.3mi	426.4mi	11.8km	686.3km		

For detailed directions see our Mount Batten to Warren Point Path Description Booklet.

This is a Section of low cliffs, much of it overlooking Plymouth Sound. Below the cliffs are extensive areas of rock platform and offshore the Great Mew Stone becomes a focal point. Caravan and chalet sites and suburban villages are never far away and this is never a lonely Section. Towards its eastern end, as the cliffs rise somewhat, is the picturesque mouth of the River Yealm, forming a dramatic wooded gap in the cliffs.

Directions

Separate bus routes serve Mount Batten and Wembury village, and also Heybrook Bay, midway along this section, all from Plymouth city centre, allowing bus-walk options. There is a popular circular walk using the Coast Path between Wembury and Warren Point and a longer, full-day circular using the waymarked Erme-Plym Trail between Wembury and Mount Batten plus the Coast Path.

Mount Batten has toilets and refreshments, as well as a direct ferry link to and from Plymouth's Sutton Harbour. From Mount Batten the Coast Path heads over the little hill and past the old fort tower to the grassy area at Jennycliff, where there are more toilets and refreshments. Keep close above the shore and at the end of the grass, from the doormat to Plymouth use the renovated steps down and stairs up again to access woodland. The path then undulates and emerges above Fort Bovisand. Descend steeply to a road and turn left; there are seasonal refreshments here. Follow round to the right and up to pass seaward of the chalets, past a cafe and toilets and on round the point and so to Heybrook Bay. There is a pub a little way up the road here, as well as a bus stop. Keep right and follow the path above the shore around Wembury Point and on to Wembury Beach. Yet more toilets and refreshments await here and the bus stop, together with pub and shop, are in the village a little way inland.

From Wembury Beach a Coast-to-Coast walk goes to Lynmouth on the north coast, following the Erme-Plym Trail and the Two Moors Way. Guidebooks are available from Ivybridge TIC.

Continuing on the Coast Path, climb seaward of the church and along the now higher cliffs to a junction of paths at the Rocket House. The path going inland from here leads to Wembury village and its facilities. For the Coast Path, bear right, downhill, to reach the ferry point. Note that operating times on this ferry can be limited – see page 19 and Walk 49.

Mountbatten Point

Week 6 - Day 5

OS Maps: Landranger 201 (western end); Landranger 202 (remainder); Explorer OL20

	This Walk	Cumulative	This Walk	Cumulative	Grading	Timing
Ascent	2,450ft	83,099ft	747m	25,329m	Easy then strenuous	5.75 hours
Distance	13.5mi	439.9mi	21.8km	708.1km		

For detailed directions see our Noss Mayo to Mothecombe and Mothecombe to Thurlestone Path Description Booklet.

This is a fine Section of high-level coastal cliffs, cut mid-way by the substantial and extremely picturesque estuary of the River Erme. The western end is a particularly good length, since the superb cliff coastline is easily accessed by a scenic former carriage route. Beyond that a series of descents and ascents, some quite steep, accentuate the dramatic landscape of the coastline. At the eastern extremity is the tidally insular Burgh Island, a focal point on this part of the coast. Because of its remoteness and strenuous nature, much of this section has a quiet character which will specially appeal to those in search of a lonely coastline.

Directions

This remote length of coast only has public transport at its western end, so no bus-walks are feasible. There is a very popular local walk using the Coast Path on the carriage drive from Noss Mayo.

The ferry at Wembury's Warren Point operates three ways over the River Yealm and its tributary Newton Creek. Warren Point is thus linked with both Newton Ferrers and Noss Mayo, and these two points with each other. For the Coast Path the link between Warren Point and Noss Mayo is needed. The ferry operates seasonally and at limited times – telephone 01752 880079. For ferry details see page 19.

There is a signal board to summon the ferryman by the steps at Warren Point or the slipway at Noss Mayo. Alternatively, telephone beforehand.

Because of the somewhat limited nature of the ferry it may be necessary to make alternative arrangements to reach Noss Mayo. Both Wembury and Noss Mayo have a regular bus service to and from Plymouth, so it is possible to use these services as a link, perhaps combining with an overnight stop in Plymouth. Alternatively, local taxi companies are available: Eco-Taxi, based in Kingsbridge, will carry walkers between Plymouth and Dartmouth and from all estuaries in South Devon; telephone 01548 856347 or 07811 385275. Ivy Cabs, telephone 01752 895555, will also carry walkers round the South Devon estuaries as will John Pitcher at Wembury Cabs, details page 103.

It is also possible to walk round the Yealm Estuary from ferry point to ferry point. This is a distance of some 9 miles/14.5km, effectively adding an extra day or half day to the itinerary.

Walk around the Yealm Estuary

Walk uphill inland from the ferry steps to the house at the top, the Rocket House. Continue inland along the track, which in turn becomes a road. Where the road bears sharp right go ahead along a public footpath into a field, then keep ahead alongside a high wall. At the end of the wall, after two gates, bear left (bearing 330) across fields, then go down a few steps. The now enclosed path goes left then right to arrive at a road. This is Knighton, on the outskirts of Wembury. The bus stop for Plymouth is a little way to the left, just before the pub.

To continue the walking route around the estuary cross the road at Knighton to a minor lane, following it left to another junction. Turn right here and continue until the road meets another, more major, road. Cross this road, going ahead and left for a short way then turn right on a signed footpath. This is part of a waymarked route, the Erme-Plym Trail, and is shown on the OS Explorer OL20 map. Follow the waymarked route across fields, over Cofflete Creek, next to a lane and on to the village of Brixton. Turn right and follow the road through the village to Brixton Church then back on the Erme-Plym Trail up Old Road, along a suburban road, over fields, along a minor lane then over more fields to arrive at another village, Yealmpton. On reaching the A379 road at Yealmpton the Erme-Plym Trail is now abandoned. Here, turn right along the A379 then quickly left, into Stray Park. At the bottom bear right along a tarmac path then, when it arrives at a road, turn left along a stony track. At the footpath sign continue ahead, eventually emerging at a road by a car park. Turn left along the road to cross Puslinch Bridge then follow the road up the hill. Take the footpath on the right near the top of the hill, crossing a couple of fields to a road. Turn right and continue to meet a more major road, which is followed ahead to Newton Ferrers. At the edge of the village turn left down the road signed to Bridgend and Noss Mayo, and at the junction at the head of the creek keep to the right. Follow the riverside road, forking right into Noss Mayo. Keep on the road round Noss Creek and continue on the creekside road out of the village until this becomes a track. A signed path on the right leaves the track for the ferry point.

Coast Path, Noss Mayo-River Erme

From the ferry point, follow the path westward through the woods as it climbs to meet a track, an old carriage drive. The drive continues through woods, past a row of former coastguard cottages, into more woods, then on a superb cliff-face shelf round Mouthstone Point. Further on keep right where the more obvious path bears left inland to a car park, the drive continuing round Stoke Point and on to Beacon Hill. A series of ups and downs now ensues as the path approaches the estuary of the River Erme, which has been fairly described as England's most unspoiled river estuary, and is possibly the most attractive. The path crosses the top of a small beach then passes through a short woodland stretch to arrive at Mothecombe slipway on the Erme. There are seasonal refreshments a little way inland.

There is no ferry at the River Erme. It is usually possible to wade the river 1 hour either side of low water along the old ford and, under normal conditions, at low tide the water is about knee deep and the river bed is of sand with pebbles. The crossing is between grid references 614 476 and 620 478, ie the road by the row of coastguard cottages at Mothecombe and the end of the inland road to Wonwell Beach. However, great care should be taken as heavy rains or high seas can make conditions dangerous. Low water is approximately at the same time as at Devonport; see tide tables on pages 21-23.

If timing makes wading impossible there are local taxi companies Eco-Taxi telephone 01548 856347 or 07811 385275, or Ivy Cabs, telephone 01752 895555.

Alternatively, it is possible to walk round the estuary. There are no riverside rights of way and for the most part minor roads must be used. The distance is approximately 8 miles/13km, adding an extra half day to the itinerary.

Walk round the Erme Estuary

From the slipway follow the road inland, following signs to Holbeton. Go through the village and leave on the minor lane to Ford and then Hole Farm. At the sharp bend after this farm follow the waymarked Erme-Plym Trail to the A379 and across the River Erme at Sequer's Bridge. Then leave the waymarked trail, continuing very carefully along the A379 for a couple of hundred yards/metres, before turning right on the lane signed to Orcheton. Follow this for about 2 miles/3km then turn right, following signs for Wonwell Beach. Follow the lane downhill to arrive at the estuary.

Coast Path, River Erme-Bigbury-on-Sea

Just inland of the Wonwell slipway a path leaves the lane into the woods then continues above the shore, emerging on cliffs which rollercoaster up and down to the holiday park at Challaborough. There are toilets here and also the year round Venus Café. On Burgh Island offshore, reached by walking across the sands or by unusual sea tractor, is a pub.

Week 6 - Day 6 (half day)

OS Maps: Landranger 202; Explorer OL20

	This Walk	Cumulative	This Walk	Cumulative	Grading	Timing
Ascent	876ft	83,975ft	267m	25,596m	Moderate	2.75 hours
Distance	5.7mi	445.6mi	9.2km	717.3km		

For detailed directions see our Mothecombe to Thurlestone and Thurlestone to Salcombe Path Description Booklet.

This is a well-used and popular Section, never far from residential and holiday accommodation. It is a length of low cliffs and sandy beaches, the coastline providing some interesting seascapes. These include views of the tidal Burgh Island, the estuary of the River Avon, the distinctive holed Thurlestone Rock and the headland of Bolt Tail. At the end of the Section, Hope Cove is a charming little settlement with a picturesque harbour and an old centre of historic cottages.

Directions

A regular, if infrequent, bus service links Thurlestone and Hope Cove, making a bus-walk option possible. There is a popular short circular walk using the Coast Path between Bantham and Thurlestone.

From the main facilities at Bigbury-on-Sea the Coast Path goes along the road, turning right immediately after the car park entrance to follow a short cliff-top length which re-joins the road further up. Cross the road and follow the path along the field edge next to the road. Leave the field where signed and cross the road, passing through Folly Farm and down the cliffs to the flat open area of Cockleridge Ham. At the edge is the ferry point for the crossing of the mouth of the River Avon.

The ferry is seasonal and operates at limited times – telephone 01548 561196. For ferry details see page 20. The ferryman is alerted by waving. It must be noted that if the ferry is not operating on arrival the river should NOT be forded, despite its sometimes benign appearance. There are local taxi services, ie: Eco-Taxi, telephone 07811 385275; or Ivy Cabs, telephone 01752 895555.

Alternatively, there is a waymarked walk round the estuary between Bigbury-on-Sea and Bantham on the opposite bank. This route, the Avon Estuary Walk, is signed with blue waymarks and adds about 8 miles/13km to the route, or another half day to the itinerary. The route is shown on OS Explorer map OL20.

Avon Estuary Walk

The route is accessed by continuing up the road, without turning into Folly Farm, for a further 60 yards/55m and then turning right. The path reaches the golf course, turning left on a track then off this to the right, down another track past Hexdown Farm. Follow this track to the bottom then go left along a drive which eventually arrives at a road. There is a permissive path alongside the road and at the end of this a path goes right over a field, through the top of a wood then downhill over another field to a road alongside the estuary. This tidal road is then followed to Aveton Gifford on the A379. At high tide there is a waymarked diversion which crosses the tidal road on arriving at it and re-joins it next to the village. From Aveton Gifford cross the Avon on the A379 then

Burgh Island

take the first lane on the right, which becomes a track and continues to Stadbury Farm. Bear left approaching the farm onto a footpath, following field edges towards the valley bottom to cross Stiddicombe Creek. Enter the wood on the right and climb to leave at the far top corner. Follow the top edge of fields then cross a farm track and a stream to a junction of paths. Turn right and continue to Bantham village, where there is a pub, shop, toilets and seasonal refreshments as well as the ferry point.

Coast Path, Bantham-Hope Cove

From the ferry point go through the car park and round the edge of the dunes of Bantham Ham. Follow the shore, leaving the dunes and climbing past the edge of Thurlestone Golf Club to descend to Thurlestone Sands. Cross a long footbridge at an inland lagoon (South Milton Ley), pass public toilets and seasonal refreshments then join a road for a short stretch before turning back to the shoreline and over low cliffs to Outer Hope, where there are all facilities in season. Follow the path behind the little harbour and down to the old lifeboat station at Inner Hope, where the bus stop is situated. Buses to Kingsbridge leave from here. A little inland is the old village centre of Inner Hope, at The Square, a picture-postcard location worth seeing before leaving.

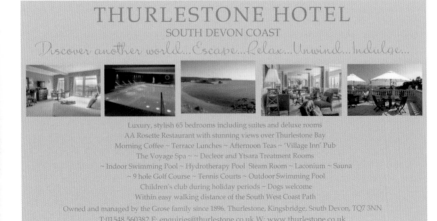

Week 6 - Day 6 (half day)

OS Maps: Landranger 202; Explorer OL20

	This Walk	Cumulative	This Walk	Cumulative	Grading	Timing
Ascent	1,506ft	85,481ft	459m	26,055m	Strenuous	4 hours
Distance	8.0mi	453.6mi	12.9km	730.2km		

For detailed directions see our Thurlestone to Salcombe Path Description Booklet.

This is a very scenic Section of the coast, largely comprising quite spectacular high cliffs soaring above tiny, mostly inaccessible coves. Near both ends are dramatic headlands, Bolt Tail in the west and Bolt Head in the east, offering superb coastal views in their respective directions. At the eastern end this Section turns into the mouth of the estuary of Salcombe Harbour, and there is the contrast of softer, sandy bays. This is a length which is never really remote, but never really busy.

Directions

Separate bus routes serve Hope Cove and Salcombe from Kingsbridge, a few miles inland, making a bus-walk feasible from there. However, there are numerous popular local circuits using the Coast Path which are based on Hope Cove and Salcombe.

Leave Hope Cove from the old lifeboat station at Inner Hope up the signed Coast Path and out to the magnificent viewpoint of Bolt Tail, where the ramparts of an Iron Age cliff fort are crossed to reach the end. The path doubles back along the cliff top over Bolberry Down and then down to the splendid little Soar Mill Cove. Climbing from the cove a long level stretch of easy walking follows. Keep along the cliff top and as the path approaches Bolt Head pass through a couple of gates, staying on the closest path to the cliff top as possible. A steep descent will then lead to the headland, where a sharp turn leads to the cliff-face path round Starehole Bay and then on to the Courtenay Walk below rocky pinnacles. Passing into woodland at the National Trust's Overbecks property

the path joins a road which is followed past South Sands and North Sands – toilets and seasonal refreshments at both – and then on into Salcombe town centre. For a variation, there is a summer ferry service between South Sands and Salcombe. The town is a renowned yachting centre and has all facilities.

Hope Cove

Week 6 - Day 7

OS Maps: Landranger 202; Explorer OL20

	This Walk	Cumulative	This Walk	Cumulative	Grading	Timing
Ascent	2,251ft	87,732ft	686m	26,741m	Strenuous	6.75 hours
Distance	12.9mi	466.5mi	20.8km	751.0km		

For detailed directions see our Salcombe to Torcross Path Description booklet.

This is a superb section of walking. Part of it is on exposed cliff faces, the sometimes stark cliffs contrasting with numerous tiny sandy coves below. A significant length in the middle is on an old "raised beach", a low shelf a little above the sea giving an easy passage here. In the east the path crosses the rocky spine of Start Point, behind its lighthouse, a dramatic stretch, before following a lush, sheltered length into Torcross.

Directions

Salcombe and Torcross are both on regular bus routes to and from Kingsbridge, a little inland, making a bus-walk possible from that town. There is also a popular local circuit using the Coast Path from the Salcombe Ferry.

Salcombe has all necessary facilities. The ferry across the estuary leaves from steps next to the Ferry Hotel, a little way downstream from the town centre. The ferry operates all year; telephone 01548 842061 or 01548 560558. For ferry details see page 20.

From the ferry point on the eastern side, where there are toilets and refreshments, the Coast Path follows the road down the estuary side then, after crossing the rear of the beach at Mill Bay (toilets), passes the refreshment facilities at Gara Rock (call 01548 844810 for details), then follows a clear cliff path to Prawle Point. The path goes to the Coastwatch lookout at the very end, then descends to follow the "raised beach" shelf just above the waves before a short inland length to avoid a cliff fall leads to Lannacombe Beach. Beyond here a dramatic length goes along and up to the rocky ridge leading to Start Point, the path dropping to the lighthouse access road. From the car park at the top the path bears off right down the cliff face to Hallsands, passing above the old ruined village. A short diversion to the viewpoint is both instructive and interesting.

The path continues over low cliffs to Beesands, where there is a pub, toilets and seasonal refreshments. Continue along the shingle ridge then behind an old quarry to descend into Torcross, with a panoramic view of Slapton Ley ahead on the descent. Torcross has all facilities, and buses to Plymouth, Kingsbridge and Dartmouth.

Start Point Lighthouse

If you enjoy sleeping, eating or drinking at any business on the Path please suggest they join us as Business Members so that we can share their brilliance!

The businesses listed here are all supporters of the South West Coast Path, they have joined as Business Members and it would be great if you could show your support for them too. Additional Businesses are listed on **www.southwestcoastpath.org.uk** with links to their own sites for more information.

DO

Samantha Short **Kingsbridge Tourist Info Centre,** The Quay, Kingsbridge, TQ7 1HS	info@welcomesouthdevon.co.uk www.welcomesouthdevon.co.uk 01548 853195

EAT & DRINK

Mandy & Steve Shephard **The House on Props Restaurant,** Talland Street, Polperro, PL13 2RE	houseonprops@btinternet.com www.houseonprops.co.uk 01503 272310
Christine Colmer **The Odd Wheel,** Knighton Road, Wembury, Plymouth, PL9 0JD	theoddwheel@btconnect.com www.theoddwheel.co.uk 01752 863052

SLEEP

Bella Alexander **Hormond House B&B,** 55 Fore Street, Polruan, PL23 1PH	bella@chrisbella.demon.co.uk www.hormondhouse.com 01726 870853 • 07703 170969
Mandy & Steve Shephard **The House on Props B&B, Polperro,** Talland Street, Polperro, PL13 2RE	houseonprops@btinternet.com www.houseonprops.co.uk 01503 272310
John Prinn **Hannafore Point Hotel,** Marine Drive, Hannafore, West Looe, PL13 2DG	stay@hannaforepointhotel.com www.hannaforepointhotel.com 01503 263273
Stephen Morton **The Sail Loft Studio,** Vine Street, Princes Street, West Looe, PL13 2ER	sailloftstudio@seasidecottagesincornwall.co.uk www.seasidecottagesincornwall.co.uk 0756 4525132
Fiona Harvey **The Bungalow B&B,** Cliff Road, Portwrinkle, PL11 3BY	fiona.harvey334@btinternet.com www.portwrinklebedandbreakfast.co.uk 01503 230334
Linda Dunstone **Maker Camping,** 6 Old Coastguard Cottage, Cawsand, Torpoint, PL10 1LN	makerevents@hotmail.com www.makerfestival.co.uk 07900 994231
Mrs Jeanette King **Coombe House,** Coombe Farm, Fourlanesend, Cawsand, PL10 1LR	info@coombehouse-cawsand.co.uk www.coombehouse-cawsand.co.uk 01752 823925
Ann Heasman **Cliff House,** Devonport Hill, Kingsand, PL10 1NJ	chkingsand@aol.com www.cliffhouse-kingsand.co.uk 01752 823110
Sue Broad **Trelidden Farm,** Downderry, Torpoint, PL11 3DP	www.treliddon-farm.co.uk 01503 250288
Carla Williams **Edgcumbe Guest House,** 50 Pier Street, West Hoe, Plymouth, PL1 3BT	enquiries@edgcumbeguesthouse.co.uk www.edgcumbeguesthouse.co.uk 01752 660675
Jan Kirsop-Taylor **The Rusty Anchor Guest House,** 30 Grand Parade, Plymouth, PL1 3DJ	jankirsoptaylor@me.com www.therustyanchor-plymouth.co.uk 01752 663924
Rod Davies & Ann Young **Raleigh Stile B&B,** 1 Raleigh Stile, Hexton Hill Road, Hooe, Plymouth, PL9 9WA	roddaviesofcornwall@yahoo.co.uk www.raleighstile.co.uk 01752 492232
Phil Greenwood **Wembury Bay B&B,** 2 Warren Close, Wembury, PL9 0AF	pwgreenwood59@gmail.com www.wemburybaybedandbreakfast.yolasite.com 01752 863392

Sam Philpott **Churchwood Valley,** Wembury Bay, Plymouth, PL9 0DZ	info@churchwoodvalley.com www.churchwoodvalley.com 01752 862382
John & Lorraine Pitcher **Ferrystop B&B,** 1 Barton Close, Wembury, PL9 0LF	lorraine.pitcher123@btinternet.com 01752 863710
Sue Spooner **Cellars,** Passage Wood Road, Noss Mayo, PL8 1EU	suespoonerrogers@btinternet.com 01752 872771
Jackie Rogers **Worswell Barton Farmhouse,** Noss Mayo, Near Plymouth, PL8 1HB	info@worswellbarton.co.uk www.worswellbarton.co.uk 01752 872977
Mark Walker **Blackadon Barn Holiday Cottages,** Blackadon Farm, Ivybridge, PL21 0HB	info@blackadonbarns.co.uk www.blackadonbarns.co.uk 01752 897034
Richard & Jane Baker **Kimberley B&B,** Ringmore, Near Kingsbridge, TQ7 4HJ	bakerjanem@hotmail.co.uk www.kimberley-annex.co.uk 01548 811115
Pat Dolby **1, Coastguard Cottages,** Challaborough Bay, Near Kingsbridge, TQ7 4HT	patdolby1951@hotmail.co.uk 07517151635
Kim Roberts **Summerwinds,** Marine Drive, Bigbury on Sea, TQ7 4AS	pritchard212@btinternet.com 01548 810669
Mr Vanstone **Holywell B&B,** St Ann's Chapel, Bigbury, Near Kingsbridge, TQ7 4HQ	holywellstores@msn.com www.holywell-bigburybedandbreakfast.co.uk 01548 810308
Jane Griffiths **The Old Post Office,** South Milton, Kingsbridge, TQ7 3JQ	toposouthmilton@hotmail.co.uk www.theoldpostofficesouthmilton.co.uk 07760 225717
Sarah Ireland **The Cottage Hotel,** Hope Cove, Kingsbridge, TQ7 3HJ	info@hopecove.com www.hopecove.com 01548 561555
Sandra Wilson **Kings Arms Cottages,** Fore Street, Kingsbridge, TQ7 1AB	stay@kingsarmscottage.co.uk www.kingsarmscottage.co.uk 01548 854023 • 07989394704
James Norton **Toad Hall Cottages,** Elliott House, Church Street, Kingsbridge, TQ7 1BY	james@toadhallcottages.co.uk www.toadhallcottages.co.uk 01548 853089
Sue & Richard Agar **Ashleigh House,** Ashleigh Road, Kingsbridge, TQ7 1HB	reception@ashleigh-house.co.uk www.ashleigh-house.co.uk 01548 852893
Val Mercer **Old Walls,** Slapton, Kingsbridge, TQ7 2EJ	val.slapton@gmail.com www.slaptonbandb.co.uk 01548 580516
Valerie Johnson **Valseph,** Beesands, Near Kingsbridge, TQ7 2EJ	valseph@btinternet.com www.beesandsbandb.co.uk 01548 580650 • 017890197673
Rachel Wood **The Cricket Inn,** Beesands, Near Kingsbridge, TQ7 2EN	enquiries@thecricketinn.com www.thecricketinn.com 01548 580215
Judy Foss **Down Farm Holidays,** Down Farm, Near Start Point, Kingsbridge, TQ7 2NQ	downfarm@btinternet.com www.downfarm.co.uk 01548 511234
Mrs Anne Petty Brown **Rocarno B&B,** Grenville Road, Salcombe, TQ8 8BJ	rocarno@aol.com www.rocarno.co.uk 01548 842732
Pauline Snelson **Waverley B&B,** Devon Road, Salcombe, TQ8 8HL	paulinesnelson@icloud.com www.waverleybandb.co.u 01548 842633

Week 7 - Day 1

OS Maps: Landranger 202; Explorer OL20

	This Walk	Cumulative	This Walk	Cumulative	Grading	Timing
Ascent	1,493ft	89,225ft	455m	27,196m	Easy then strenuous	4.75 hours
Distance	10.2mi	476.7mi	16.4km	767.4km		

For detailed directions see our Torcross to Kingswear Path Description Booklet.

Something like a quarter of this Section consists of the low shingle ridge known locally as the Slapton Line, cutting off the freshwater lake of Slapton Ley from the sea. Most of the remainder of the Section is cliffs and coves, partly looking to the sea and partly to the outer reaches of the picturesque wooded Dart Estuary.

Directions

A regular bus service runs along the coast road which is, for much of the Section, adjacent to the Coast Path. With stops at most obvious locations this gives numerous bus-walk options. There is also a very popular and scenic circular walk using the Coast Path between Dartmouth and the mouth of the Dart Estuary.

From Torcross, with all facilities, the Coast Path runs along the shingle ridge. The official route is on the landward side but it is possible, if more tiring, to walk along the seaward side. After the Strete Gate car park, look out for the fingerpost signing the new section of Coast Path, opened in summer 2015. Follow the path along the cliff top and through the woods to the A379. It is now necessary to walk along this and for the next 400 yards/365m.

Follow the main road through Strete village (pub and shop) then, just after the village end, take the path to the right which passes over fields and a footbridge to reach a high point above the sea. Continuing parallel to the coast for a while it then heads inland over a deep valley, crossing the main road and over more fields to a lane. Descend the lane then leave it across more fields until, after crossing the main road again, the picturesque cove of Blackpool Sands is reached. There are toilets and seasonal refreshments. Follow the path uphill through the woods then the route enters and meanders along various paths in the village of Stoke Fleming (pub, shop and toilets), arriving at the village hall. Cross the main road again and follow a lane to a National Trust car park. From here a

scenic cliff path proceeds, latterly through woods, to reach the Dart Estuary and arrive at Dartmouth Castle. An estuary-side path passes the adjacent church and joins the road which is followed into the town. Look out for some steps on the right just after the public toilets before reaching the centre; the steps lead down to Bayards Cove through its little castle and on to the Embankment at the town centre. Dartmouth, of course, has all facilities.

Near Strete looking at Slapton Sands

Week 7 - Day 2

OS Maps: Landranger 202; Explorer OL20

	This Walk	Cumulative	This Walk	Cumulative	Grading	Timing
Ascent	2,992ft	92,217ft	912m	28,108m	Strenuous	5.75 hours
Distance	10.8mi	487.5mi	17.3km	784.7km		

For detailed directions see our Kingswear to Brixham Path Description Booklet.

This is a Section of superb cliff scenery, tough going in places and often quite lonely. In the west, near the mouth of the Dart, are substantial wooded areas but further along the cliffs become higher and more open. This makes for a dramatic, steeply undulating landscape ending at the sea in steep cliff faces.

Directions

A regular bus service links Brixham and Kingswear, on the east side of the Dartmouth Ferry, making a bus-walk possible. There is also a popular circuit using the Coast Path based on Kingswear.

Walkers have two ferry options from Dartmouth town centre to cross the river, the Lower Car Ferry, which also carries foot passengers, and the Dartmouth Passenger Ferry. The Lower Car Ferry operates all year on a continuous service telephone 01803 752342. The Dartmouth Passenger Ferry also operates all year on a continuous service telephone 01803 555872. For ferry details see page 20.

From either ferry landing point in Kingswear, follow the Coast Path signposts, turning left along Beacon Road then right up Church Hill and down Beacon Lane. Continue out of the village. After some 1.25 miles/2km turn right down steps and undulate sometimes steeply into and through woodland to the old Battery buildings at Froward Point. Here the path descends steeply to the right from the corner of an old lookout building, passing World War II searchlight and gun positions before continuing along the cliffs. Pass Pudcombe Cove, by the National Trust Coleton Fishacre Gardens, and then on over Scabbacombe Head and past Scabbacombe Sands and Man Sands and over Southdown Cliff to Sharkham Point – this is a particularly strenuous length. Passing holiday accommodation the path arrives at Berry Head, a Napoleonic fortified area. Divert to the end of the headland to see the unusually squat lighthouse. Berry Head has toilets and seasonal refreshments. From here descend past an old quarry to a road, where there are further refreshment facilities at the Guard House Cafe (01803 855778). Turn right then go right again through the Shoalstone Car Park and along above the shoreline, returning to the road before descending steps to Brixham Breakwater. Follow the promenade to the harbour. Brixham has all facilities.

Week 7 - Day 3

OS Maps: Landranger 202: Explorer OL20 (western half); Explorer 110 (eastern half)

	This Walk	Cumulative	This Walk	Cumulative	Grading	Timing
Ascent	1,972ft	94,189ft	601m	28,709m	Moderate	6 hours
Distance	12.8mi	500.3mi	20.5km	805.2km		

*For detailed directions see our Brixham to Torquay and Torquay to Shaldon
Path Description booklets.*

This is mostly an urban Section, passing along the shoreline of the "English Riviera", or Tor Bay. There is a mixture of grand terraces, open green parkland, amusement parks and the elegant white buildings overlooking the sea at Torquay. At the western end there is also the old fishing town of Brixham and at the other end the almost rural wooded cliffs around Babbacombe. All in all, this is a surprisingly diverse Section.

Directions

A range of bus routes runs throughout the Torbay area, including one which follows the coast road between Brixham and Torquay, and another linking Torquay to Babbacombe. As a result, a wide variety of bus-walks is possible. A pleasant alternative is the Torquay to Brixham ferry which runs regularly.

Leaving Brixham by the fish market, the Coast Path initially passes a car park and gardens before passing two small coves and climbing into woodland which takes the path to Elberry Cove. From here it passes behind the sweep of Broadsands, climbing by the railway viaduct at the far end to proceed alongside the steam railway line to the promenade at Goodrington. At the far end climb through ornamental gardens and go down a road to Paignton Harbour and so along the promenade. Paignton's railway station is inland of the pier. Turn inland at Hollicombe, at the far end of Preston Sands, going through a park to the main sea-front road which is followed to Torquay Harbour. Torquay Station is inland a little before the harbour.

Cross the pedestrian bridge across the harbour and climb the hill, turning right at the Imperial Hotel on the signed path which leads to the open area at Daddyhole Plain. Descend to the sea-front road at Meadfoot Beach, climbing again at Ilsham Marine Drive. Take the cliff path round Thatcher Point to Hope's Nose. A cul-de-sac path goes to the end of this low headland.

From Hope's Nose follow the path inland of the road, crossing the road to the Bishop's Walk, which in turn arrives at a car park above Anstey's Cove. The path now goes round the edge of the grassy downs on Walls Hill, bearing off right to descend to Babbacombe Beach. Cross a wooden footbridge to Oddicombe Beach then climb by the cliff railway to reach Babbacombe's facilities at the top.

Oddicombe Cliff Railway, Babbacombe

Week 7 - Day 4 (half day)

OS Maps: Landranger 202; Explorer 110

	This Walk	Cumulative	This Walk	Cumulative	Grading	Timing
Ascent	2,090ft	96,279ft	637m	29,346m	Strenuous	3.75 hours
Distance	6.4mi	506.7mi	10.3km	815.5km		

For detailed directions see our Torquay to Shaldon Path Description booklet.

This is a tough Section of almost constant ups and downs. The characteristic red cliffs of this part of Devon are often quite high and quite sheer, though unfortunately the terrain is such that sea and cliff views are perhaps less frequent than would be wished. Its strenuous nature makes it a relatively quiet Section, except for the two ends, although it is never far from roads or housing.

Directions

A regular bus service links Babbacombe and Teignmouth, making a bus-walk an option.

From Babbacombe, a pleasant suburb of Torquay with all facilities, the Coast Path descends next to the cliff railway and then soon climbs again to avoid a cliff fall. This diversion takes the path up a grassy area to a main road where it turns right, then right again into Petitor Road. At the bottom turn left on the Coast Path again, which soon descends onto a cliff face before reaching the wooded valley at Watcombe. Cross the track running down the valley and on through a wooded length to a short rocky stretch, turning right at a junction before reaching the car park at Maidencombe. There is a pub and toilets here. Turn right after the car park and keep on the rollercoaster path which eventually climbs to go alongside the coast road, then quickly leaves it to pass alongside fields to a track. Turn right and go round the wooded Ness headland, with super views ahead, descending to the promenade at Shaldon, on the estuary of the River Teign.

The ferry service across the River Teign operates throughout the year, weather permitting - mobile: 07896 711822. For ferry details see page 20.

Walk, Shaldon-Teignmouth

If the ferry is not operating, continue inland along the riverside roads to Shaldon Bridge and cross the Teign. On the Teignmouth side turn right into Milford Park, through Bitton Sports Ground into Park Hill, cross into Bitton Avenue then into Clay Lane and right into Willow Street. At the end bear left then right into Quay Road, then right to go along the Strand and right to the Harbour Beach and the ferry point. Teignmouth has all facilities, including a mainline rail station and buses to Exeter.

Teignmouth Beach

Week 7 - Day 4 (half day)

OS Maps: Landranger 192; Explorer 110

	This Walk	Cumulative	This Walk	Cumulative	Grading	Timing
Ascent	488ft	96,767ft	149m	29,495m	Easy	3 hours
Distance	7.9mi	514.6mi	12.7km	828.2km		

For detailed directions see our Shaldon to Exmouth Path Description booklet.

This Section primarily comprises two fairly large seaside towns, flanked by a coastline of high red cliffs at one end and marshes and a sand bar at the other. Running through it, often next to the Coast Path, is possibly the most scenic part of Brunel's GWR railway line, the embankment of which forms the sea wall for much of this length. This is a busy, largely urban and much used Section with an historic importance to the tourist trade.

Directions

A regular bus service links Teignmouth and Starcross, the ferry point for Exmouth, and also passes through Dawlish and Dawlish Warren. As there are also stations on the railway line at these places, bus or train-walks are options here.

From the ferry point at Teignmouth, or from the town centre, go to the car park at The Point, jutting out into the Teign Estuary, and begin by walking along the promenade. Leaving the town the Coast Path continues between railway and sea below the red cliffs to the end, where it descends steps to pass under the railway and then up Smugglers Lane to the A379 road at the top.

High water route, Teignmouth-Smugglers Lane

With a high sea and an onshore wind the far end of the promenade can become very wet, and for about an hour either side of high tide the steps at Smugglers Lane become impassable. In these cases, immediately after leaving the town fork left and cross the railway on a footbridge on Eastcliff Walk, and this path eventually reaches the A379 which is then followed ahead to meet the official path at the top of Smugglers Lane.

Coast Path, Smugglers Lane-Dawlish Warren

Use the footway on the inland side of the A379 and walk for about 150 yards/135m before turning right into Windward Lane, going immediately left on a path which skirts fields before returning to the A379. Bear right into Old Teignmouth Road, which in turn returns to the A379 then, very soon, turn right by some railings on a path which zigzags down to the shoreline. Follow the sea wall through Dawlish, past the station – all facilities are found beyond the railway here. The Coast Path then continues on the sea wall between railway and sea, again below the red cliffs, to Dawlish Warren. Just before the amusement area cross the obvious railway footbridge to a car park, turn right and follow to the main road.

High water route, Dawlish-Dawlish Warren

Occasionally, at the highest tides, it becomes impossible to proceed along the sea wall for a short stretch just beyond the station. In this case, cross the footbridge immediately after the station and follow the path up to the A379. Turn right and continue alongside

Dawlish looking down on the town

the road until the path bears slightly away from the road (opposite Henty Avenue). Here follow the path that bears off right, going right at a fork to descend to another footbridge over the railway and return to the sea wall.

Coast Path, Dawlish Warren-Starcross

The Coast Path does not go around the large sand spit at Dawlish Warren itself, jutting out into the mouth of the River Exe, or the marshes behind it, but if there is time this can be an exhilarating experience. Otherwise continue along Warren Road on the pavement, then opposite the entrance to Dawlish Warren Sandy Park join the cycleway and footpath to Cockwood Harbour. After following the road around the harbour join the A379. Cross the road and follow the footpath and cycleway to Starcross, and the ferry point to Exmouth. Starcross has all facilities.

The ferry operates mid-April – end October, telephone 01626 862452 or 07974 022536. For ferry details see page 20. If there is no ferry operating on arrival at Starcross, there are several options to reach Exmouth.

Option 1: Explorer Water Taxi – this runs daily 1st April until 31st October. Check their web site before travelling as times vary: www.exeplorerwatertaxis.co.uk

Option 2: Bus or train from Starcross to Exeter, bus or train from Exeter to Exmouth.

Option 3: Walk from Starcross to Turf Lock following the waymarked Exe Valley Way on the riverside road and footpath (3 miles/5km), then ferry Turf Lock-Topsham and bus or train from Topsham to Exmouth.

Ferry operates seasonally – telephone 07778 370582. For ferry details see page 20.

Option 4: Walk from Starcross to Topsham Lock following the waymarked Exe Valley Way on the riverside road and footpath and Exeter Canal towpath (4.5 miles/7km), then ferry Topsham Lock-Topsham and bus or train from Topsham to Exmouth.

Ferry operates seasonally – telephone 01392 274306 (office) or 07801 203338 (ferryman). For ferry details see page 20.

Week 7 - Day 5 (half day)

OS Maps: **Landranger 192; Explorer 115**

	This Walk	Cumulative	This Walk	Cumulative	Grading	Timing
Ascent	722ft	97,489ft	220m	29,715m	Moderate	3 hours
Distance	6.2mi	520.8mi	9.9km	838.1km		

For detailed directions see our Exmouth to Sidmouth Path Description booklet.

This is a well-used and popular Section, never far from houses and passing a large caravan site and a golf course on the way. Most of this length is on relatively low cliffs, and in the west these give excellent views over the mouth of the Exe and the great sandy bar of Dawlish Warren. Further east, the high point of West Down Beacon gives exceptionally fine panoramic views, while beyond the Beacon the path becomes more enclosed. It is an easy-going Section of some variety, ideal for those not wishing to explore remote or strenuous lengths.

Directions

A regular bus service links Exmouth and Budleigh Salterton, making this a good bus-walk option. In addition, a summer service links Exmouth with Sandy Bay, approximately mid-way along the section, giving another, shorter bus-walk.

Exmouth has all facilities, including a railway station on a branch line from Exeter. The obvious route for the Coast Path is to walk along the promenade from the former, now redeveloped, docks area at the mouth of the Exe, which is also the ferry landing point. Continue to the cliffs at Orcombe Point then climb the steps and continue on the cliff top, passing the Jurassic Coast marker and on to the Devon Cliffs Caravan Site at Sandy Bay. Follow the fence line inland of the Straight Point rifle range then climb to the high point at West Down Beacon. The path then descends steadily, seaward of the golf course though offering relatively few sea views on this stretch. Approaching Budleigh Salterton, a charming and traditional small town, the path turns inland then almost immediately, at a junction, goes right to descend to the end of the promenade. The shops, pubs and other facilities are immediately inland of the path, which continues towards the distinctive line of pine trees to the east of the town.

Red sandstone - Budleigh Salterton

www.southwestcoastpath.org.uk

127

Week 7 - Day 5 (half day)

OS Maps: Landranger 192; Explorer 115

	This Walk	Cumulative	This Walk	Cumulative	Grading	Timing
Ascent	1,037ft	98,526ft	316m	30,031m	Moderate then strenuous	3.5 hours
Distance	6.9mi	527.7mi	11.1km	849.2km		

For detailed directions see our Exmouth to Sidmouth Path Description booklet.

This pleasant Section is mostly on relatively low red cliffs with attractive views inland over an undulating pastoral countryside as well as to seaward. However, there are contrasts at both ends. The western end skirts the narrow, marsh-fringed estuary of the River Otter while the eastern end includes a wooded cliff top and high cliffs on the appropriately named High Peak and Peak Hill. This is a pleasant and quietly popular Section.

Directions

A regular bus service links Budleigh Salterton and Sidmouth, making a bus-walk a possibility.

Budleigh Salterton, a town with something of an olde-world air, has all facilities.
The Coast Path goes along the promenade to the car park at the eastern end. Progress east seems tantalisingly close, but the River Otter, with no bridge at its mouth, bars the way. The path therefore passes through a gate at the rear riverside corner of the car park and follows the riverside path until it meets a road. Turn right and cross the River Otter on the road bridge, then bear right to follow the path back downriver to the sea, bearing round to the left on reaching the cliffs.

The path is clear to the caravan site at Ladram Bay, where there are toilets and seasonal refreshments. Here, descend across a field to the beach access track, going left then immediately right, past a pub and on to climb into woodland at High Peak. Here, the path goes behind the very top, emerging on a track. Turn right and climb again to the open land at Peak Hill. Follow the path down the cliff through woodland to a road, turn right then keep right along an old road length then onto a large grassy area down to a zigzag path next to the white Jacob's Ladder. At the bottom follow the seafront path to reach the main esplanade. Sidmouth is an elegant Regency town and has all facilities.

Sidmouth

Week 7 - Day 6

OS Maps: Landranger 192; Explorer 115 (most); Explorer 116 (eastern end)

	This Walk	Cumulative	This Walk	Cumulative	Grading	Timing
Ascent	2,408ft	100,934ft	734m	30,765m	Severe then strenuous	5.5 hours
Distance	10.4mi	538.1mi	16.7km	865.9km		

For detailed directions see our Sidmouth to Lyme Regis Path Description booklet.

This is a Section of lofty cliffs cut by deep and narrow valleys, making for a magnificent coastal landscape but a testing one to walk. In the west the cliffs are characteristically red, but this changes quite abruptly along the length as the Section reaches the most westerly chalk cliffs in England, appropriately bright white. Add an elegant Regency town, a charming picture-postcard village and a picturesque fishing town and the result is a length of great attraction.

Directions

A regular bus service links Sidmouth with Seaton, making a bus-walk an option. There are also regular, if less frequent, bus links to Branscombe and Beer, along the length, giving further options.

The Coast Path passes along the elegant esplanade at Sidmouth to the footbridge over the mouth of the River Sid at the eastern end. Some dramatic cliff falls have occurred just east of Sidmouth and a well-signed diversion is necessary past housing until, at the top of Laskeys Lane, it turns back to the cliff top. A steep climb up Salcombe Hill is soon followed by an equally steep descent and climb through the Salcombe Regis valley. The path skirts behind the hollow of Lincombe then descends to the beach at Weston Mouth. A short way along the beach the path leaves to climb steeply back to the cliffs and a good level stretch which eventually turns inland to meet a track. This descends to Branscombe Mouth, where there are refreshments and toilets. Beyond Branscombe the official path passes among some holiday chalets then along an undercliff path, with the cliffs rearing massively above, before climbing to the cliff top at Beer Head. These are the most westerly chalk cliffs in England. An alternative route from Branscombe Mouth climbs up the valley side and proceeds directly along the cliff top to Beer Head.

Follow the signed path from Beer Head, past a caravan site and into the village behind the beach. Beer, an attractive fishing village, has all facilities. Climb the path on the east side of the beach to the cliff top, descending to a road and down to Seaton Hole. If the tide is low, walk along the beach to the end of the promenade at Seaton. If not, an inland diversion must now be taken. A cliff fall caused by the extreme wet weather in 2012 has created a very large hole in Old Beer Road, necessitating permanent closure of the previous Coast Path route. At Seaton Hole one must now turn left on to Old Beer Road and walk approximately 220 yards/200m inland towards Beer. At the junction with the B3172 Beer Road, turn right towards Seaton. After approximately 985 yards/900m, leave the Beer Road and take the path on the right through the chine and on to the promenade and so into Seaton, which has all facilities, including bus services to Exeter, Weymouth and Poole.

The businesses listed here are all supporters of the South West Coast Path, they have joined as Business Members and it would be great if you could show your support for them too. Additional Businesses are listed on **www.southwestcoastpath.org.uk** with links to their own sites for more information.

EAT & DRINK

Rebecca Prideaux **Kings Arms,** Dartmouth Road, Strete, TQ6 0RW	kingsarmsstrete@gmail.com www.kingsarmsstrete.co.uk 01803 770380

SLEEP

Ingrid Sidell **Roxburgh House,** Dartmouth Road, Strete, TQ6 0RW	ingrid@roxburghhouse.co.uk www.roxburghhouse.co.uk 01803 770870
Shirley Tonkin **Fairholme,** Bay View Estate, Stoke Fleming, Dartmouth, TQ6 0QX	stay@fairholmedartmouth.co.uk www.fairholmedartmouth.co.uk 01803 770356
Mrs E Helyer **Eight Bells B&B,** South Embankment, Dartmouth, TQ6 9BB	lizhelyer20@gmail.com www.dartmouthbandb.com 7813803472
Roger Jordan **Cladda House,** 88-90 Victoria Road, Dartmouth, TQ6 9EF	BandB@cladda-dartmouth.co.uk www.cladda-dartmouth.co.uk 07967 060003 • 01803 835957
Valerie Ruddle **Estuary View,** 11 Horn Hill, Dartmouth, TQ6 9RA	vjruddle@gmail.com www.estuaryview.co.uk 01803 834066 • 0795 0852014
Jean Wright **Camelot B&B,** 61 Victoria Road, Dartmouth, TQ6 9RX	jjwright@talktalk.net 01803 833805
Nigel Makin **Beacon House B&B,** Prospect House, South Furzeham, Brixham, TQ5 8JB	enquiries@beaconbrixham.co.uk www.beaconbrixham.co.uk 01803 428720
Helen Barrow **South Bay Holiday Park,** St Mary's Road, Brixham, TQ5 9QW	hsbarrow@uwclub.net 01626 821221
Mandy Tooze **Elberry Farm B&B,** Broadsands, Paignton, TQ4 6HJ	enquiries@elberryfarm.co.uk www.elberryfarm.co.uk 01803 842939
Julia Frost **Garway Lodge Guest House,** 79 Avenue Road, Torquay, TQ2 5LL	info@garwaylodge.co.uk www.garwaylodge.co.uk 01803 293126 • 07711 552878
Sheila Brewer **Coastguard Cottage,** 84 Babbacombe Downs Road, Babbacombe, TQ1 3LU	sheila.besidethesea@gmail.com 01803 311634 • 0778 0661381
Jacqui Blenkinsopp **Aveland House,** Aveland Road, Babbacombe, Torquay, TQ1 3PT	avelandhouse@aol.com www.avelandhouse.co.uk 01803 326622
Tracy Howell **Babbacombe Palms,** 2 York Road, Babbacombe, TQ1 3SG	reception@babbacombepalms.com www.babbacombepalms.com 01803 327087
Kate Wood **The Downs,** 41-43 Babbacombe Downs Road, Babbacombe, TQ1 3LN	enquiries@downshotel.co.uk www.downshotel.co.uk 01803 328543
Palle & Rose Jessen **Quentance Farm,** Salterton Road, West Down Beacon, Exmouth, EX8 5BW	palleandrose@hotmail.com www.quentancefarm.co.uk 01395 442733 • 07584 165900
Jane Simmonds **Chapter House,** Westbourne Terrace, Off Jubilee Park, Budleigh Salterton, EX9 6BR	chapterhouse@fsmail.net 01395 444100 • 7817849512
Caroline Thomas **Bidwell Farm Cottages,** Upottery, Near Honiton, EX14 9PP	caroline@bidwellfarm.co.uk www.bidwellfarm.co.uk 01823 259138 • 07984 628718
Alistair Handyside **Higher Wiscombe,** Southleigh, South Devon, EX24 6JF	info@higherwiscombe.com www.higherwiscombe.com 01404 871360 • 07772 630104 • 07771 678028

What it feels like to be alive!

Week 8 - Day 1 (half day)

OS Maps: Landranger 193; Explorer 116

	This Walk	Cumulative	This Walk	Cumulative	Grading	Timing
Ascent	1,401ft	102,335ft	427m	31,192m	Moderate	3.5 hours
Distance	6.8mi	544.9mi	11.0km	876.9km		

For detailed directions see our Sidmouth to Lyme Regis Path Description booklet.

This unique length of the Coast Path was made impassable by the storms of winter 2013-14, which badly impacted on the still-active landslip which forms the National Nature Reserve of the Axmouth-Lyme Regis Undercliffs. We anticipate a new route will be in place in the near future, in which case follow the waymarked route. Check on the Association web site at www.southwestcoastpath.org.uk/walk-coast-path/trip-planning/route-changes/ for the latest position. While there is a regular bus service between Seaton and Lyme Regis (X53), the Association recommends a very attractive inland alternative for use as a stop-gap until a coastal route can be re-established.

Directions

Leave Seaton on the Coast Path route which crosses the River Axe and turns right up the golf course access road and past the club house. Continue due east over the fairway and along a bridleway. Keep ahead where the Coast Path turns off to the right, soon arriving at a road (Stepps Lane).

Turn right along this quiet lane and continue for approximately 1.5 miles/2.5km to a junction in the hamlet of Dowlands. Follow the lane signed to Rousdon then turn right at a telephone box onto a public bridleway. Pass through a gate and under an arch into the Rousdon Estate. Follow the straight access road for 0.5 mile/0.8km and exit through the arch on the other side.

The bridleway then becomes a lane. At the junction after Charton Farm, by a large grey barn, turn left and continue to a crossroads. Cross this fairly busy road (A3052) and continue on the road opposite for another 0.5 mile/0.8km before turning right at a crossroads, signed to Shapwick. Keep on this lane to its end and here turn left, signed Uplyme.

After approximately 100 yards/91metres take the public bridleway on the right just past Shapwick House. Cross the field, heading for the cream coloured house, go through a gate and follow the bridleway to the left of the house. Follow this for approximately 0.25 mile/0.4km.

Just after some footpaths to the left, take the signed public footpath to the right, just past a cottage. Follow this up and round the cottage and over a stile then follow along the side of a field for about 100 yards/91metres before the path turns left and over another stile. After two more stiles the path emerges in Gore Lane. Turn right. At the Ware crossroads re-cross the A3052 and follow the lane opposite for just over 0.5 mile/0.8km, passing two paths leaving on the right. Turn right off the lane at the 30mph speed limit sign, just before a sharp left-hand bend, signed "to Coast Path – the Cobb 0.75 mile".

Follow the well-marked path down the valley, through a gate; bear right at the finger post marked "to Coast Path" and at the next junction of paths follow that signed for the Coast Path to Lyme Regis. Pass through a kissing gate and down the steps to the Cobb, Lyme Regis's harbour. Lyme Regis is a charming and attractive town and has all facilities.

Week 8 - Day 1 (half day)

OS Maps: Landranger 193; Explorer 116

	This Walk	Cumulative	This Walk	Cumulative	Grading	Timing
Ascent	1,883ft	104,218ft	574m	31,766m	Moderate then strenuous	3 hours
Distance	6.7mi	551.6mi	10.9km	887.8km		

For detailed directions see our Lyme Regis to West Bay Path Description booklet.

A major feature of this Section is the large number of cliff slippages caused by a combination of wet weather and geology. This means that as things currently stand there is effectively no proper coastal path between Lyme Regis and Charmouth (approximately 3 miles/4.5km), nor, indeed, immediately east of Charmouth. However, the remainder of this Section is a superb coastal experience, climbing as it does over the top of Golden Cap, the highest point on the entire south coast of England, with views to match as well as an energy requirement of a high level!

Directions

A regular bus service which could be used as a basis for a bus-walk links Lyme Regis, Charmouth and Chideock, which is about 0.75 mile/1.25km inland of Seatown.

Major diversions have had to be put in place in this Section, especially between Lyme Regis and Charmouth, to avoid the considerable cliff falls that have occurred. It looks likely that these diversions will remain in place for 2015. However, for up-to-date details check the Association's website (www.southwestcoastpath.org.uk).

Lyme Regis is a charming and attractive town with all facilities. From the Cobb Harbour proceed along the esplanade to the small car park at Cobb Gate and the Millennium Clock Tower: the town centre is on your left. Continue along the new sea wall for approximately 500m to steps on left. Go up the steps and continue on the footpath. Cross Charmouth Road car park to the main road (A3052), then turn right uphill past the Football Club, beyond which there is a gate at the corner of a lane to a footpath across fields to a lane where the route turns left for 100 yards/90m. Turn right at a sign up through woods and near the top is a path junction.

Official Coastal Route, Lyme Regis-Charmouth

Follow the route along the new sea wall and then down onto the beach, walking along the beach as far as the Charmouth Heritage Centre/Café. Due to landslides the route is very narrow and SHOULD ONLY BE ATTEMPTED AT LOW WATER. Many people are cut off by the tide on this stretch each year and have to be rescued. The mid-section is quite difficult due to large rocks and boulders, with no clear path through.

Official Diversion, Lyme Regis-Charmouth

Dorset County Council have installed and waymarked their official diversion. At the path junction in the wood (at GR 3456 9330) turn left for 130 yards/120m to meet Timber Hill. Turn right here to join in some 440 yards/400m the A3052 road and continue on this for 110 yards/100m. Turn eastwards on a public footpath signposted to Fern Hill, crossing the golf course then north-east through woods to re-join the A3052. Turn right to the roundabout with the A35 and fork right, signposted to Charmouth, following the road into the village for 760 yards/700m. At the second road junction turn right into Higher Sea Lane. When the road bends right take a footpath south-east and continue for about 650 yards/600m to re-join the official Coast Path at GR3640 9305.

Official Diversion, Charmouth West

If the official route from Lyme Regis to the edge of Charmouth is in place, there may still be the necessity for a diversion at the western end of Charmouth. This will take the route from the west end of Old Lyme Hill north-eastwards to the main road through the village. It then turns right and, after 110 yards/100m right again into Higher Sea Lane as above.

Preferred Diversion, Lyme Regis-Charmouth

The Association recommends a preferable alternative to the official diversion above, which deviates from it at the A3052/A35 roundabout. Take the road signposted to Charmouth and shortly after the junction take steps on the right to a stile and public footpath. Follow the waymarked direction up the field to the former Lily Farm, now holiday accommodation. Cross a stile and pass between the buildings and the Dutch barn on the left and after the buildings cross a field to arrive at a tarmac lane (Old Lyme Hill). Turn right and after 90 yards/80m turn left to arrive at Old Lyme Road.

Go left along Old Lyme Road and after 80 yards/70m turn right into a private road, Westcliffe Road. Descend steeply for 330 yards/300m to a junction with Five Acres. Bear right here and at the end of the cul-de-sac take a footpath going forward into a narrow lane. Shortly it reaches a wider road (Higher Sea Lane). Turn right and continue ahead, ignoring various signs pointing off the lane, continuing round the bend to the west in the lane that rises for some 130 yards/120m to an oak signpost on the left. Here leave the lane through a metal gate to re-join the Coast Path, descending over grassy slopes to Charmouth Beach, with its toilets and refreshments.

Official Route, Charmouth East

The official route crosses a footbridge and climbs the obvious green path ahead. This is unlikely to be available for 2015.

Diversion, Charmouth East

From the approach to the footbridge go north-east along a tarmac lane (River Way) and at the end continue along a gravel path to Bridge Road. Continue to the main village road (The Street) then turn right, cross the bridge and fork right into Stonebarrow Lane. Continue up this narrow lane for nearly 0.75 mile/1.25km. At the car park at the top turn sharp right to a signpost then take a grassy track as signed south-westward to re-join the Coast Path.

Coast Path, Charmouth East-Seatown (Chideock)

There is a hefty climb to Golden Cap, the highest point on England's south coast, but the views from the top are spectacular. At the top go slightly left to the trig point which then leads to the long and steep descent. There is a minor diversion on the approach to Seatown, taking the Coast Path slightly inland then back to the coast along the access road. Seatown has toilets and refreshments. Other facilities are at Chideock, 0.75 mile/1.25km inland.

Towards Golden Cap

Week 8 - Day 2

OS Maps: Landranger 193 (western half); Explorer 116 (western half)
Landranger 194 (eastern half); Explorer OL15 (eastern half)

	This Walk	Cumulative	This Walk	Cumulative	Grading	Timing
Ascent	1,489ft	105,707ft	454m	32,220m	Strenuous then moderate	6.25 hours
Distance	12.4mi	564.0mi	19.9km	907.7km		

For detailed directions see our Lyme Regis to West Bay and West Bay to Abbotsbury Path Description booklets.

This is a Section of two contrasting halves. West of West Bay is a rollercoaster of steep and high cliffs, giving far-reaching views along the coast and also inland, over the deeply dissected pastoral countryside. East of West Bay a sheer red sandstone cliff rises from the sea, looking almost artificial in its straight lines, and then the coastline subsides to a low level and the Coast Path loses its ups and downs, though not its hard work, as the shingle of what is the far western end of Chesil Beach tests the legs.

Directions

A regular bus service links Chideock, which is 0.75 mile/1.25km inland of Seatown, with Abbotsbury, and also calls at West Bay and Burton Bradstock which are along the length of this Section, giving various bus-walk options. A popular circular walk based on Abbotsbury uses the Coast Path as well as the South Dorset Ridgeway.

From the pub and toilets at Seatown the Coast Path climbs the cliff slope on its way to the high point of Thorncombe Beacon. There is a descent to the little beach at Eype then a further climb and descent to the harbour at West Bay, which has most facilities. Go round the back of the harbour, pass to the right of the church and ahead to the West Bay public house, opposite which is the Coast Path sign pointing to the surprisingly steep cliff. Arriving at Burton Freshwater the path runs between the caravan park and the beach and is well signed. Following major cliff falls in the summer of 2012 the Coast Path has been reopened along Burton Cliff, although a short inland diversion is necessary around the hotel leading to Burton Beach, where there are refreshments and toilets. Further on, the path passes inland of Burton Mere before coming to West Bexington, where there are toilets and seasonal refreshments.

See Section 71 for details of the alternative Inland Coast Path (South Dorset Ridgeway) between West Bexington and Osmington Mills.

The Coast Path continues along the back of the beach, later passing another car park with toilets and seasonal refreshments and some 200 yards/185m beyond this it turns inland to Abbotsbury. There are alternative routes either going into the village or going south and east of Chapel Hill and missing the village. A permissive path alternative leaves the Coast Path and leads direct to the famous Swannery. Abbotsbury is a beautiful stone-built village with much of historic interest and most facilities.

Burton Bradstock

Week 8 - Day 3

OS Maps: Landranger 194; Explorer OL15

	This Walk	Cumulative	This Walk	Cumulative	Grading	Timing
Ascent	955ft	106,662ft	291m	32,511m	Easy. Chesil Beach route strenuous	4 hours official route
Distance	10.9mi	574.9mi	17.5km	925.2km		

For detailed directions see our Abbotsbury to Ferry Bridge Path Description booklet.

This is an untypical Section of the Coast Path. In the west, there is an inland rural high-level field route, giving views over the unusual feature of Chesil Beach and the landlocked Fleet behind. To the east, the path runs along the banks of the Fleet, with pleasant views over this attractive feature, but with views of the sea largely cut off by the shingle bank of Chesil Beach. Although never far from houses or roads, this is often a very quiet Section.

Directions

Buses to and from Abbotsbury and Ferry Bridge link at Weymouth for a potential bus-walk.

It is possible to walk direct from the beach near Abbotsbury to Ferry Bridge at Wyke Regis along the length of Chesil Beach. If this is intended, start at the beach at the inland turn (Day 2) to Abbotsbury, continuing along the beach. However, note that:

1. It is not possible to get off the beach before Ferry Bridge.
2. It is extremely hard and slow walking.
3. It is necessary to check that firing is not scheduled at the nearby Chickerell Rifle Range; telephone Major Hazard on 01305 783456, ext.8132.
4. The beach is closed to visitors from 1st May to 31st August for the bird nesting season.

Although the Coast Path does not pass through Abbotsbury most walkers will visit the attractive village and its facilities. From the village leave West Street on the path going south adjacent to Chapel Street Stores. Continue on to Nunnery Grove to the signed Coast Path, which now goes inland but is well signed and enjoyable with some excellent views. After Horsepool Farm on the edge of Abbotsbury the path climbs onto the ridge. After about a mile/1.5km turn right off the ridge then left after Hodder's Coppice. Cross a minor road then follow the field headland east then south to the north-east corner of Wyke Wood. The path then heads for the edge of the Fleet – be aware approaching

Rodden Hive that the path suddenly goes through a hedge on the left. From here the path follows the edge of the Fleet. At Tidmoor Point follow the red and white posts, unless it is necessary to divert inland because of firing. The diversion is well marked. Approaching Wyke Regis there is a minor deviation behind an MOD Bridging Hard, then the path arrives at the A354 road adjacent to Ferry Bridge, the access for the Isle of Portland, at Wyke Regis, a suburb of Weymouth.

Tidmoor Point Rifle Range

Week 8 - Day 4

OS Maps: Landranger 194; Explorer OL15

	This Walk	Cumulative	This Walk	Cumulative	Grading	Timing
Ascent	1,112ft	107,774ft	339m	32,850m	Moderate	6 hours
Distance	13.2mi	588.1mi	21.3km	946.5km		

For detailed directions see our Portland Path description booklet.

Portland is different. Different from the rest of Dorset and from the rest of the Coast Path. An almost-island, jutting out into the English Channel, joined to the mainland only by the end of Chesil Beach, it has an isolated air. Formed of limestone, it has been extensively quarried and these workings, some still operational, characterise much of the landscape. Elsewhere, former military buildings and those of Verne Prison and the Young Offenders' Institution are prominent. Portland is rugged rather than pretty, but it is well worth exploring with superb views and a rich natural and historic heritage.

Directions

Bus routes run the length of Portland, making a variety of bus-walks possible. This Section is, in any event, a circular walk in its own right. However, at the time of going to print there were suggestions that the service all the way to the Bill may be discontinued. Check on local bus information.

It is possible to omit this section and continue from Wyke Regis directly into Weymouth. However, Portland is officially part of the National Trail and its interest and sense of being different make it well worth the day's walk.

From Ferry Bridge cross the causeway onto Portland; this is done by simply following the shared footway/cycleway alongside the A354 road or alternatively by crossing the bridge on the A354 to beyond the boatyard and then walking along the raised bed of the old railway on the eastern bank to near the end of the causeway at the roundabout for the access road to Osprey Quay and here returning to the footway/cycleway. At the southern of the two roundabouts at Victoria Square take the main road south and shortly turn right into Pebble Lane then left just before the public toilets. Continue to the Cove House Inn and bear right up onto the promenade. About half way along, at the floodgates, cut back sharp left then right, following Coast Path signs up a steep tarmac path, past the school and up the steep path in the grass incline to the steps to the terraced path that was once the old road. Bear off right onto the signed path running between quarry banks and the cliff face, leading to 3 miles/5km of airy cliff-top walking to Portland Bill. Two short lengths of the Coast Path above West Wears have remained closed since January 2013 following movement in the cliffs. Follow the signed diversions as you proceed along the old quarrymen's tramway. At Portland Bill, as well as the lighthouse, are refreshments, toilets and buses (but see above).

Continue around the end of the low headland then start northwards, seaward of the wooden chalets, to follow a winding path along the top of low cliffs to join a road above Freshwater Bay after about 1.5 miles/2.5km. Turn right on the road (use the footway on the west side of the road) for 600 yards/550m, past Cheyne Weares car park to a signpost on the right. Follow the zigzag path into the undercliff area and follow the waymarking through disused quarry workings to Church Ope Cove.

Ascend the stepped and signed path up to Rufus Castle. Here the South West Coast Path also becomes the England Coast Path, the first section of which, from here to Lulworth Cove, was formally opened on 30th June 2012. The signposting now usually indicates simply "Coast Path". Some, but not all, of the improvements to the route that the Association sought on Portland can now be walked and the new route is described below. Unfortunately the major alignment around the north-east corner of Portland was not resolved because of legal complications with Portland Ports plc and security issues.

After Rufus Castle the Coast Path soon joins the track bed of the former Weymouth to Easton railway line. This is then followed northwards for some 1,585 yards/1,450m to a pair of signposts. Here turn left to follow a rocky path that climbs up the cliffs to what appears to be an isolated chimney seen on the skyline above. At the top turn sharp right along the prison road northwards and through a gap in a high wall. On the right is the Old Engine Shed, soon to be converted into a visitor centre. On reaching a narrow road the official route is signed across the road and takes a route across open ground passing disused quarries to reach the perimeter fence of the Verne prison. However, the Association's preferred route here, which is all on public rights of way, can be followed thus:

At the road turn right and just over the brow of a hill turn left on an access track to compounds. Continue ahead on a grassy path towards a large pinnacle of rock (Nichodemus Knob) after which, at the "rock falls" sign, bear left steeply up onto the higher escarpment, heading for a large communications mast. At the high wire perimeter fence turn left and follow it along then round to the right, to reach the south entrance to Verne Prison. Here rejoin the route of the England Coast Path.

Take a path through a little gap to the left of the entrance, passing beside railings and down steep steps. Bear right along a path that traverses under the grassy banks.

The path drops downhill towards houses to a waymark post. Ignore the left fork and continue on the level on a grass path which then passes through an underpass below a road. Descend steeply down the Castletown Incline (a former quarry tramway), crossing two footpaths and a road. Pass under a footbridge and through another underpass to reach an access road and turn left to a roundabout.

Continue ahead for some 30 yards/27m and then cross to turn right down Liberty Road, signposted to Portland Castle. Go past the castle entrance to the car park and turn

right towards the harbour, heading for five black posts. Here join the footway/ cycleway to follow the harbour-side to the Sailing Academy, the venue of the sailing events at the 2012 Olympics. Continue on the footway/cycleway to reach the roundabout on the A354 road. From here follow the former railway trackbed to the boatyard before the bridge over the mouth of the Fleet and follow the footway alongside the road to Ferry Bridge.

Hikers along the Coast Path on Portland

Week 8 - Day 5

OS Maps: Landranger 194; Explorer OL15

	This Walk	Cumulative	This Walk	Cumulative	Grading	Timing
Ascent	2,385ft	110,159ft	727m	33,577m	Easy to moderate to strenuous	6.25 hours
Distance	14.1mi	602.2mi	22.7km	969.2km		

For detailed directions see our Ferry Bridge to Lulworth Cove Path Description booklet.

This section is part of the first section of the England Coast Path. The signposting generally only refers to "Coast Path".

The western part of this Section is an urban walk along the various lengths of Weymouth's sea front. East of the town is a length of relatively low cliffs but then at White Nothe, two thirds of the way along the section, the coastal geology changes. East of here is a rollercoaster of often sheer white cliffs, the length punctuated by the iconic landmarks of Durdle Door and Lulworth Cove. Both ends of this Section are busy, but in the centre is an often quiet and remote length.

Directions

A regular bus service links Weymouth with Lulworth Cove, also serving Osmington, close to the Coast Path mid-way along this Section, allowing some bus-walk options.

From Ferry Bridge the signed Coast Path follows the footway/cycleway on the old railway trackbed, passing behind the sailing centre. Shortly afterwards bear off right to continue into Old Castle Road. Ignore the footpath sign to the right, a cul-de-sac as the onward cliff path is closed due to a landslip. However, except at high tides the beach can be used to reach a flight of new timber steps that rejoin the former Coast Path beyond the landslip. Instead, continue along the road and 260 yards/240m beyond turn right into Belle Vue Road. Continue for about 600 yards/560m to a crossroads and turn right into Redcliff View. At the end of this road a path leads across a grassed area back to the coast at GR 682 781. Continue on the path to Nothe Fort and bear sharp left then turn down steps on the right to Weymouth harbourside. This is followed to the Town Bridge, which is crossed and the opposite side of the harbour followed back to the Pavilion complex. Bear left to join the Esplanade.

From April, Ferries operate (rowing boats) to cross the harbour, slightly shortening the route, but they are weather dependent. Telephone 01305 838423. For ferry details see page 20.

Leave Weymouth along the promenade then, at Overcombe, go up the minor road to Bowleaze Cove. After passing the Spyglass Inn the route now bears right to cross the crest of the grass public open space to reach the Beachside Centre. With the new public access rights now provided the Coast Path follows a signed route through the Beachside Leisure Centre to take a narrow path that squeezes between the Riviera Hotel and cliff edge and follows a new signed route to Redcliff Point. A little further on, beyond an education and adventure centre, follow the signed route on a re-established length of the Coast Path. On the downhill approach to Osmington Mills the route avoids another landslip by bearing away from the cliff edge over a stile and down the edge of a field, then crosses two further stiles to meet a narrow road down to the coast.

See Section 71 for details of the alternative Inland Coast Path (South Dorset Ridgeway) between West Bexington and Osmington Mills.

The path goes slightly inland at Ringstead. Beyond the wooden church the route of the Coast Path near Holworth House is now signed to deviate north-east and south although the original route (which is a public right of way) can still be used as a more direct route.

Further on, at the coastguard cottages at White Nothe, take the left fork of the two yellow arrows. The path now traverses some quite severe gradients on its way to Lulworth Cove, passing behind Durdle Door to Hambury Tout. Follow the waymarking here – the route sometimes shown on older maps going south here is not usable. Approaching Lulworth Cove a stone-pitched path leads down through the car park to the Heritage Centre. Turn right here along the cliff past the view into Stair Hole. Pass the Jurassic Coast commemorative stone then turn down towards the Cove in front of the boathouse. Lulworth Cove has toilets and refreshments and most facilities are found here or at West Lulworth a little way inland.

Durdle Door

Week 8 - Day 6 (half day)

OS Maps: Landranger 194 (most); Landranger 195 (eastern end); Explorer OL15

	This Walk	Cumulative	This Walk	Cumulative	Grading	Timing
Ascent	2,002ft	112,161ft	610m	34,187m	Severe	4 hours
Distance	7.3mi	609.5mi	11.8km	981.0km		

For detailed directions see our Lulworth to Kimmeridge Path Description booklet.

The coast of this Section is of geological interest and importance, largely having been formed by lines of relatively hard limestone having been breached at intervals to form coves and bays as the sea erodes the softer rocks behind. The result is a dramatic coastline of white cliffs and darker coloured coves, some prominent headlands and a succession of extremely steep slopes. Inland, the landscape of the military ranges has been unchanged by farming for some seventy years, though it is perhaps a little too obviously military in a few places.

Directions

Lulworth Cove and Kimmeridge village (inland from Kimmeridge Bay) have extremely limited bus services to Wareham, Corfe Castle and Swanage, which could provide a bus-walk option.

IMPORTANT: Note that this Section passes through the Lulworth Army Firing Ranges. Before deciding to walk this Section, check that the Ranges are open. PLEASE BE AWARE THE OFFICIAL COAST PATH FOR THIS SECTION MAY BE CLOSED TO WALKERS DURING THE WEEK. However most weekends and during school holidays it is normally open, but please read the section below to check the dates when walkers are allowed access along the official Coast Path.

The Lulworth Range walks, including the Coast Path between Lulworth Cove and Kimmeridge Bay, plus access to Tyneham village, are open to the public every weekend.

LULWORTH RANGE WALKS AND TYNEHAM VILLAGE - OPENING TIMES 2016

The Lulworth Range walks and Tyneham Villages are open to the public every weekend with the exception of the following:

| 16/17th Jan | 13/14th Feb | 12/13th Mar |
| 08/09th Oct | 19/20th Nov | 10/11th Dec |

Non firing days open for public access for 2016 are as follows:

EVENT	CLOSED FROM	REOPENS
Easter	25 MAR 16	04 APR 16
Bank Holiday	30 APR 16	03 MAY 16
Spring Break	28 MAY 16	06 JUN 16
Summer	30 JUL 16	05 SEPT 16
Christmas	19 DEC 16	08 JAN 17

Please note that the exhibitions in Tyneham School and Tyneham Church are open from 10.00 until 16.00. When no firing is taking place the gates to the walks are opened as near to 0900 hours on the Saturday morning as possible and remain open until 0800 hours on Monday morning. The Elmes Grove gate that allows vehicle access to Tyneham is opened at 0900 hrs daily when no firing is taking place and is closed at dusk each evening.

The abandoned village and its historical exhibition are 0.5 mile/800m inland of the Coast Path, and worth the diversion. The gates to the walks are opened as near to 09.00 on the Saturday morning as possible and remain open until 08.00 on the Monday morning when open only at weekends. The gate to Tyneham is locked each night at dusk. For any further information telephone 01929 404819 or 01929 404712, 0800-1700, Monday to Friday.

If the Ranges are closed, it is strongly recommended that schedules are re-arranged so that the Coast Path is walked when open. If, however, this is not possible, two alternative inland diversions are shown below. If using these routes you are strongly advised to carry OS 1:25,000 Explorer Map OL15 (Purbeck and South Dorset).

Coast Path – Lulworth Cove-Kimmeridge Bay

The eastbound Coast Path from Lulworth Cove no longer leaves from behind the café adjacent to the beach – both the café and the adjacent cliffs were destroyed in the storms of the winter of 2013-14. Instead, take the road inland up through the village and after passing the entrance to the main car park and café take the narrow higher road northward past the properties on the east side of the road. After the last house take a signed footpath eastwards steeply uphill to join a path southwards that contours around the hill to re-join the old Coast Path route as it climbs around the cliff edge at the top of the cove. The Coast Path then turns south-eastwards and descends to the east side of the cove. As an alternative, tide permitting, walking the beach avoids considerable ascent and descent. At most states of the tide this is possible. Then take the path going up from the far side of the cove beach to re-join the Coast Path which rises steeply on the eastward cliff edge to the beginning of the Army Ranges. The route onward is straightforward – just follow the yellow topped posts through the ranges to arrive at Kimmeridge Bay. Here are toilets and seasonal refreshments (or all year refreshments in the village 0.6 mile/1km to the north).

If Ranges Closed – Alternative Option 1 (13.5 miles/22.0km)

This route is safer and quieter but more strenuous than Option 2; it uses mainly rights of way plus some permissive paths. It should be noted that this route is not specifically signed or waymarked as an official alternative to the Coast Path. However the Association is hopeful that some specific waymarking as an alternative route may be installed for 2016.

Leave Lulworth Cove as described above for the Coast Path and where the revised route of the Coast Path leaves to the east continue ahead on a footpath parallel to the B3070 road. At the end of the footpath return to the road and follow it inland, forking right, before taking the next road on the left just after a bus shelter (GR 825 807). In 100 yards/90m turn right on to a footpath that heads uphill for 0.75 mile/1.2km. At the second junction of paths turn right (east) and after 100 yards/90m turn left (north) to pass Belhuish Coppice and Belhuish Farm. On reaching the B3071 road at GR835 832 cross the road and take the track opposite. Ignore the first path junction to the north-east and continue downhill to the eastern boundary of Burngate Wood (GR 845 828). Turn north-east on a permissive path (blue) past Park Lodge and go across the road at GR 855 832 onto a bridleway. Continue along the bridleway for just over 2 miles/3.4km to GR 866 856 to join a minor road from Highwood veering north and later north-east to meet an east-west road at GR 871 861. Walk east along the road then fork right (signposted Stoborough) at GR 883 856. Go over the crossroads (seat) with the B3070 road at GR 886 855 (Route Option 2 joins this route at this location) and walk east for a further 1.5 miles/2.5km along Holme Lane to GR 909 854 (about 330 yards/300m before railway underbridge) and turn southwards onto diverted Doreys Farm bridleway (see Option 1A below), which is followed for 1.25 miles/2.1km before turning right onto Creech Road.

Turn right and in 0.9 miles/1.5km after Creech Grange the road climbs steeply for 0.6 miles/1.0km to the Steeple viewpoint car park. Just before the car park turn left at GR 905 817 on a bridleway that falls steeply southwards to re-join the same road. As the road levels out, at a left hand bend at GR 907 812, take the bridleway/access road ahead that leads south through Steeple Leaze Farm. About 200 yards/185m south of the farm take the narrow footpath that heads up steeply south through woods to a bridleway on the ridge. Turn left through a gate and look for a narrow path on the right raking steeply downhill and then across three fields towards the coast ahead and Kimmeridge Bay, where the Coast Path is joined at a T-junction.

Option 1A (This avoids 0.6 miles/1.0km of road walking.)

On Doreys Farm bridleway (see above), after emerging from Bridewell Plantation (GR 914 839), (where a fine house comes into view through trees on the left), go through the first field gate on the right onto the east side of Grange Heath. Initially the route is indistinct and the ground can be wet in and after inclement weather. However, head south-west across the heath and in some 160 yards/146m a good gravel path will be found that winds its way across Grange Heath. Although this is described as a permissive path on some maps legal access is as shown, as this area is designated as Access Land. Follow the path south-west across the heath to join a bridleway that runs south-east passing a farm to join Creech Road by a telephone box. Turn right on the road and in 0.3 miles/0.5km pass Creech Grange and then follow the details set out in the final paragraph of Option 1 above.

If Ranges Closed – Alternative Option 2 (12 miles/19km)

This option is mainly road walking, and care is needed on narrow bends. Leave the Cove to West Lulworth on the B3070, then turn right to East Lulworth and beyond, keeping to the B3070 for some 3 miles/5km to GR 886 855. Here turn right along Holme Lane to GR 911 854. From here, follow the route described from (*) in Option 1 above.

Taxi operators: Mike Whittle, Silver Cars, tel. 01929 400409, mobile 07811 328281 and K Bay Taxi, tel.01929 480669, all offer their services in the Lulworth/Kimmeridge area.

Week 8 - Day 6 (half day)

OS Maps: **Landranger 195; Explorer OL15**

	This Walk	Cumulative	This Walk	Cumulative	Grading	Timing
Ascent	1,059ft	113,220ft	323m	34,510m	Severe	3.25 hours
Distance	5.2mi	614.7mi	8.3km	989.3km		

For detailed directions see our Kimmeridge to South Haven Point Path Description booklet.

This is a Section of steeply undulating cliffs, often with quite sheer faces and frequently with rock ledges at the cliff face. Houns-tout Cliff, near the eastern end of the Section, is especially steep. There are some very attractive bays formed by these cliffs, particularly at the eastern end. The tough terrain means that this Section often has a remote character, accentuated by the lack of neighbouring houses and roads.

Directions

Bus-walks are not easily undertaken on this Section. Circular walks using the Coast Path, based on inland villages such as Kimmeridge or Kingston, are possible.

The Coast Path from Kimmeridge Bay eastwards is straightforward, although care may be needed where small lengths have slipped, cracked or may be close to the cliff top. Just beyond Kimmeridge the Clavell Tower has been relocated 27 yards/25m inland and an improved Coast Path installed. There is a very steep climb to Houns-tout and the descent beyond turns inland to avoid dangerous terrain at Chapman's Pool. (For those aiming to end at Worth Matravers, which is about 1.2 miles/2km inland, the Coast Path is left where it crosses the valley at Hill Bottom Cottages. For the village head inland then turn right up a steep track past Renscombe Farm. Worth Matravers has a pub, shop and cafe.) The route up from Chapman's Pool is hazardous and is avoided by following the official Coast Path inland via Hill Bottom – see Section 69.

Kimmeridge

Week 8 - Day 7 (half day)

OS Maps: Landranger 195; Explorer OL15

	This Walk	Cumulative	This Walk	Cumulative	Grading	Timing
Ascent	1,195ft	114,415ft	364m	34,874m	Severe then Moderate	4 hours
Distance	8.1mi	622.8mi	13.1km	1,002.4km		

For detailed directions see our Kimmeridge to South Haven Point Path Description booklet.

The western part of this Section is dominated by St Aldhelm's Head, a flat-topped headland of limestone surmounted by an old chapel. There are extensive views, especially along the coast to the west. East of the headland the cliffs become increasingly disturbed by the remains of small-scale quarrying activity until the Country Park at Durlston Head marks the approach of Swanage.

Directions

Numerous footpaths cross the cliffs to the Coast Path from the outskirts of Swanage and the inland village of Langton Matravers. This allows for bus-walks which combine these link paths with the Coast Path.

(For those starting in Worth Matravers village, walk along the lane westwards past Weston Farm and Renscombe Farm then turn into the valley and on to the Coast Path at Hill Bottom Cottages.)

From the valley at Hill Bottom the Coast Path climbs on a well-signed route steeply up West Hill and on to Emmett's Hill. The path goes out round St Aldhelm's Head, with excellent coastal views west, and on as a fine high level walk to Durlston Head. Signing in Durlston Country Park is limited; keep on the low level path all the way round Durlston Head then, coming up on the north side take the second turning right (the first is a cul-de-sac to a quarry). Durlston Castle has now been converted to a Jurassic Coast Gateway Centre and includes refreshment facilities.

After leaving Durlston Castle follow a broad stony path north through the woods for some 760 yards/700m to a barrier and sign. From here there is a permanent diversion following a cliff fall. Turn left on a good path for some 125 yards/115m to reach Durlston Road at a gate. Turn right and in 185 yards/170m turn right again into Belle Vue Road. Follow the road north-eastwards to the grassed open space leading to Peveril Point. In bad weather or at high tides use the roadway and then down to the footpath at the end of the coastal buildings, otherwise use the foreshore. Continue along Swanage's sea front promenade. Swanage has all facilities.

Local taxi company Swanage & Purbeck Taxis' are offering a 10% discount to readers of this Guidebook. Contact Martin on 07969 927424.

Towards Dancing Ledge

Week 8 - Day 7 (half day)

OS Maps: Landranger 195; Explorer OL15

	This Walk	Cumulative	This Walk	Cumulative	Grading	Timing
Ascent	492ft	114,907ft	150m	35,024m	Moderate	3.5 hours
Distance	7.6mi	630.4mi	12.2km	1,014.6km		

For detailed directions see our Kimmeridge to South Haven Point Path Description booklet.

This is an excellent and scenic Section. The southern, Swanage end comprises increasingly high cliffs, culminating in the length between Ballard Point and Handfast Point, with its offshore stacks. This is an exhilarating length with superb views over Poole Bay to Bournemouth and across the Solent to the matching cliffs of the Needles on the Isle of Wight. The northern end passes along a long sandy beach before arriving at the mouth of Poole Harbour, an enormous enclosed water area and the second largest natural harbour in the world.

Directions

A regular bus service, half hourly in summer and hourly in winter, links Swanage with South Haven Point, making a bus-walk a good option. There are also popular local circuits using the Coast Path in the Swanage-Ballard Down-Studland area.

Swanage has all facilities. The Coast Path passes along the town's sea front, following the main road (Ulwell Road) at the north end by the telephone box where it bears left and on ahead into Redcliff Road at a one-way system. At a shop and post-box turn sharp right into Ballard Way – do not be put off by "Private Estate" signs. Continue forward into the chalet estate and follow signs for the Coast Path, to emerge on a grassed area on the cliff edge. However, from the sea front road, except at very high tides or in severe weather it is possible to keep along the narrow promenade then 200 yards/185m along the beach turn up some rough steps to re-join the official route in a little valley.

The path climbs out to Ballard Down, then the obvious high-level route continues out to Handfast Point and the much-photographed rocks of Old Harry before turning west towards Studland. Studland has toilets and refreshments. For the pub turn up the road from the toilets, otherwise turn right (east) on the outskirts of the village along the signed stony path to South Beach. On reaching the shore, turn left (north) along a terrace in front of beach huts to a seasonal cafe. The route ahead was diverted in 2013 inland up a track to join the road by the public toilets. Turn right here past the pub and right again to re-join the Coast Path above the beach huts. If this short diversion is no longer necessary then continue along the beach for another 90 yards/82m and look for a Purbeck stone waymark between beach huts numbers 59 and 60B, to find a narrow path that ascends steeply up the low cliff. At the top, at another sign, turn right and follow the cliff edge past Fort Henry to join the Middle Beach access road by a barrier. Turn sharp right down to the beach then left by another cafe.

The final 2.6 miles/4.3km are on the sandy beach. Note that further along this beach a length is used by naturists – do not be surprised if nobody else is wearing clothes! There is an alternative, the Heather Walk, through the dunes, marked by yellow-topped posts, but the soft sand is tiring walking and part of the naturist area is still visible. The beach

Old Harry Rocks

route curves round to the point at the mouth of Poole Harbour. This is South Haven Point, the end (or beginning) of the Coast Path, with an impressive commemorative marker. A ferry links the Point with Sandbanks on the opposite shore, which is linked to Poole and Bournemouth.

The ferry operates all year daily every 20 minutes, from Shell Bay (South Haven Point) 07:10 to 23:10; from Sandbanks 07:00 to 23:00; Christmas Day every half hour – telephone 01929 450203; website www.sandbanksferry.co.uk.

Note that the ferry is usually scheduled to undergo maintenance during late October or November and may be closed for approximately four weeks. If you intend to use the ferry at this time check the Association's website under Path News or the ferry company's website above. For ferry details see page 21.

Postscript

For those who have been with us all the way from Minehead, be it in one go or in bits and pieces over a period, a final few words seem appropriate. Alfred Wainwright, at the end of his work on the Pennine Way, said; "You have completed a mission and satisfied an ambition. You have walked the Pennine Way, as you have dreamed of doing. This will be a very satisfying moment in your life. You will be tired and hungry and travel stained. But you will feel great, just great." Just substitute the South West Coast Path for the Pennine Way and Wainwright's words will doubtless ring true. You will be glad and proud that you have walked and finished Britain's longest and finest footpath. As Wainwright said of the Pennine Way, it's a longer step than most take in their lifetime!

Alternative Inland Coast Path

OS Maps: Landranger 194; Explorer OL15

	This Walk	This Walk	Grading	Timing
Ascent	2,290ft	698m	Moderate	8 hours
Distance	16.8mi	27.0km		

For detailed directions see our West Bexington to Osmington Mills Path Description booklet.

This is a very scenic walk, parallel to the coast and a varying distance inland. For most of its length quite extensive coastal views are obtained beyond a green and rural foreground. Substantial lengths follow chalk ridges and these give impressive views north as well. Coastal features such as Portland and Chesil Beach are clearly seen, as are the flanks of the enormous Iron Age Maiden Castle inland. This is a quiet route, often feeling quite remote, and with usually no refreshments on its length it requires preparation. It is, nevertheless, a superb experience.

Directions

A regular bus service links Swyre (for West Bexington) and Osmington Mills, making this a perfect opportunity for a bus-walk.

The Dorset element of the Coast Path is unique in having an official alternative route for part of its length. This was often referred to by the apparently contradictory name of the "Inland Coast Path". It is, however, now known as the South Dorset Ridgeway (SDR) and the signposting now uses that name almost throughout. The waymarking has also been replaced and incorporates the name of the South Dorset Ridgeway. The length of the Section, and the fact that the two ends are linked by a regular bus service, make it an ideal long day's walk. However, be aware that other than one seasonal mobile refreshment van if the timing is right, no facilities are found anywhere along the route other than at the two ends, so it is necessary to be well prepared. A detailed route description is given below.

At West Bexington car park turn inland up the road and where the road turns left continue forward up the stony track, signposted "SDR. For Hardy Monument 6 Osmington Mills 16".

Near the top of the hill take the right-hand fork to reach a lay-by on the B3157 road. Take the gate or stile to the right and follow a faint path that follows the edge of the escarpment of the hill passing three waymark posts. After passing through a wall start to bear upwards to the left towards a signpost near the road. Continue eastwards through the field to reach a gate by the corner of a wall. Continue through the gate and almost immediately emerge on the B3157 road at a signpost. Cross and leave through a gate, again signposted "Hardy Monument".

Approaching Abbotsbury Castle prehistoric hill fort, where the grass path divides, take the upper, slightly right-hand fork along the top of the southern earthwork of the fort, past the trig point, from where there are superb views in all directions. It should be possible to see the Hardy Monument clearly in the distance.

Continue eastwards along the top of the earthwork and cross a minor road, signposted "SDR Hardy Monument". Proceed in an approximately easterly direction along the ridge of Wears Hill and the crest of White Hill for about 2 miles/3.2km, following the signing. Be careful not to follow any signs indicating routes down to the village of Abbotsbury in the valley below and its adjacent hilltop chapel. At the east end of White Hill bear north-east as signed and leave the field in the north-east corner through a gate on to a minor road. Continue north-east along this road for some 50 yards/46m and then turn right as signposted.

Follow the narrow and rough bridleway along the wire fence above the scrub to a path junction; where the bridleway bears right take the yellow waymarked footpath to the left and cross a stile. At the end of this short section take a headland path north-east. At the far side of the field the track then leads approximately 50 yards/46m to a further gate with a stile and waymark. Immediately adjacent to this gate is a prehistoric stone circle, a scheduled ancient monument. Continue forward on the track, leaving a small wood to the left, to reach the road between Portesham and Winterbourne Steepleton. Turn left along the road for about 60 yards/55m and then turn right over a stile into a field, signed "Hardy Monument". Continue eastwards through four fields. At a small wooded area before Black Down Barn (ruin) turn north at a signpost to Hardy Monument. Climb through the woods to the recently renovated monument. In season it may be possible to find a mobile refreshment van here.

To continue find a roadside signpost 30yards/32m east of the car park entrance. Cross the road and descend eastward on a narrow path through the bracken. Reaching the same road again, ignore the signpost "Bridleway to Coast Path" and the track opposite and turn left along the road then in another 30 yards/32m turn right, signposted "Inland Route or SDR to Bincombe".

Now there is a good ridgeway path for some 3 miles/4.8km, with excellent views to seaward. At a point some 550 yards/500m after passing under the second set of HV power lines take the gate north of a large tumulus to stay on the north side of the fence running along the ridge. On reaching the B3159 road, marked by the Borough of Weymouth boundary stone, continue across as signposted and towards the A354 road.

Major road construction has now been completed and a new section of the busy A354 road opened over Ridgeway Hill. The former very difficult crossing of the old road has been replaced with a fine new bridleway bridge (locally known as Green Bridge). Cross the new bridge and take a new bridleway south, that at first rises and then falls, down the perimeter fence on the east side of the new road. About halfway down the hill look out for and take the old bridleway on the left.

Continue eastwards, then before the farm, with its adjacent radio mast, take care to go through the gate on the right, marked with a blue arrow. After crossing the field, leaving two tumuli on the left, reach a metalled road and turn right. At the junction at the corner of Came Wood turn right at the signpost "Bridleway to Bincombe".At the end of the path join a metalled lane and at the road junction turn left, signposted "South Dorset Ridgeway".

Drop down the road into the village of Bincombe and where the road turns right take the track forward leaving the small church on the right. Where the path splits take the left-hand fork, marked with a blue arrow and acorn. After the overhead HV power lines, pass through a small signposted wooden gate and then proceed forward through one field, into the next to a footpath sign. Here turn left and there is a choice of routes for the next couple of hundred yards/m.

For the best option, at a waymark post turn sharp right down a steep grassy slope to a stile at a road ahead. Cross the road to go over another stile to follow a grassy path that contours around the south and east sides of Green Hill. On reaching a road at a gate and stile turn left and in 50 yards/46m turn right through a gate signposted "White Horse Hill – Osmington Mills". The path is now easy to follow with extensive views to seaward over Weymouth and Portland. On passing a ruined building on the left the route reaches a broad track; here turn right, signposted "Osmington" and after about 200 yards/185m go through a gate as signposted. Shortly afterwards pass a trig point on the right and at the next field gate bear left and follow the field boundary along White Horse Hill. Just beyond the next gate fork right, signposted "For Osmington".

Descend to Osmington and follow the signs through the village. On reaching the main Weymouth road near the Sun Ray Inn turn left and in about 250 yards/230m turn right at a signpost, over a stile and footbridge. Follow the field boundary on the left through two fields - at the top look back to see the Hardy Monument in the distance and the white horse on the hillside. Go over the stile to the footpath sign, then turn half right to cross the field at an angle to a further stile. Cross it and turn left along the hedge side to the bottom. At the end of the field there is a very short length of enclosed footpath to the road; turn right along it, descending to Osmington Mills.

Hardys Monument

If you enjoy sleeping, eating or drinking at any business on the Path please suggest they join us as Business Members so that we can share their brilliance!

Seaton to South Haven Point

The businesses listed here are all supporters of the South West Coast Path, they have joined as Business Members and it would be great if you could show your support for them too. Additional Businesses are listed on **www.southwestcoastpath.org.uk** with links to their own sites for more information.

SLEEP	
Owen Lovell **Lucerne,** View Road, Lyme Regis, DT7 3AA	stay@lucernelyme.co.uk www.lucernelyme.co.uk 01297 443752
Jennifer Thomson **Westley B&B,** Lyme Road, Uplyme, Lyme Regis, DT7 3UY	westleybandb@btinternet.com www.westleybedandbreakfast.wordpress.com 01297 445104
Lisa Tuck **Broadlands B&B,** Doghouse Lane, Chideock, Bridport, DT6 6HX	enquiries@broadlandschideock.co.uk www.broadlandschideock.co.uk 01297 489543
Anna Dunn **Chideock House,** Main Street, Chideock, DT6 6JN	annachideockhouse@yahoo.co.uk www.chideockhouse.co.uk 01297 489242
Mrs C Crawford **Mervyn House,** Chideock, Near Bridport, DT6 6JN	callbrig@gmail.com www.chideockandseatown.co.uk 01297 489578
Glenis French **Eypes Mouth Hotel,** Eype, Dorset, DT6 6AL	info@eypesmouthhotel.co.uk www.eypesmouthhotel.co.uk 01308 423300
Angela Munro **Southfield,** West Bay, Bridport, DT6 4JB	angela@southfield-westbay.co.uk www.southfield-westbay.co.uk 07983 611193
Andrew & Chrissie Bailey **Graston Farm,** Burton Bradstock, Bridport, Dorset, DT6 4NG	info@grastonfarm.co.uk www.grastonfarm.co.uk 01398 897603 • 07766 912403
Steve & Maria Peach **Peach's,** 6 Market Street, Abbotsbury, DT3 4JR	enquiries@abbotsburybandb.co.uk www.abbotsburybandb.co.uk 01305 870364
Irene Donnelly **Cowards Lake Farmhouse,** 13 West Street, Abbotsbury, Weymouth, DT3 4JT	cowards-lakebandb@btconnect.com www.abbotsbury.co.uk/cowardslake 01305 871421
Clare Rawlings **Upalong B&B,** 8 West Street, Abbotsbury, DT3 4JT	candcrawlings@gmail.com www.upalingwestdorset.co.uk 01305 871882
Rocky Dibben **Sea Barn Farm Camping Park,** Fleet Road, Fleet, Weymouth, DT3 4ED	enquire@seabarnfarm.co.uk www.seabarnfarm.co.uk 01305 782218
Keith Smith **Swallows Rest B&B and Martleaves Farm Campsite,** Martleaves Farm, South Road, Wyke Regis, Dorset, DT4 9NR	info@swallowsrestselfcatering.co.uk www.swallowsrestbedandbreakfast.co.uk 01305 485244
Christina Moody **Mariners Cottage,** 181 Brandy Row, Chiswell, Dorset, DT5 1AP	christina181@live.co.uk www.portlandbandb.com 01305 826665
Giovanni Bisogno **Alessandria,** 71 Wakeham, Easton, Portland, DT5 1HW	01305 822270

Angela Monaham & Sharon Arnold **Greenwood Guest House,** 1 Holland Road, Weymouth, DT1 0AL	greenwoodguesthouse@hotmail.com www.greenwoodguesthouse.co.uk 01305 775626
Mrs M Acton **Maribel's,** 28 Alma Road, Weymouth, DT4 0AJ	maribelacton@gmail.com www.maribelsweymouth.co.uk 01305 781921
Mike Clark **Oaklands Edwardian Guest House,** 1 Glendenning Avenue, Weymouth, DT4 7QE	stay@oaklands-guesthouse.co.uk www.oaklands-guesthouse.co.uk 01305 767081
Kate Rickard **Dream Cottages,** 4 & 5 Hope Square, Weymouth, DT4 8TR	admin@dream-cottages.co.uk www.dream-cottages.co.uk 01305 789000
Peter Banks **Harbour Lights Guest House,** 20 Buxton Road, Weymouth, DT4 9PJ	harbourlights@btconnect.com www.harbourlightsguesthouse.com 01305 783273
Alison Stamper **East Fleet Farm Touring Park,** East Fleet Farm, Chickerell, Weymouth, DT3 4DW	enquiries@eastfleet.co.uk www.eastfleet.co.uk 01305 785768
Hope Horvath **1 Old Coastguards,** Osmington Mills, DT3 6HQ	hope.horvath68@live.co.uk 01305 832663
Joanne Selfe **The Dairy House B&B,** Chaldon Herring, Dorchester, DT2 8DN	joanneselfe@hotmail.com 01305 852138 • 07968 255269
Susie Mitchell **Alford House B&B,** 120 East Street, Corfe Castle, BH20 5EH	info@alfordhouse.com www.alfordhouse.com 01929 480156
David Ensor **Chiltern Lodge,** 8 Newfoundland Close, Worth Matravers, BH19 3LX	densor@btopenworld.com www.chilternlodge.co.uk 01929 439337
Tim Arnold **Post Office Cottage,** Worth Matravers, Isle of Purbeck, BH19 3LQ	office@worthmytravels.co.uk www.worthmytravels.co.uk 01929 439442
Sarah Wootton **Tom's Field Campsite & Shop,** Langton Matravers, BH19 3HN	tomsfield@hotmail.com www.tomsfieldcamping.co.uk 01929 427110
Ian Bell **Allnatt Stop and Stay**, 35 Ulwell Road, Swanage, BH19 1LG	enquiries@stopandstay.co.uk www.stopandstay.co.uk 01929 421075
Lyn Fegan **The Limes,** 48 Park Road, Swanage, BH19 2AE	info@limeshotel.net www.limeshotel.net 01929 422664
Elaine North **The Laurels,** 60 Britannia Road, Poole, BH14 8BB	info@thelaurelsbandb.com www.thelaurelsbandb.com 7837737368

South West Coast Path
Association

CHALLENGE

What will your Challenge be?

It costs at least £1,000 every year to look after one mile of Coast Path

Take part in October and help support the Path
Register your interest now
www.southwestcoastpath.org.uk

There is an amazing variety of Youth Hostels along the South West Coast Path, all offering comfortable, friendly accommodation.

You don't have to be a member of the YHA but membership enables you to take advantage of more than 4000 Youth Hostels world wide, and discounts online and high street retailers as well as local tourist attractions.

YHA annual membership costs are currently:

Under 26 - £10, Individual - £20, Household £30. Discounts for direct debit payments.

Buffet breakfasts, lunches and evening meals all available, but you can still prepare your own food in most of the hostels.

Book directly with the Youth Hostel of your choice or for further assistance, please contact YHA Customer Services:

Tel: 0800 0191700

Website: **www.yha.org.uk**

Email: **customerservices@yha.org.uk**

Youth Hostels

Town	Address	Phone	OS Ref
Minehead	Alcombe Combe MINEHEAD TA24 6EW	0845 371 9033	973 442
Ilfracombe	Mullacott Farm, ILFRACOMBE EX34 8NA	01271 866 877	513 452
Elmscott	Hartland, BIDEFORD EX39 6ES	0845 371 9736	231 217
Boscastle	Palace Stables BOSCASTLE PL35 0HD	0845 371 9006	096 915
Tintagel	Dunderhole Point TINTAGEL PL34 0DW	0845 371 9145	047 881
Treyarnon	Tregonnan Treyarnon PADSTOW PL28 8JR	0845 371 9664	859 741
Newquay	Mor Lodge, Mount Wise NEWQUAY TR7 2BP	01637 877776	809 613
Perranporth	Droskyn Point PERRANPORTH TR6 0GS	0845 371 9755	752 544
Portreath	Nance Farm, Illogan, PORTREATH TR16 4QX	01209 842244	668 443
Land's End	Letcha Vean ST JUST TR19 7NT	0845 371 9643	364 305
Penzance	Horneck, PENZANCE TR20 8TF	0845 371 9653	457 302
Lizard	The Lizard HELSTON TR12 7NT	0845 371 9550	704 116
Coverack	Parc Behan, School Hill COVERACK TR12 6SA	0845 371 9014	782 184
Boswinger	GORRAN PL26 6LL	0845 371 9107	991 411
Beer	Bovey Combe, BEER EX12 3LL	0845 371 9502	223 896
Litton Cheney	Litton Cheney DORCHESTER DT2 9AT	0845 371 9329	548 900
Portland	Castle Road, Castle Town PORTLAND DT5 1AU	0845 371 9339	685 741
Lulworth Cove	School Lane WEST LULWORTH BH20 5SA	0845 371 9331	832 806
Swanage	Cluny Crescent SWANAGE BH19 2BS	0845 371 9346	031 785

Tourist Information Centres

Town	Address	Phone	Website
Minehead	The Beach Hotel, The Avenue, Minehead TA24 5AP	01643 702624	www.visitminehead.org
Porlock	West End, Porlock TA24 8QD	01643 863150	www.porlock.co.uk
Lynton	Town Hall, Lee Road, Lynton EX35 6BT	01598 752225	www.lynton-lynmouth-tourism.co.uk
Combe Martin	Museum, Cross Street EX34 0DH	01271 889031	www.visitcombemartin.com
Ilfracombe	Landmark Theatre, Ilfracombe, EX34 9BZ	01271 863001	www.visitilfracombe.co.uk
Woolacombe	The Esplanade, Woolacombe EX34 7DL	01271 870553	www.woolacombetourism.co.uk
Braunton	Bakehouse Centre, Caen Street EX33 1AA	01271 816688	www.visitbraunton.co.uk
Barnstaple	The Square, Barnstaple EX32 8LN	01271 375000	www.staynorthdevon.co.uk
Bideford	Burton Art Gallery, Kingsley Rd EX39 2QQ	01237 471455	www.burtonartgallery.co.uk
Bude	The Crescent, Bude EX23 8LE	01288 354240	www.visitbude.info
Boscastle	The Harbour, Boscastle PL35 0HD	01840 250010	www.visitboscastleandtintagel.com
Padstow	North Quay, Padstow PL28 8AF	01841 533449	www.padstowlive.com
Newquay	Marcus Hill, Newquay TR7 1BD	01637 854020	www.visitnewquay.org
Perranporth	Westcott House, St Pirans Road TR6 0BH	01872 575254	www.perranporthinfo.co.uk
Hayle			www.hayle.co.uk
St Ives	The Guildhall, Street An Pol TR26 2DS	0905 252 2250	www.stivestic.co.uk
Penzance	Station Approach, Penzance TR18 2NF	01736 335530	www.purelypenzance.co.uk/tourism
Falmouth	Prince Of Wales Pier, 11 Market Strand TR11 3DF	01326 741194	www.falmouth.co.uk
Mevagissey	St George's Square, Mevagissey PL26 6UB	01726 844440	www.mevagissey.net
Fowey	5 South Street, Fowey PL23 1AR	01726 833616	www.fowey.co.uk
Looe	The Guildhall, Fore Street, Looe PL13 2AA	01503 262072	www.visit-southeastcornwall.co.uk
Plymouth	3-5 Plymouth Mayflower, Barbican PL1 2LR	01752 306330	www.visitplymouth.co.uk
Ivybridge	The Watermark, Ivybridge PL21 0SZ	01752 897035	www.ivybridgewatermark.co.uk
Salcombe	Market Street, Salcombe TQ8 8DE	01548 843927	www.salcombeinformation.co.uk
Kingsbridge	The Quay, Kingsbridge TQ7 1HS	01548 853195	www.welcomesouthdevon.co.uk
Dartmouth	The Engine House, Mayors Ave TQ6 9YY	01803 834224	www.discoverdartmouth.com
Brixham	Hobb Nobs Gift Shop, The Quay TQ5 8AW	01803 211211	www.englishriviera.co.uk
Paignton	Garfield Road, Paignton, TQ4 6ED	01803 551959	www.englishriviera.co.uk
Torquay	Torbay Road, TQ2 5EZ	01803 211211	www.englishriviera.co.uk
Shaldon	Shaldon Car Park, Ness Drive TQ14 0HP	01626 873723	www.visitsouthdevon.co.uk
Teignmouth	The Den, Sea Front, Teignmouth TQ14 8BE	01626 215666	www.visitsouthdevon.co.uk
Dawlish	The Lawn, Dawlish EX7 9PW	01626 215665	www.visitsouthdevon.co.uk
Exmouth	42 The Strand, Exmouth, EX8 1AL	01395 830550	www.exmouth-guide.co.uk
Budleigh -Salterton	Fore Street, Budleigh Salterton EX9 6NG	01395 445275	www.visitbudleigh.com
Sidmouth	Ham Lane, Sidmouth EX10 8XR	01395 516441	www.visitsidmouth.co.uk
Seaton	The Underfleet, Seaton EX12 2TB	01297 21660	www.seatontic.com
Lyme Regis	Guildhall Cottage, Church Street DT7 3BS	01297 442138	www.lymeregis.org
Bridport	Town Hall, South Street, Bridport DT6 3LF	01308 424901	www.visit-dorset.com
Swanage	The White House, Shore Road BH19 1LB	01929 422885	www.visit-dorset.com
Poole	Poole Museum, 4 High Street, Poole BH15 1BW	01202 262600	www.pooletourism.com
Not on Coast Path			
Truro	Municipal Buildings, Boscawen St, Truro TR1 2NE	01872 274555	www.visittruro.org.uk
Weston Super Mare	The Winter Gardens, Royal Parade BS23 1AJ	01934 417117	www.visitsomerset.co.uk

1973–1979

The Association was officially formed at a public meeting held in Newton Abbot on the 5th May 1973 and we were called the South West Way Association. We were registered as a charity in 1974.

During this inaugural period we were mainly engaged in campaigning for a complete Coast Path. During the 70s the Path was created in stages and we attended the official openings; Cornwall (1973), South Devon and Dorset Paths (1974), Exmoor Coast (1975) and the final section through Somerset & North Devon (1978).

1980–1989

As a mark of our growing standing, we entered a dialogue with the Countryside Commission in 1980 over the deficiencies with the Path at that time.

Improvements followed thick and fast in the 80s, many following the Association's campaigns.

Notable successes in this decade were a Public Enquiry at Bude to prevent development adjacent to the footpath (1987); Branscombe Public Enquiry for a true Coast Path (1987) and at Wembury where the Royal Navy proposed to erect locked gates across the Coast Path (1989).

By the end of the 80s the Coast Path as we now see it existed, although it was far from ideal.

1990–1999

It was during the 90s that we came of age. Our growing standing with local authorities and the National Trust meant that our suggestions for alternate routes and other improvements were often adopted.

As 1998 was our Silver Jubilee year, the Association set up a fund to raise money for markers at Minehead and South Haven Point.

As early as 1994 we were invited by Countryside Commission to become a member of the South West Coast Path Steering Group and to review the management of the Path. This was final recognition that we were an important supporter of the Path. At the end of the decade, at our AGM in Dorchester, our members voted in favour of adopting the name we have today, in recognition of the official name for the Path.

In 1994 our first Chairman and founder, Philip Carter, stepped down and Brian Panton became Chairman. Philip's contribution both to the Association and the Path cannot be underestimated. In another sign of changing times, the Path and Association were put on the Internet by Andrew Lack, a member from London who was looking to learn more about web-site creation.

2000–2009

The first decade of the 21st century saw us build an impressive number of members to over 5,000. During this period we started to fund improvement works for the first time, thanks largely to the income we were receiving from our members. In 2007 we pledged a substantial amount (£30,000) to move the Path off a busy road at Watermouth in North Devon.

We continued to press the local authorities and National Trust for changes to the route. Notable improvements secured in the millennium were at Crock Pits where the Exmoor National Park installed our recommended coastal route (2000); at Chynhalls Cliff (2003); Tregantle Cliff where the MoD created a permissive path (2003), and at Thatcher Point where our requested realignments were adopted (2007).

The Path Markers, which were an idea to celebrate our 25th anniversary, were finally installed at Minehead in 2001 and at South Haven Point in 2002. The mid-way marker at Porthallow was installed in 2009.

In 2003 the Isle of Portland was added to the official route, making the Path 630 miles in total, plus the 18 miles of the "inland route" between West Bexington and Osmington Mills.

To celebrate the re-opening of the Coast Path in 2001 after the Foot and Mouth outbreak, we organised the first of two "walk the whole path in a day" events. The second such walk took place in 2003 to celebrate 25 years since the completion of the Coast Path in 1978 when the Somerset and North Devon sections were opened.

Eric Wallis, who became our Hon. Secretary in 1986 was recognised for his contribution to the Association by being awarded an MBE in 2009.

2010–present

The decade opened with the very sad news of the death of Eric Wallis in 2010 after a short illness. Eric's contribution to the Path and Association was formally recognised in 2013 with the opening of Eric's Steps at the Royal William Yard in Plymouth.

We stepped up our funding of Path improvements in 2012 with twelve projects funded.

To celebrate our 40th anniversary, we organised the Great South West Walk in 2013. This consisted of two relays of walkers, one starting from Minehead and the other from South Haven Point, meeting at Land's End on 11th May. We raised £250,000 towards further improvement projects.

In January 2014 the South West Coast Path won South West Tourism's award for the Outstanding Contribution to Tourism 2013–14. Members of the Association and Team were at the ceremony in Plymouth to collect the award.

In August 2014 our bid for £1m to the Government's Coastal Communities Fund was successful. The bid, submitted in partnership with the South West Coast Path Team, but with us leading, provided roughly £0.5m for 38 Path improvement projects, plus £0.5m to build the capacity of the Association.

Following requests from members to be more involved with practical help with the Path, Trustees established over 50 Local Reps to assist with the reporting the condition of the Path. In 2015 the Association equipped the Local Reps with tablet computers to allow them to carry out the first detailed survey of the whole path by volunteers.

Following legal advice the Association changed its legal status from an unincorporated charity to a Charitable Incorporated Organisation in 2015. A resolution proposing the change was approved by our members at the AGM held in Ilfracombe in March and on the 4th September the Charity Commission approved our application. The Association will be operating under the new status from January 2016.

Funding Improvements to the South West Coast Path

The Coastal Communities Funding achieved by the South West Coast Path Association in 2014 has enabled 35 significant storm damage repair projects to be successfully completed in 2015, ranging from small reroutes to the Path to avoid erosion, up to the construction of a new flight of steps at Kynance Cove.

A major project completed this year has been at Strete Gate – after 40 years of planning and negotiating, collaboration from local landowners and funding from Natural England, Devon County Council and Strete Parish Council, improvements to the Coast Path at this beautiful spot have allowed the route to be taken off the very busy road, and opened up wonderful views for walkers across Start Bay.

The Association has utilised its own funding to complete a number of other improvement schemes with various partners along the length of the Path, and now, more than ever, we are reliant on subscriptions, donations and other help from Association members as funding cuts bite from traditional sources.

Funds raised through the South West Coast Path Challenge 2015 will help the Association to deliver more improvement projects in the coming year, and memorial donations have increased this year and been used for some lovely projects to remember loved ones.

As always, we are extremely grateful for the support that Members' contributions provide to help us improve and maintain the South West Coast Path.

We'll keep you up to date on our projects through regular features in our newsletters. You can sign up for e-newsletters at www.southwestcoastpath.org.uk

Clothing

There's no such thing as bad weather, only unsuitable clothing

Alfred Wainwright

Prices include p&p

We have some great clothing and accessories to help you keep dry, cool/warm and comfortable, a few suggestions are here and there are plenty more online at **www.southwestcoastpath.org.uk**

Your Comments

Just received calendar with beautiful coast path photos. It will remind us of many of the fantastic places we have walked through on the coast path so far. **P Browning, Manchester**

Thank you, just arrived and am really pleased with everything! Great service. **N.McGuirk, Barnstaple**

Received my books today, they look wonderful! Can't wait to get out on Path. Thanks for all your help, it's been a real pleasure. **T. Guglielmo, U.S.A.**

Love this map, can't wait until all coastline is coloured in! **Willand**

Does what it says on the tin. Beautifully organised and laid out, bristling with useful current information. **Notts**

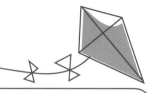

Hoodie
£32.50
Fantastically easy to wear this double fabric hoodie is embroidered with the South West Coast Path logo and available in a range of stunning colours.

Backpack
£15.00
Available in 11 exciting colours this roomy backpack has an easy access pocket at the front and is great for a variety of activities.

Sleeveless Fleece
£28
Ideal for those days when it's not hot and not cold. Also great for wearing as a layer on really cold days.

Light Weight Jacket
£39
Waterproof and windproof jacket, with concealed hood. Lightweight so great for Path adventures.

Gifts

Prices include p&p

If you Love the Path, want to support it, embrace it, share it and celebrate it, there is no better way to do all of this than to buy our gifts – every single purchase supports the Path.

Fridge Magnets • Tea Towels • Map Posters • Mugs • Badges...

and so much more online at www.southwestcoastpath.org.uk

Dog Leads
£15
Ideal for dog lovers and dogs who love the Path. Stitched with 'I ♥ walking the South West Coast Path', soft web lead.

Drawstring Bag
£9.00
Brilliant for shoes, gym kit, wet swim gear or as a school bag. Comes in a range of colours.

Water Bottles Blue and Green
£8.50 & £10.50
Sit back and drink in the scenery. Light weight bottles 350ml or 770ml with carabiner clip.

Notelets
£6.50
8 beautiful notelets showing stunning images of the Path by Gary Holpin. Be inspired as you write.

Books & Guides

Maps, guides, information and more. We have a range of publications that we find really useful for walking the Path or just plain lovely to have. Every publication you buy helps the Path.

Prices include p&p

Walking Guides
£1.50 - £2 each
Packed full of Path details including wildlife, heritage, geology and history, these guides cover every section of the Path. Great to carry with you so you don't miss a thing.

Little Yellow Log Book
£4.50
Keep a memory of each day walking, log conditions, particular things you see and points of note. This Little Yellow Log Book fits neatly into your pocket so it can be scribbled in when you're inspired.

Reverse Guide
£5.50
Whether you have walked the Path already or simply feel like doing it the other way this guide is perfect for anyone wanting to keep the sea on their left and walk from Poole to Minehead.

A-Z Maps
£9.50
To keep you on track don't leave home without one of these A-Z Maps that give a detailed 1:25 scale Ordnance Survey mapping. Five different maps cover the whole of the Path.

Artists

We are really lucky to be supported by some very talented, local artists and are always on the look out for emerging talent that has a coastal theme especially around the Path. Please contact us at **hello@southwestcoastpath.org.uk** if you're an artist or know someone who is, we'd love to hear more.

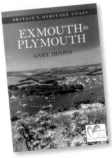

Exmouth – Plymouth by Gary Holpin £14.99
This beautifully illustrated and informative book, signed by Gary, provides a wealth of fascinating history and folklore, taking the reader on a journey along the entire length of the South Devon coast, revelling in its heritage, with interesting facts and photos.

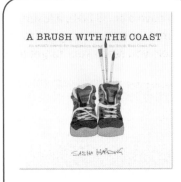

Sasha Harding
A Brush with the Coast Path is a beautiful coffee table book by Sasha, telling the story of her experience walking the whole Path using words and illustrations.

Anna Ventura
Anna designed our stunning Christmas card for winter 2015. She is a talented artist who works in a number of mediums.

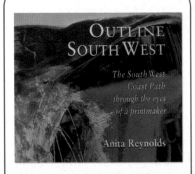

Anita Reynolds
Anita is a painter and print maker who has created a collection of work done while walking the whole 630 miles of the Coast Path.

The South West Coast Path attracts over 8.6m tourists a year...

... and these visitors spend over £436m with local businesses

If you have a small b&b, a luxury hotel, a fantastic place to eat and drink or something great to see, our Business Membership can help you reach your target audience.

By joining us you will get:

- Targeted advertising to an audience of nearly 1 million
- Adverts on our website with links to your site
- Direct communication with an audience who are interested in the Path
- South West Coast Path Guides at a reduced price
- A window sticker to show your support
- Leaflets about the Path and Association for your customers
- Opportunities to offer members' discounts
- The satisfaction of supporting the South West Coast Path

Visit www.southwestcoastpath.org.uk or call 01752 896237 to find out more

South West Coast Path Association

It costs as little as £60 a year depending on the size of your business

We're asking for your support to help us look after and love the Path.

The South West Coast Path Association is the voice of the Path, we are striving to promote and protect it for future generations. If you aren't already a member, we would love you to join us and be a part of the Association, whether you enjoy the Path for an occasional stroll, plan to walk all 630 miles or simply want to make sure this stunning trail is loved.

If you are already a member please encourage a friend to join; the more members we have the more we can do for the Path.

For less per month than the price of a pint or a pasty, you can support the Path and the work of the Association. Our membership rates for 2016 are:

Single Membership	**£20**
Joint Membership	**£25**
International Membership	**£25**

Membership benefits include:

◍ Being a friend of the South West Coast Path and helping to conserve this stunning coast line ◍ Car Sticker ◍ 2 Newsletters a year ◍ e-newsletter every month ◍ Solo walker network ◍ Offers at the South West Coast Path shop ◍ Offers with other retail outlets ◍ Events and activities throughout the south west and we hope the satisfaction of knowing that you are helping us to protect and conserve this beautiful Path

To join us please visit www.southwestcoastpath.org.uk or call for a chat on 01752 896231

Cooling off in the River Erme

We are really lucky to have a huge range of supporters who help us to deliver our promises and look after the Path, conserving it for future generations and promoting it for the enjoyment of everyone.

Ways that we are supported are shown below and we always welcome new supporters of all kinds.

Members

We have a membership base of well over 5,000 dedicated South West Coast Path lovers, a handful of these members have been supporting us since the very beginning in 1973. Some are individual members and some joint, we also have a number who live overseas and want to enable us to continue the good work from afar. Whatever the reason for being a member, you are always welcome. See opposite for more details.

Volunteers

We have a core group of volunteers who have positions such as Trustee, Area Rep and Local Rep, these volunteers are vital in the Association's work and their help and dedication is often unseen but never unappreciated. We also have many volunteers who help us with jobs such as stewarding at events, manning the stand at shows, packing Christmas cards even! Everyone is welcome whatever your interest or availability.

Business Members

We are lucky enough to have a range of local businesses who support us in through a business membership scheme which offers advertising for businesses, support for them to be walker friendly and much more. South West Coast Path walkers contribute approximately £436m to local businesses, which supports the equivalent of 9,771 full-time jobs.

To ensure that these businesses continue to support us or advertise with us try and use them so that they find their support for us worthwhile.

Business Supporters

Our main business supporter is South West Water who has been contributing to the Coast Path since 2014. The partnership works incredibly well and helps the South West Coast Path Association deliver our aims to promote and protect the Path. You can see us out and about at shows together and at our events including the Challenge event in October.

We also have a number of other business supporters – Toad Hall Cottages and hotels including Thurlestone, Mullion Cove, South Sands, Yarn Market and more.

Home before dark

Whitsand Bay Sunset